The Days of the Beloved

Mahbub Ali Pasha wearing the Star of India

The Days
of the Beloved

HARRIET RONKEN LYNTON
and MOHINI RAJAN

UNIVERSITY OF CALIFORNIA PRESS
BERKELEY, LOS ANGELES, LONDON

University of California Press
Berkeley and Los Angeles, California
University of California Press, Ltd.
London, England
Copyright © 1974, by
The Regents of the University of California
ISBN: 0-520-02442-7
Library of Congress Catalog Card Number: 73-76106
Designed by W. H. Snyder
Printed in the United States of America

To the memory of
MAHBUB ALI PASHA,
    whose name means Beloved
    and who is still so remembered
    by his people
    and
    to all those of his people
    who shared their memories
    with us.

"My sovereign's name is Beloved.
  Could any title be more important? "

                Persian couplet by
         MAHARAJAH KISHEN PERSHAD

Preface

"Facts are the enemy of truth," says the Man of La Mancha. In that sense the understanding most Americans have of things Indian is distorted. Isolated pieces of information may be correct, but their interpretation is often misleading because it is drawn from too narrow a context or because it has missed the particular flavor of India. Not for lack of interest or intelligence, Americans and Asians, despite all the news coverage in recent years, are really strangers. Historical perspective is absent. The history of India is long, complicated, and as full of confusing names as a Russian novel; only those who have some acquaintance with the culture can make much of it.

Out of an urge to know India better, the idea for this book was born. It attempts to make personal one small slice of the Indian past to bring it alive, to populate it with individuals who ate, slept, made love, pursued their will-o'-the-wisps, did their duty as they saw it, kept up with fashion and ran into debt in doing so, even as you and I. But they did these things in a way of life so different from ours as to seem straight out of the Arabian Nights. That way of life is now gone, swept out by the political and social changes of this century which laid the foundation for the democratic society that now exists in India.

Hyderabad moved from a feudal to an industrialized society within the span of one generation, many of whom are alive today. From a personal administration to the impersonal rule of law, from a monarchy to a republic, from an agricultural to an industrial economy, from people-helpers to mechanical helpers—such moves are generally considered signs of progress. Whether liking the changes or not, people are having to accommodate themselves to a quite altered way of life. To see how they are managing, the book concludes with a brief look at the present. We hope in this process to get some impression of what the changes have cost and what got lost along the way that could still be useful.

To knit together the raveled and disjoined pieces of a society is a good thing. When one is young and groping for an identity, the central question is "Who am I? What may I become?" As one grows older, the focus shifts to "Who were we? What did we come from?" A society as well as an individual may draw strength from knowing that others in the historical lineage have had similar problems and have coped.

In choosing which small slice of the past to look at, Hyderabad suited our purpose admirably as a culture recognizably Indian in all its significant essentials. Yet far from being just any small slice, it is a distinctive one. The North and South, the East and West are sections of India with their own distinguishing characteristics; Hyderabad is at the crossroads of them all. The sixth city in the country, it is one of the two major ones (Lucknow being the other) in which Muslim and Hindu cultures have profoundly influenced one another, giving the lie to the often-repeated assertion of a traditional enmity between the peoples of the two religions. It is a city in which many cultural strains are intermingled: Persian and northern Islamic, with the Hindu culture of the South, itself a blend of Maratha, Telegu, and Tamil influences, and last of all a little of the Western world. Through all the changes of wars and social upheaval, Hyderabad's continuity has remained solid and is, if anything, more disturbed now by modern industrialization and the political shuffling following independence than it was by events of the intervening centuries.

Mahbub Ali Pasha, whose reign spanned the turn of the century, was the last ruler of Hyderabad to live in the style that the West is pleased to think of as "Oriental Potentate," wielding a power that acknowledged no democratic limitations. The social organization was still feudal, but not in any sense primitive. It was highly cultivated, with a grace of manner and, above all, a tolerance and mutual respect between components which could speak to our generation if we would listen.

THE DAYS OF THE BELOVED is neither traditional history nor traditional biography. It is a book about people: it attempts to re-create the atmosphere of the days of Mahbub Ali Pasha by depicting the lives and manners of a cross section of the people of Hyderabad. Individuals have been chosen for this as representatives of their class or rank. That the very poorest are omitted is not to suggest that they did not exist. Rather, as was common in the nineteenth century, they were not particularly influential in determining the tone of the society. Moreover, although their lives have probably changed less than those of any of the levels of society at which we have looked, it is now almost impossible to get first-hand information on them pertaining to the years around 1900. As usual, extreme poverty was not productive of either longevity or legends.

This book has been written by two persons: one an American for whom Hyderabad is a second home, the other an Indian whose heritage is the culture written about. Apart from a certain amount of necessary background reading, it is by and large oral history, based on conversations with all the traceable eighty- and ninety-year-olds in the city and many sixty- and seventy-year-olds who remember their earliest childhood and the stories their parents told and retold them as children.

What the book relates is true, not in the sense of scientific accuracy but in the sense that people today do believe that things happened in the way told here. For the most part, we also believe; where memory has re-formed history, it has surely done so in the direction of the heart's desire. If the memories are not completely accurate as to "the facts," then they tell us all the more clearly about the things that people valued in a society which is now gone. Our method in approaching this work has been shaped by that understanding, together with our consciousness that the memories of a generation that knew the days of Mahbub Ali Pasha at first or even at second hand are a treasure which is rapidly being eroded by time.

Gossip, of course, can also survive in people's memories. Over a few questions we had a difficult task to sift reports that had a basis in fact from those that seemed to be only unsubstantiated hearsay. Occasionally this process involved giving up tantalizing leads, for laws pertaining to libel in India protect the dead as well as the living, and with the type of material dealt with here, the odds are heavily against finding hard evidence so many years after an event. For some readers this cautiousness may leave an impression of partiality, but that at least is closer to our design than the opposite position: we are not out to write a sensational exposé but to capture the spirit of an era.

In a different attempt to capture the original spirit, we owe apologies to the late Maharajah Kishen Pershad and to his fellow poet, Fani, for the liberties we have taken in translating their work. To people who know only the literal rendition of the words, Persian poetry sounds either platitudinous or nonsensical. Rather than this, we risked having it sound like the insides of greeting cards in order at least to be suggestive of the poet's philosophy or sentiment. To give them their due, what we have translated is considered skillful poetry in the original language.

In the matter of spellings, a considerable latitude has been exercised. Because translation from Indian languages involves transliteration, the same word may appear in a variety of English spellings. In the case of proper names we have followed the spelling favored by the individuals to whom they belonged. Thus Maharajah Kishen Pershad spelled his title with a final *h*, whereas the Raja of Wanaparthy did not. In common usage are four different spellings for Husain, a name which is about as popular among Muslims as Joseph among Christians. For words other than names we have consulted three guides: dictionaries, which sometimes vary from one another; the form that sounded to our ears phonetically the most accurate; and general usage in Hyderabad. In the end, one simply makes a choice.

The people who so generously shared their memories with us, or who led us to others who could, prefer to remain anonymous. Those whom we can acknowledge publicly are Nawab Ghazi Jung Bahadur, who died in September, 1971, at the age of ninety-four, and Roy Mahboob Narayan of the Guna Bharat Vardhak Library in Hyderabad, without whose unstinting help much of our task would have been more difficult. To them and to all the others we owe a debt of gratitude, not only for helping us with this book but, in the process, for broadening our understanding and increasing our knowledge of the city which they and we love.

All data from the British point of view are from the India Office Records, Foreign and Commonwealth Office, 197 Black-friars Road, London SE 1. To that staff we express our gratitude for their numerous trips up and down to search out records and their patient explanations of the complex systems for retrieving the data.

Of non-Hyderabadis who have given generously of their time to read and criticize the manuscript, mention must be made of James M. Bray, in Hyderabad, and Robert G. Kirkpatrick, Jr., of the University of North Carolina at Chapel Hill. Rolf Lynton's guidance has been invaluable in establishing priorities and in sustaining our focus, partly through his ability consistently to cut through to what is significant. Isabel Kingsley Arms, by her painstaking comments on each chapter, has greatly increased the readability. To Daphne Reddy, who cheerfully took on the job of typing interview notes and manuscript that often resembled squirrel tracks, our special thanks.

Finally, we salute our spouses and children—husband Rolf and children Maya, Nandani, and Devadas in Chapel Hill; and husband Rajan and son Mohan in Hyderabad—for their qualities of perceptivity, enthusiasm, and endurance, which allowed us to indulge our passion for this work. In a very real sense they have been partners in this enterprise. Now that it is completed, we hope they will also share our sense of satisfaction at having attempted it. To them we say now, Salaam Aleikum, Peace be with You!

Chapel Hill, North Carolina   H. R. L.
Hyderabad, Deccan   M. R.

Contents

SOCIAL PYRAMID OF MAHBUB ALI PASHA'S HYDERABAD

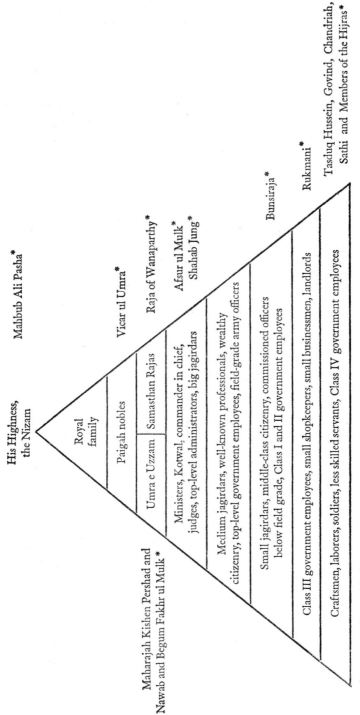

His Highness, the Nizam
Mahbub Ali Pasha*

Royal family

Paigah nobles
Vicar ul Umra*

Umra e Uzzam | Samasthan Rajas
Raja of Wanaparthy*

Ministers, Kotwal, commander in chief, judges, top-level administrators, big jagirdars
Afsur ul Mulk*
Shahab Jung*

Medium jagirdars, well-known professionals, wealthy citizenry, top-level government employees, field-grade army officers

Small jagirdars, middle-class citizenry, commissioned officers below field grade, Class I and II government employees
Bunsiraja*

Class III government employees, small shopkeepers, small businessmen, landlords
Rukmani*

Craftsmen, laborers, soldiers, less skilled servants, Class IV government employees
Tasduq Hussein, Govind, Chandriah, Sathi and Members of the Hijras*

Maharajah Kishen Pershad and Nawab and Begum Fakhr ul Mulk*

* Representative persons in text

Chapter I

The City

On a summer day in 1908, an old woman was picking her way carefully through the colorful throngs that filled the narrow streets of Hyderabad, Deccan. The once-black burqa which covered her from head to ankle-bracelets, now turned gray from long exposure to sun and dust, scarcely hid the frailty of her shoulders. She stepped along purposefully despite her limited view of the world through the net of the eyehole. Near the palace a ragged fellow whose face was scarcely visible under his dirty turban jostled her so that the brass food-carrier nearly flew out of her hand. "Room enough for a hundred here, but not for you and me," she snapped.

Before the words were out, she felt a strong, steadying hand under her elbow, while a pleasant voice soothed her with polite apologies. "It is hot for you to be out, mother," the stranger continued gravely. "Where do you go at this hour?"

"Aiee! I am taking food to my son who is a guard at the palace of the Nizam, may God protect His Highness," she replied. "He should have come home hours ago, when the gates opened. No doubt that swine of a relief hasn't turned up again, may mud fall in his mouth! So old women have to be running about in the heat. He will be wanting his food."

"I also am hungry," the man commented wistfully. "It is a long time since I have eaten."

"I am sorry for you, baba," the old woman said, "but my son—"

"He is fortunate; he has someone to care about him," interrupted the stranger, eyeing the stack of brass containers which made up the toshdan in the woman's hand.

Suddenly her tone changed, charged with pity. "Arrai! There is enough for two if you don't eat too much." Stepping back to the crumbled remains of a mud-and-thatch hut, she invited him to follow. "Come, sit here and eat a mouthful." She handed him the toshdan and he squatted near her, back respectfully turned while he ate. Then, reassembling the container and returning the toshdan to her with expressions of gratitude, he disappeared again into the crowd.

The old woman looked after him for a moment, shaking her head, and then continued on her way until she found her son at his station near the palace gate. Scolding him gently for not coming for his food, clucking over the unreasonableness of guards who did not show up for duty, and explaining in a few words why he would find less food than usual, the mother stooped and cleared a spot on the floor of his shelter, smoothing the dust from it with her hands before setting the toshdan there and opening it to spread out the dishes for her son's meal.

With a sharp intake of breath she stopped in mid-gesture, staring at the container in which the food had been replaced with gold pieces. Comprehension dawning, she sank to her knees, murmuring, "Huzoor (His Highness)!" And she was right, for it had been the Nizam himself whom she had fed. It was a known thing that occasionally Mahbub Ali Pasha disguised himself as a poor man and wandered among his people, learning their woes, rejoicing in their well-being, discovering what they needed or feared and what was good among them.

By the time the woman and her son had penetrated his disguise, Mahbub Ali Pasha was far away. He was headed in the direction of Char Minar, the four-towered structure astride the intersection of the four main streets of the city. It had been built in 1589 by Mohammad-Quli Qutub Shah, the king whose seat was Golconda Fort some fifteen miles away, to commemorate the spot where he caught his first glimpse of Bhagmati, the Hindu girl who captured his heart and in time became his queen. When the Golconda kingdom fell to Emperor Aurangzeb in 1687, followed shortly by the virtual dissolution of the Moghul Empire, Asaf Jah I chose the green and park-filled city of Hyderabad, rather than the walled fort of Golconda, for his capital, and Char Minar became the heart of the city.

Reaching his destination, Mahbub picked his way among the scribes who filled the ground-floor area. On pieces of carpet or on rush mats, they sat cross-legged about a central fountain, their glazed earthenware inkpots and stacks of paper around them. The affluent among them had low, slanting desk-tops on which to write; others used a smooth wooden board balanced on a knee. Business was always brisk; the illiterate majority needed not only letters to relatives in the villages, but also chits to their economic betters to seek relief or favors. Even if a man could read and write, the odds were heavily against his being able to use the flowery, highly Persianized phrases required for petitions. Mahbub stood to watch one being written. The quill glided smoothly over the handmade paper, the calligraphy making a handsome design. "After kissing your feet, your humble slave begs to bring to your honor's worthy notice . . ."

Turning away, Mahbub climbed the uneven stairs that spiraled to the mosque at the very top, passing the several stories where schools of philosophy had once been housed so that the students could look down on the bustle of life below and realize that all was vanity. "Vanity, indeed," he said to himself with a smile,

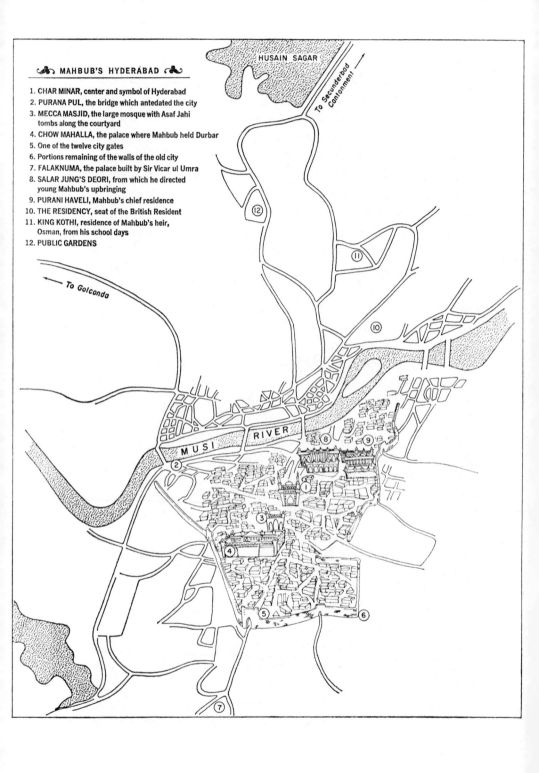

MAHBUB'S HYDERÁBAD

1. CHAR MINAR, center and symbol of Hyderabad
2. PURANA PUL, the bridge which antedated the city
3. MECCA MASJID, the large mosque with Asaf Jahi tombs along the courtyard
4. CHOW MAHALLA, the palace where Mahbub held Durbar
5. One of the twelve city gates
6. Portions remaining of the walls of the old city
7. FALAKNUMA, the palace built by Sir Vicar ul Umra
8. SALAR JUNG'S DEORI, from which he directed young Mahbub's upbringing
9. PURANI HAVELI, Mahbub's chief residence
10. THE RESIDENCY, seat of the British Resident
11. KING KOTHI, residence of Mahbub's heir, Osman, from his school days
12. PUBLIC GARDENS

HUSAIN SAGAR

To Secunderbad Cantonment

To Golconda

MUSI RIVER

letting his thoughts follow his gaze down the streets. Facing west he looked into Lud Bazaar, named for a spoiled and petted Qutub Shahi princess. On the right-hand side for a distance of at least a furlong, every shop was a bangle shop, walls lined from floor to ceiling with the brightly colored circlets of glass, enameled brass, or lac, plain or studded with beads or stones, until it seemed as though every conceivable color could be matched and every taste satisfied there.

Facing these was a succession of small shops selling the myriad essentials for a fastidious woman's toilet: sandalwood paste, perfumed oils for the hair, the long black strands of cotton ending in decorative tassels which the girls braided into their plaits to make them look thicker and longer, the red powder for the bride to put into the parting of her hair, the glitter with which her eyelids and forehead were decorated. Beyond these were displayed bright saris and cloth of every color, and sequins and beads for embellishing them. In short, here were available innumerable things to help a new bride make her husband happy. It was truly said that no bride in Hyderabad was sent from her father's house without at least ten trips on her behalf to Lud Bazaar.

Turning southward, Mahbub could see the high roof of Mecca Masjid, the great mosque where the crowd at noonday prayers on Fridays spilled out into the streets. In its broad courtyard, idlers gathered to spend a sociable hour, while others came to feed the doves that flew down from their nests under the high eaves and covered the flagstones like a carpet whenever grain was scattered there. Without actually being able to see them at the edge of the courtyard, Mahbub could visualize the graves of his ancestors in a long row, each protected by a low marble fence, while behind the mosque and back-to-back with it stretched the acres of Chow Mahalla, his late father's residence, which was now used mainly for durbar. From beyond the great entrance arch of the mosque came the noise of the makers of gold and silver leaf used for decorating food. They filled the air with the hypnotic sound of wooden hammers pounding on the leather wallets within which the leaf was beaten to tissue-paper thinness.

Leaning over the balcony railing, Mahbub stretched his neck to see the flower stalls opposite the mosque, imagining he could smell their heady scent even at that distance. Jasmines and roses, marigolds and scented lilies lay heaped in baskets big enough for a child to curl up in. Nimble fingers had strung and tied them for all the different needs they served: garlands for officers who were newly appointed or retiring; garlands for travelers arriving or departing; garlands for the little boy who had been circumcised, for the tiny girl who sat for the ceremony of the first braid, or for children who took the name of Allah for the first time; garlands to put round the neck of a god, and loose flowers for puja; garlands heavy with tinsel for the bride, along with small circlets for her arms and wrists; the sehra for the groom, a band of flowers to tie around his forehead from which strings of jasmine fell from head to toe, forming a curtain in front of his face; half-moons of fat buds to tie round a lady's chignon, the buds opening with the warmth of her body to release their perfume. No beauty was fully realized or emotion fully expressed without the aid of flowers.

Recalling himself from his reverie, Mahbub walked across to the east balcony, from where he looked into the street of the gold- and silversmiths and the dealers in pearls and gems. The shops on the right-hand side were built against the walls of the deoris of the great Shia nobles, chief among them the Salar Jungs, whose domain stretched all the way down to the river. Above the shops on the left of the street, a second story held the houses of pleasure from where the singing girls were summoned to entertain the wealthy with their music and dancing—or were just summoned.

Down below were made jewelry and ornaments of all kinds, magnificent pieces turned out by craftsmen sitting cross-legged on the floor and blowing through their slender pipes to direct the flame from their burners precisely at the spot on the work where it was required. They sorted precious gems with delicate pincers, hammered intricate designs into gold and silver, threaded pearls, and fashioned the beautiful jewelry for which Hyderabad was famous. The silversmiths produced every conceivable article and ornament, from cooking vessels to buttons, from elaborately woven or embossed belts to elaborately carved bridal bedsteads.

Beyond the smiths were the bookshops, supplying for the intellect the enchantment that the smith supplied for the eye. The standard assortment was there, but the most desired were books of philosophy and poetry to help the soul either weep or sing, and songs for the heart to sing of the beloved.

Finally, from the north side of the balcony, Mahbub looked down to his left at the delicatessen shops. At the entrance to one a man sat grilling ground, spiced mutton wrapped about long skewers; beside him, another fried hot, savory puffs in a deep pan. From the dark regions at the back a boy emerged with a huge tray piled high with hot, freshly baked kulchas, large flat buns which the customers seized, also helping themselves from a big brass platter heaped with finely sliced raw onions, chopped fresh mint leaves, and quartered limes to give zest to the appetite. Across the road he could see the sweetmeat shops. His mouth watered at the sight of piles of golden jellabies, their pretzel shapes filled with heavy syrup; brown balls of gulab jamun bobbing in rose-scented syrup; lacy doilies of almonds ground with sugar and baked; pak, green with pistachio; or sweetened milk solids cut into squares on which silver leaf caught the sunlight. Some of the sweetmeats contained a trace of the local derivative of hashish, to produce in the consumer a mild glow of well-being.

"Truly," His Highness murmured to himself, quoting a popular saying, "happiness radiates from Char Minar." Of the thirteen million people in the Nizam's Dominions, the happiest no doubt were the half million who lived in its shadow. With all the different levels of society symbiotically related to each other, Hyderabadis existed in a nearly self-sufficient pyramid. At the apex were the wealthy and powerful, whose tastes and interests determined and employed the efforts of those below them. In return for supplying the goods and services which allowed the uppermost families to live in luxury, the others were assured of a reasonably secure existence with leisure to enjoy the fruits of their labors and to take part in the culture to which they all belonged.

From his vantage point on Char Minar, Mahbub Ali Pasha could see homes representing many levels of this pyramid, snuggled against one another, often sharing a wall. Many of the shops and dwellings of the simple people were actually let into the walls of deoris, the city palaces of the wealthy which often covered an entire block each. Hidden behind their high walls and the shops, the deoris consisted either of a number of separate buildings set in gardens, or of a single extensive building made up of successive quadrangles, each containing a courtyard with garden and fountains. The word "deori" originally meant a hut; through long usage as a deprecating way to refer to one's mansion, it had come to refer specifically to this style of architecture.

In the spaces between the deoris were more modest dwellings. Groups of thatched huts sheltered laborers, porters, cartmen, itinerant jugglers and acrobats, village craftsmen. More substantial dwellings, roofed with country tiles and sometimes huddled together to share walls, housed the families of artisans, domestics, soldiers in the army of the Nizam or of one of the Paigah nobles, clerks on the first rung of the ladder of government service, or small shopkeepers. Here and there a slightly larger, more solid construction with a tiled or flat roof bespoke a shopkeeper who had done well, an officer, or a white-collar worker such as the pyrokar, who ran about in offices and courts submitting petitions and obtaining copies of documents for his customers. Interspersed among all these were lines of tiny shops, many of them no more than booths set against the high wall of a deori, catering to the daily needs of the surrounding populace.

Satisfied with his reconnoitering, Mahbub bounded down the stairs and reentered the rabbit warren of lanes and alleys which, aside from the clear pattern of the four streets, made up the city's traffic-ways. Plunging into the crowd, he exchanged a word here, stopped there to buy a cup of tea from a street vendor and to listen to the conversations among the other customers. Intent on their own errands, few people gave a second glance to the ragged fellow strolling among them. Far more noteworthy were Chaoushes, descendants of Arab mercenaries, with their daggers and long muskets; Pathans with hands and belts full of the five weapons which constituted their standard armory; merchants in their gaily painted palanquins, followed by runners bearing their hookahs, pandans, and other items similarly essential to a deskbound day; nobles on horseback, with grooms running alongside and holding onto the horses' tails, preceded and followed by armed retinues of mounted and foot soldiers.

More elephants than any other single city could boast picked their way gingerly down streets so narrow that two of them could barely pass, while the more privileged children returning from school, or ministers from their offices, called greetings to one another from comfortable howdahs atop the beasts. The most prestigious ministers sat in elaborate amaris, the canopied howdahs of a particular design whose use was restricted to those few on whom the Nizam had bestowed that signal honor and, often, the amari itself as a gift. Camels, saddle blankets flapping in the breezes, strode the streets on their long legs and gazed superciliously on the more earthbound creatures around them, while their masters dozed atop their load. Threading their own way through this traffic were packs of pariah dogs, sacred bullocks wandering at will, and goats—first assistants to the scavengers: all jostled and shouted at by coolies with head-baskets of cabbages, of bangles, of fruits from the hills or dung from the streets or stones for a building under construction.

As he moved away from Char Minar, Mahbub stopped idly by a kirana shop selling grain and sugar, spices from a stack of small drawers built up one wall, oil from bulk tins where settling dust made a black film on the covers, and brilliant red chilies arranged like rosettes in big baskets. He watched the shopkeeper weigh an order. The scales stood dead even. "What, Sait Sahib, are you weighing pearls?" complained a woman who had come to buy. "Put in a little more, in Allah's name. It is for a sick child."

A boy and a man waiting their turn guffawed. "These are the

pearls that are building the Sait Sahib's new house!" the man teased.

The shopkeeper frowned. "All right, sister, take!" he said grudgingly as he threw in a few more grains, tipping the scales a fraction in her favor.

Further along toward the outer ring of the city, Mahbub turned in at the opening in a wattle fence to watch a carpenter working on a rath, one of the bullock-drawn canopied carts that provided much of the transport for the middle and poorer classes. He struck up a conversation, squatting to watch the carpenter drill a hole with a bit moved by a bowstring while holding the wood in place with his toe. Nearby a tree trunk had been balanced on high saw-horses. One workman stood on top of it, pulling upward a cross-cut saw which his partner underneath then pulled down again. Their day had been spent producing planks in this way and the sweat glistened on their bare torsos. The logs had come in from the districts by bullock—one or two good-sized logs balanced between a pair of wheels—while the bullocks' owner walked alongside his animals. Young boys, sons of the carpenters or apprentices of the same caste, were busily chipping off the bark and throwing it on a heap for sale as kindling.

On the next street were the blacksmiths, long rows of them working at their anvils, each in his own tiny space. The smithies were low sheds, completely open on one side, where soot-blackened apprentices called sociable insults to one another as they worked the bellows.

Further on the clacking of wooden looms, made by local workmen, proclaimed the huts of the weavers, who produced coarse cloth for workmen and their families to wear, to sleep on, or to sit under in the raths. Outside the huts, women and girls carded and spun, while men stirred copper cauldrons of dye boiling over wood fires.

The day was cooler by now. The colorless, almost yellow sky of midday had given way to the returning blue of evening. Like horses headed for the stable, people in the streets quickened their pace. Work was over for the day and now was the hour for pleasure, even for the poorest. Gardens in the city and along the river began to blossom with saris and turbans in the bright blues, greens, oranges, and purples and checkered red and blacks that were favored by the people. Mahbub stopped to listen to the betting on a cockfight which had attracted a noisily enthusiastic crowd, refused to have his fortune told, and caught bits of a discussion of a famous singer who could be heard that evening.

A wrestling enthusiast, he stopped longest at a local gymnasium to watch a match in the wrestling pit. These neighborhood gymnastic centers, he knew, were maintained by the patronage of one or another noble and were open to anybody without fee. If young men who came there regularly for instruction and exercise gave presents of clothing or sweets to the coaches on festival days, that was their pleasure, not a condition of participation. The young men in the pit were evenly matched and clearly not beginners. Presently the coach intervened. "That's enough now," he admonished the athletes. "Always remember, you do not wrestle in order to put your opponent down but to develop your own chests."

Another few minutes' walk brought Mahbub Ali Pasha to the big yellow wooden gate set in the entrance arch of his own palace, Purani Haveli. He walked nonchalantly past the guards, elated by the hours he had spent among his people. But his contact with them was not quite over for the day, as it turned out. By the time he had bathed and dressed and was ready to appear once more in his regal aspect, the palace ears had picked up and its whispers had reported to him the sequel to the story of the guard whose meal was turned to gold. Fortune such as that does not remain secret for long. When the news reached Tipu Khan, that wily captain of the guard thought to cash in on it himself, so he went to his underling and asked about it. Alternately pretending not to believe the story and dropping hints about what would happen to a man possessing stolen *ashrafis,* he had managed to relieve the guard of his windfall. In a fury, Mahbub Ali Pasha summoned Tipu Khan and, whip in hand, recovered the full amount from the frightened and repentant captain. This time it was publicly restored to the guard so that no one should be able to question his title to it.

What Mahbub Ali Pasha did not see on this day's outing was any part of the newer sections of the city. The old walled town had burst its shell and expanded across the river and beyond, in the direction of the tank bund which connected it with Secunderabad. Not only had great nobles built palaces outside the walls—such as Sir Vicar ul Umra, Fakhr ul Mulk, and Afsur ul Mulk. Institutions had also grown up across the river, in the new sections of the city—the general hospital, the Residency, and the big Anglo-Indian church and the school associated with it. Merchants had established themselves in this growing area and there were busy, teeming bazaars on both banks.

Joining these two sections were four bridges. The first, Purana Pul, was built in 1578 by Sultan Ibrahim Qutub Shah. According to legend, on an occasion when the river was in flood, his son Mohammad-Quli had forced his steed across the roaring torrent to keep a romantic appointment. The king decided not to give the prince any further opportunity to prove his passion by endangering his life, and ordered the bridge built, to be completed before the next monsoon season. Eventually the young prince married his love and built Char Minar to commemorate the spot where he had first seen her. This story has survived repeated denials by scholars and become a much-loved part of popular folk-lore. In fact, Purana Pul gave access to a new and open area for a carefully-planned capital city, with Char Minar as its focus. The plans, drawn up under Mohammad-Quli in the 1580s, included provision for 14,000 shops and for baths, caravanserais, and other public facilities.

So Purana Pul existed before Hyderabad, and long before the coming of the first Nizam. It was customary to record the date of public works and other important buildings by means of a chronogram in Persian verse. A chronogram is an inscription in which certain letters are made to stand out. Those letters, if put together, reveal the date. Once a chronogram is translated it completely loses its original function of dating a structure but may give interesting clues as to its purpose or importance. The chronogram which establishes 1820 as the date when Purana Pul was repaired describes the bridge as "safe from flood like a pearl in the oyster," and so it was, for when the floodwaters of 1908 subsided and it once again became visible, it proved to be the only one of the four bridges not to have sustained major damage.

People crossing these four bridges, which were all on a level with the banks, looked down twenty feet or more to see the River Musi (Moses). During most of the year it was a peaceful stream, small enough in many places for an agile man to jump across. Except during monsoon, most of its four-hundred-foot bed was dry, a fruitful place for growing melons, as the steep banks absorbed the warmth of the sun and poured it out during the cool nights. Washermen laid out their laundry on the river bed to dry and bleach in the sun. The river had its source only fifty miles to the northwest of the city: between those two spots its water was detained in no less than 788 tanks (artificial lakes) which supplied the water by which the second annual crop of paddy was irrigated. It was a working stream, a useful, contributing member of society, pleasant and undramatic. No one would have suspected it of treachery.

But on Monday, September 28, 1908, there occurred a flood of such catastrophic proportions that it still haunts the imagination of Hyderabadis. The rainfall had been less than normal since June, usually the period of the rainy season. In the third week of September a cyclonic storm formed in the Bay of Bengal, crossing the coast and reaching Hyderabad on the 26th. It brought rain which fell unceasingly for forty-eight hours, now building up to a downpour, now settling in to a steady soaking rain, until the ground was saturated and the tanks were full. The river rose more than twenty feet in six hours, and by Sunday evening was lapping at the doorsteps of the houses along the banks.

Sometime in the night, the storm suddenly became a cloudburst. One after another, the tanks gave way. When the two largest were breached in quick succession, their combined waters rushed down the valley in an uncontrollable mass and hurled themselves against the bridges, buildings, and rampart wall of the ill-fated city. Water headed up behind Purana Pul and breached the city wall about three o'clock in the morning.

From the pen of an eyewitness we have the following account:

Nobody thought that the water would be able to come right into the city. . . . With astonishing speed and strength it took on the aspect of an ocean which wound its way with great noise and grew in every direction. To describe the scene the pen has no strength, language has no words, the tongue has no power. That dead of night, at the end of the days of the moon, was blacker than can be described. On top of this the all-pervading waters from the sky, billowing upon the earth like a blanket of smoke, were a dreadful calamity, no less than doom upon the sleeping, unwitting city. . . . The water was flowing from the roofs of those great houses of which the steps had never thought to be wet. Even in the streets and thoroughfares far away, the water was high enough to drown an elephant. Those who had climbed on the roofs of houses and the tops of trees to save themselves were being washed away with those very houses and those very trees. Children saw with their own eyes their parents, husbands their wives and children, brothers their sisters, friends their friends, washed away, gasping their last. Nobody could help anybody else; each was concerned for his own life and the flood was increasing every moment. And on this terror and confusion the dawn broke but the dawn was no less than doom.[1]

[1] The eyewitness descriptions of the flood have been translated directly from the Urdu of Syed Khursheed Ali in *Adeeb,* Toofan Number, September–December, 1908, published by the Sahifa Press, Chaderghat, Hyderabad. The entire number deals with the flood and consists of a detailed account written by Syed Ali, along with several poems by other contributors. In his conclusion to this special issue, Syed Ali writes, "I am ashamed . . . because the magazine is being issued after a lapse of four full months. . . . The flood of the River Musi, along with half of Hyderabad, took into the abyss of destruction the office of *Adeeb* and all its contents, together with the number for September, which was ready for publication, and of the property of the magazine nothing is left save the name of

Mahbub Ali Pasha was out early that Monday morning to assess the disaster. Possibly to keep a roof over his head in the continuing downpour, he chose to go in a motor car, which was still something of a novelty. The driver, perhaps relying too heavily on his name, Dolphin, stalled the car in deep water and a crowd quickly gathered to push it out. Even in the emergency their help was not taken for granted; their names were secured so that they could later on be called to the palace and given a sherwani and 50 rupees each. Those people who put their shoulders to the car, and many others who sent messages to Purani Haveli, began a continuous petition to their sovereign that he should take refuge at his hilltop palace, Falaknuma. About nine o'clock he bent to their pressure, but this did not mean that he left them, for in the midst of the crisis and on succeeding days he was at the flood scene many times, on horseback or elephant, or on foot among the suffering people. When at the palace, he was described as "restless and feverish," receiving almost minute-by-minute reports and issuing orders for whatever immediate relief appeared possible.

As soon as the seriousness of the crisis became apparent, Sir Afsur ul Mulk, the commander in chief of the army, set out on horseback to join his Nizam on the other side of the river. Three of the four bridges were impassable and, by the time Sir Afsur reached the last, Chaderghat, water was already pouring over it. Our eyewitness reports:

Hyderabad's first soldier was determined to use all his strength and pit his courage against the storm to serve his beloved sovereign. Without hesitation, he spurred his horse into the waters and eventually, struggling with all his strength against the sweeping waves, he overcame the wall of water and reached the other side when a crack of doom announced that the Afzul Bridge had collapsed and the same waves which had torn its bricks apart reached the Chaderghat Bridge.

Adeeb. Since we wanted the number concerning the flood to contain the full historical facts of the deluge and to be printed with special care, we decided to combine four issues in our Storm Number." The entire issue is printed on black-bordered paper.

But this courage was to be expected from the great commander in chief of Hyderabad.

By the time Sir Afsur reached there, the center of the city was one sea of water, spreading to a width of three-quarters of a mile. India's foremost hydraulic engineer, Shri Visvesvaraya, observed that "On account of obstruction and the great rush of water, the crest of the stream at the bridges rose several feet higher than along the adjoining banks. This was an extraordinary hydraulic phenomenon." In place after place along the banks, the city walls collapsed, carrying with them hundreds of people who had sought safety on their broad tops. Trees were tossed like jackstraws and people who had clung to them as suppliants rode them downstream as corpses.

About mid-morning the Brahmin pandits who frequented the palace and who were consulted about horoscopes and good and bad omens made bold to advise the ruler. "The river is an angry goddess and must be sent away," they said. "Your Highness should bid her farewell as you would a daughter, with the gifts and ceremony required for the occasion." Accordingly a golden tray was prepared containing a sari, pearls, yellow rice, condiments, the red kumkum powder used in worship, two coconuts encased in gold and silver, and a small oil lamp.

With this offering, Mahbub Ali Pasha mounted his horse and rode once again into the city in the pouring rain, heedless of the rivulets which streamed from his sideburns or were detained by his long hair until his collar soaked them up. Donning the sacred thread and joining his palms in a namaste salute of reverence to the river, he stepped carefully into the swirling waters as far as the slippery footing would allow and performed arati, moving the tray in a circular pattern as before the image during puja. Then he gently placed the tray upon the seething waters and immediately, so runs the story, the flood began to subside. Shri Visvesvaraya recorded that the fall was much more rapid than the rise: first noticed at 11:45 in the morning, it amounted to one foot in the first hour. By four o'clock the river had receded to its banks, and by eight had reached the level of an ordinary high monsoon flood.

Our eyewitness gives us a picture of the toll and of people's reactions:

From the main gate of the Residency to Mukram ud Dowlah's deori the city lay ruined and desolated. Within these boundaries was a close-packed market of the dead. Those silent drowned were fortunate whom the waves of the terrible flood had folded in their mantle and consigned to the ocean . . . with their souls, their bodies were also sent to nothingness. . . . But those unfortunate creatures who were trapped beneath fallen buildings and whose burial was in the mud where they breathed their last—the thought of them made the soul tremble. Whole families were buried beneath the houses they had built themselves. . . . Here lay the corpses of young stalwarts whose arrogance would not allow a fly to alight on their noses, a prey to the vultures. There, a bride of an evening, still in her wedding apparel, slept the eternal sleep on a bed of slime instead of one of silver. . . . Alas! What an agonizing scene it was!

The condition of those who escaped with their lives was no less gruesome. Though they were without graves and winding sheets, they were as if buried alive. Thousands of grief-stricken creatures who had lost their near and dear ones, their homes, everything, and had just succeeded in saving their bare lives by flight—to see their pitiable plight froze the heart. Some, weeping and with broken hearts, searched aimlessly for the houses in which they were born and grew up; some searched for the bodies of their loved ones, calling their names in the ruined shells of houses, at heaps of stones, in caves made by the waters. Some, their minds crazed by the storm, pulled aside the heaps of bodies, trying to identify their kin; some were trying to disentangle corpses from the branches of uprooted trees or to free them from the mud under which they lay. Those upon whose heads the skies had fallen wandered about helplessly, wailing and moaning and breaking their hearts, some for two or three, some for a whole family; and the sound of their agony shook one's very being.

In the midst of this desolation, Mahbub Ali Pasha went about comforting his people, inspiring them to do the work of rescue and burial, helping where he could. He ordered that his palaces be opened to shelter all comers, while his kitchens worked around the clock to feed them. He also distributed cloth for saris and dhotis. Following his example, the nobles provided Kashmir shawls against the cold and the merchants "emptied their shops for the relief of the stricken." Many of the nobles put palaces at the disposal of the homeless, while huts were hastily erected on the parade ground and other open spaces. In opening Asad Bagh palace and filling its grounds with additional temporary shelters, Nawab Fakhr ul Mulk provided special arrangements for the miserable women who had spent all their lives in purdah and were still trying to efface themselves in ruins and caves. Countless private individuals opened their homes, whether luxurious or humble.

On his rounds, Mahbub was stopped by an old man who lamented, "Oh, Your Highness, the river has taken everything I have and in my old age I am alone and homeless!"

Mahbub touched the old man gently. "How can you say you are homeless," he asked him, "when your slave has homes that are open and waiting for you to come?"

The full toll of the flood was never known, for so many people simply vanished, but estimates of the deaths ranged from ten to fifteen thousand, while a hundred thousand people, nearly a quarter of the city's population, were left homeless. A relief fund of 500,000 rupees was voted by the state and 1,000,000 rupees more was raised by public subscription. Of this amount, 100,000 rupees came from Mahbub Ali Pasha, 20,000 from Maharajah Kishen Pershad, and 5,000 from Nawab Fakhr ul Mulk. Donations flowed in from all over India, especially from Bombay.

In order to provide opportunity for people to deal with their own crises, the government declared an official holiday of ten days. For the self-respect of government servants and to enable them to resume duty after the moratorium, the Dewan (prime minister) ordered that all should be given a month's salary in advance, to be deducted in six later installments, except in the case of those on the lower levels of salary, who were excused from repayment.

Officers of the army, police, and accounts departments worked round the clock. Ten kitchens were set up, in various parts of the city, and were in operation from September 29 to October 13. When it was discovered that people unaffected by the flood were taking advantage of the free food and that it was encouraging the avoidance of work, the main kitchens were closed after a week's notice to the public, but some kitchens were continued for many more weeks to provide for destitute purdah women and for those who were obviously in distress. In fifteen days, 625,335 people were fed, at a total cost of 37,894 rupees. Considering that in those days a bag of wheat cost 4 rupees and a hundred eggs or sixteen chickens were to be had for a single rupee, the amount of food that was prepared in the kitchens must have been staggering.

Apart from the kitchens run by government, Mahbub Ali Pasha, out of his personal funds, set up four kitchens in the city and put his old schoolmate and whipping boy, Major Mumtaz Yar ud Dowlah, in charge of them. Long after the public kitchens were closed, the Nizam's bounty continued to feed 20,000 people a day. No one else could approach this level of generosity, but many people, not only the wealthy, dug deep into their resources to follow his example and went on feeding the poor long after the government kitchens were closed.

In addition to these major relief projects, and such matters as impounding and destroying grain which had been contaminated by the flood waters and posting twenty-four hour sentries to prevent looting, the government managed to maintain its concern for individual citizens. Wedding ceremonies were performed at government expense for 383 couples whose marriages had been arranged before the flood, and 371 students were supplied with books to replace those that had been washed away.

Mahbub Ali Pasha had been actively involved in the organization and carrying out of the relief operations from the first news of the disaster. Our eyewitness comments:

At the sight of the sufferings of his beloved people, he wept tears of blood. His sorrow, his sympathy, his eagerness to assist wherever he could were such as cannot be described in words. And this attitude of his engendered an enthusiasm in all those officers who were entrusted with relief work so that arrangements were most speedily and effectively got under way and there was reason to expect that the rest of the rehabilitation work would be as well and as quickly done, as in fact it was.

For many months after the flood, wandering minstrels roamed the city with their stringed instruments, collecting alms by singing stories of the tragedy. Gradually the debris was cleared, new housing was built, life resumed its predictable course, and wounds began to heal. In the long run, the imprint of tragedy may be less enduring than the effect of love and caring. So it was with Mahbub Ali Pasha's people, who remembered how he had shared their ordeal.

One noble, now in his nineties, remembers an occasion a year or so after the flood when the people's affection nearly caused a disaster. Mahbub had just come out of the mosque after Friday prayers and mounted his elephant. The crowd surged forward to see him, get near him, feel the blessing of his presence. The elephant was becoming restless in the crush, but the guards were not able to hold the crowd back. Fearful of a stampede, the Dewan, from his seat behind His Highness, signaled to the police to unleash their whips. The old noble adds: "One fellow lost his turban, another his kerchief. One even jumped out of his shoes in his hurry to move back." But they retreated only far enough to calm the elephant and stood calling down blessings on their Nizam.

Chapter II

Cavalcade and Kulchas

MAHBUB ALI PASHA's Hyderabad, to many people in this transistorized, plasticized, homogenized world of the 1970s, seems like an elegant fairyland where His Highness's whim was law, where jewels were real and coins were gold and even a beggar might know it was not a dream when a gold piece clattered into his alms bowl. Far from being a fanciful tale, there actually was such a world, not long ago. People still live whose memories stretch back to another generation, to the days of Mahbub Ali Pasha, that charismatic monarch whose name throughout the Victorian world was a synonym for the wealth and splendor of the East. The thought of him and of the times they lived in brings a radiance to their faces and makes their old eyes flash once more.

Some of the stories they tell concern the glittering opulence of the Nizam's court, which was so famous that all over India a gem merchant who came into possession of a particularly magnificent jewel thought first of Hyderabad. Even the intimate details of Mahbub's life were lavish, sometimes shared unwittingly with his subjects. For instance, anyone wishing to indulge a taste for perfumed French soap knew exactly where to go. The Nizam imported it by the gross. Every royal bath cost him at least one fresh bar, for a servant lathered him and before starting the rubdown skidded the soap across the marble floor to the door, where a partner retrieved it and added it to the week's savings. These they sold in the bazaar on Saturdays, dividing the profits between them.

Often the poor participated in the affluence by the simple expedient of asking. There is the story of a poor farmer who wrote to the Nizam that, having successfully married off his older daughters, he was now threatened with falling into the hands of the moneylenders in order to provide the dowry for a child of his old age. If the Nizam would kindly grant him 500 rupees, he would be spared this certain financial ruin. This letter appeared in the pile of papers that the private secretary brought away from his audience with the Nizam one morning. On it was a marginal notation in His Highness's handwriting, "Rs. 5,000 is sanctioned." Noticing the discrepancy, the prudent secretary returned it with the following day's papers, pointing out that only 500 rupees had been requested. Back it came again, this time with the notation, "Rs. 15,000 is sanctioned." The prudent secretary did not risk sending it in a third time.

Not only the poorest could command the Nizam's help. Hints that a certain worthy shopkeeper was having a bit of a hard time could result in the Nizam's carriage stopping in front of the shop on some afternoon drive. When the traditional courtesies had been observed, Mahbub Ali Pasha would wave his walking stick in an arc, declaring, "I'll take that." Having thereby purchased most of the goods in the shop, he would drive off, leaving his minions behind to negotiate precisely how much of the stock "that" included and to pay the asking price.

Nor did a man need to be a suppliant. Anything that touched

Mahbub's emotions strongly was likely to become the occasion for a spontaneous gift. There is a story about the five-year-old son of the commander in chief, whose capacity to absorb teasing the monarch overestimated. When Mahbub overstepped the bounds of his tolerance, the child unloosed a string of invective which would have added luster to a sailor's reputation. The horrified father, drawing his sword, offered to avenge the insult, but the Nizam only laughed. "He is a lad of spirit," Mahbub said. "Let him draw a mansab of 250 rupees." Mansabs were monthly payments to individuals or organizations. There were many forms: some mansabs were hereditary grants from the state as a reward for service; others were bestowed for a lifetime as a token of favor and were paid from His Highness's private treasury.

On and on they roll, these stories, until we begin to discern a pattern, and to suspect that this pattern has something to say to us about our own day. To understand it, we must know something of who the Nizams were and how they came by their resplendence. For this we have to look back a bit.

We look back to 1723—nine years before George Washington was born, and while George I was king of England. In Delhi a general bearing the title Nizam ul Mulk, "Regulator of the Realm," a descendant of military men and recently appointed vizier to the Moghul emperor, was sent by his sovereign to treat with Nadir Shah, the Persian emperor who had just won a decisive victory on the northern plains. He reported the encounter thus:

When Nadir Shah, in his extreme graciousness, cast his eye on me, he offered me personally the sovereignty of the Indian Empire. I at once answered, "By this command no benefit will accrue to either of us. . . . I, as a servant, will merit the notoriety of not being true to my salt, and your August self the odium of breach of faith." He was greatly pleased with my reply and honored me with his praise.

The following year Nizam ul Mulk resigned as vizier, in disgust at the intrigue and ineffectiveness surrounding the Moghul court, and resuming his earlier appointment as viceroy of the Deccan, retired eight hundred miles south to the rocky plateau that covers most of the triangle of South India. He had been in the Deccan several times before, to subdue the warring chieftains who moved in a northwesterly direction from Madras, and to repel the Maratha raiders who were based east and southeast of Bombay. In 1724, having made the decision to settle there forever, he established control over large sections of the area and welded it into one homogeneous kingdom.

Although he acted almost entirely on his own without reference to Delhi, he remained all his life nominally loyal to the emperor. In recognition of this loyalty, combined with the reality of his power in the Deccan, the emperor conferred on Nizam ul Mulk the title of Asaf Jah—that is, equal to the rank of Asaf the Seer, who was one of Solomon's ministers. It was this title that came to identify the dynasty which the Nizam founded, and the word Nizam, or Regulator, came to designate his descendants, the Muslim rulers of the largest state in India.

Before leaving Delhi for the last time, Nizam ul Mulk went to pay a farewell visit to Nizamuddin, the saint or holy man whose devoted disciple he was, to inform him of his purpose and to entreat his prayers and blessings. Nizamuddin offered him for refreshment on his journey some of the thin, round buns called kulchas. Nizam ul Mulk took a few and, on the saint's urging, finally accepted seven, which the saint tied in a yellow cloth. In the Deccan this gift was interpreted as meaning that his dynasty would last for seven generations. Nizam ul Mulk may himself have helped to perpetuate the belief, for in his will he admonished his sons: "If you follow in my footsteps, the present expenditure remaining the same, the resources of income which I possess will suffice for the next seven generations." For his flag he chose a kulcha set on a yellow background. Above it were the words "Azmut ul Illah"—"The Greatness of God"—and below it his name. This was the flag of the seven Nizams to the end of the dynasty, only the name below the kulcha changing from ruler to

• Delhi

Calcutta •

Bombay

BERAR

NIZAM'S
DOMINIONS

Hyderabad

Madras •

ruler. Eventually the legend came also to be commemorated in the official uniform. The pips which the Hyderabad police wore on their shoulders to designate rank were in the shape of kulchas.

A vast cavalcade had set out from Delhi with Nizam ul Mulk. Besides the commanders and the army, there were four noblemen from the Moghul court with their families; various administrators, both Hindu and Muslim; a staff of clerks and accountants; and learned and holy men. These were the people he needed to fill the whole range of posts that would form the nucleus of a feudal government, the foundations of a strength that was needed at home while he himself was constantly away from his capital consolidating his kingdom and securing its borders. To these faithful he granted lands and positions and titles (jagirs and mansabs) according to their station and service, as well as the right to write Asaf Jahi after their names, an honor exercised with pride by their descendants until the end of the dynasty. These were the premier nobles of his court in the Deccan. Along with them went the camp followers, merchants and moneylenders, singing girls and eunuchs, to seek fresh pastures and build new fortunes.

Asaf Jah I was a man a little larger than life, a description of whose qualities reads like a catalogue of the attributes of a leader. A wise and redoubtable warrior, he owed much of his power to such pacific virtues as compassion, respect for ways of life and worship other than his own, a sense of justice which assured the peasants that the profits from increased efforts would be theirs and not the tax collectors'. In his dying moments, Asaf Jah I advised his sons to live their lives under canvas, for rulers ought to be in constant touch with their dominions, but not to require the common soldiers and menials to accompany the retinue too far from their homes, as this would interfere with their domestic lives and the continuation of the species. Successive generations of this great man's descendants, however, declined into habits of rapacity, indulgence, and weakness difficult to reconcile with their virile ancestry.

This descent had been down a circular staircase. The first Asifiyas necessarily relied upon their peasants both for the loyalty which would produce stability at home in case of attacks on the borders or local uprisings, and for the confidence in the future which would encourage them to greater efforts on the land and thus to increased rents and other revenue. This acted as a rough-and-ready system of checks and balances. Breaking into this delicate balance, the East India Company offered the Nizams protection against internal and external threats in return for permanent payments for the support of the troops. Control of the troops quickly passed into the hands of the company, followed several decades later by an arrangement for ceding territories with known revenue to the company in place of subsidy.

Critics of the Asifiya dynasty suggest that the British buffer freed the Nizams from reliance on their subjects and therefore constituted a license to extortion and sensuality, while at the same time it increased the temptation to oppression in order to recover the cost of the heavier military expenditures. The interpretation can also be made that the Nizams were discouraged by the unlike-lihood of reversing the trend and resuming their power. Facing what seemed like the inexorable march of empire, they dared not oppose the British as Tipu Sultan had unsuccessfully attempted to do in Mysore, and therefore retired to the consolations of the zenana. Certainly the soft arms of women were more familiar to them than the weapons of a soldier-statesman such as their ances-tor was.

When Nizam ul Mulk died, at the age of seventy-eight, his sons greatly weakened their position by fighting among themselves over the succession, wherein two sons and a grandson were killed off before a third son entrenched himself sufficiently to secure the confirmation of the emperor as Asaf Jah II. With both strength and attention so sapped by the fratricidal wars that they were no longer able by themselves to control the Maratha raiders on their borders, they were tempting targets for the English and French, who had begun to play out in India, as elsewhere, rivalry for colo-nial supremacy. The French discovered, and effectively demon-strated to the Nizams, that Indian soldiers drilled and commanded by a handful of Europeans constituted a fighting force greatly superior to wholly indigenous, often "irregular," troops common in the Princely States. The British perfected this weapon in the shape of "subsidiary forces," which in due course became contin-gents supported by the revenues from ceded territories. Providing an obvious means of interfering first in the relations between Princely States and then in their internal affairs, these forces paved the way for an age of diplomacy and intrigue.

In those dealings the British were active gamesters, easily out-maneuvering the successors of Nizam ul Mulk. In the decade after his death, in 1748, they entered the Nizam's Dominions and, by a combination of clever diplomacy, economic leverage, and naked force achieved a position of power which delicately balanced the Nizam's own.

This bifurcation of the society was symbolized by the physical arrangements. The British Resident was established at Bolarum, a settlement several hours' distance by horseback from Hyderabad City. There and in adjacent Secunderabad he was surrounded by British officers and their families. With the presence of those officers and the men of their commands, Secunderabad became the largest cantonment in India. (Even for the Westerners, this was an appropriate name for a military base: Secunder, or Sikander, is the Persian form of the name Alexander.) Later, as the accommodation between the two powers became easier, a second Residency was established just across the river from the city.

By contrast, Hyderabad City was the focus of the indigenous life in the Dominions. It was a walled area with twelve gates, at whose heart Char Minar bestrode the intersection of the main streets. In time a representation of that four-towered building was embossed on the state coinage, to become a kind of trade-mark of the city. Within the city walls were the many palaces of the Nizam, chief among them Purani Haveli, his habitual residence, and Chow Mahalla, a home of kings since the days of the Qutub Shahis though eventually used by Mahbub Ali Pasha mainly for durbar, or royal audience. Within the walls also were the city residences of most of the nobles and officials.

Some reduction in this polarization had been achieved when hands were reached across the gap by the great Sir Salar Jung I. Becoming Dewan in 1853, he advanced as close to the Resident as his suspicious sovereign would allow, while keeping it eminently clear where his primary loyalty lay. Under Salar Jung's wise and strong guidance, the state entered a period of settled prosperity. When, in 1869, the Nizam Afzul ud Dowla died, leaving a three-year-old son, Mahbub, it was in an act of more than formal symbolism that Sir Salar Jung and the Resident each took a hand of the small prince and led him to the Musnud, the ceremonial rug and bolsters which by Hyderabad tradition represented the throne.

So long as they were seeking a foothold in the subcontinent, the British employees of the East India Company were required to learn the court language of the Princely States and use it in communications with the indigenous rulers. In Hyderabad, this meant Persian with its stylized phrases and flowery imagery. The expression for requesting a royal audience, for instance, was, "———— craves to see His Highness's feet." This phrase was once used as an instrument of revenge when Afzul ud Dowla was angry with a pushy Resident. The Englishman arrived at the durbar hall, only to be greeted by the Nizam's feet stuck out from under a silken curtain. When they were withdrawn a few moments later, the audience was over. By the time of Mahbub Ali Pasha's assumption, however, the British had established themselves in the position of paramount power, and they required that the Indian rulers be educated in English.

One of the petty ways used by the British for asserting their paramountcy was that of controlling the English versions of titles permitted to Indians. Indigenous rulers were "chiefs," or the most important were "princes." Attempts to use the title of prince for Mahbub's son brought immediate correction from the Government of India. The policy was to forbid terms such as "throne," "royal," and "reign," and degrees of kingly status, which could conceivably imply the "enjoyment by Native Chiefs of independence or of the main attributes of sovereignty." Similarly the Dewan could not be known as the prime minister, there being in the British view only one prime minister, the one in London. The man filling that function in an Indian state, according to the usage of the paramount power, was a minister. (But as there were other ministers in the Hyderabad Cabinet Council, we have tried to avoid confusion by retaining the original title of Dewan.)

Mahbub Ali Pasha, by the time he assumed full powers at the

age of seventeen, had no intention of being a puppet. Some of the elements in the continuing jockeying for power between him and the British are suggested in an incident during Mahbub's visit to Delhi as a young ruler, on the occasion of a durbar. Sometime before that, H.R.H. the Duke of Connaught, the third son of Queen Victoria, was an honored guest in the Nizam's Dominions and, on taking leave, had inquired whether there were anything he could do for his host.

Mahbub Ali Pasha indicated that there was. On arriving in Delhi for the next durbar, he would like an elephant to be brought to his railway carriage, as he found it beneath his dignity to alight on the platform and walk outside the station to seek transportation like an ordinary traveler. The royal guest agreed readily enough, but ran into opposition when he reported the conversation in Calcutta, the capital of British India. The Viceroy insisted testily that he had forbidden elephants inside the station and that it was beyond the prerogative of even a royal guest to countermand the order.

When time for the durbar came, the Nizam's party pulled into Delhi Central Station to find no elephant. A messenger, sent to bring one, returned with the news that an elephant was outside the station but was not allowed in. To say that a contest of wills followed is to misinterpret the Nizam's temperament. Mahbub Ali Pasha engaged in no contest. He simply ignored the fact of his arrival. He had his meals. He played cards with his nobles. He behaved as though this were an ordinary day in his palace.

Meanwhile other trains, bearing other princes and their retinues, piled up behind, unable to reach the station because the Nizam of Hyderabad would not get down. Two days later, under pressure from the mounting fury of the other princes, the Viceroy lifted the ban. With no visible show of emotion, Mahbub Ali Pasha mounted his elephant and the station was cleared.

Chapter III

Mahbub Ali Pasha, The Beloved

ᴅᴇᴄᴇᴍʙᴇʀ, 1911, was the date set for the great Delhi Durbar. His Majesty, George V, King of Great Britain and Ireland, and of the British Dominions beyond the Seas, Emperor of India, would become the first reigning British monarch to visit India, the largest gem in the chain of empire. For a year the preparations had been going on. The British king and the Indian princes and chiefs, who would gather with their retinues to meet him, were to camp together in an elaborate tent city set up to accommodate them. A special railway line was laid to serve the durbar camp. Preparations were being made for the food, housing, protection, entertainment, and all the other services that would be required for the quarter of a million people expected to stream into the ancient city. On December 7, under a Moghlai tent erected on the field, the king-emperor would receive the homage of the Indian princes. It was the high-water mark of the British Empire.

To the south, in a Princely State nearly the size of France, the reign of Mahbub Ali Pasha, Nizam Asaf Jah VI, was the high-water mark of the Nizam's Dominions. In his capital at Hyderabad, Mahbub had been making his plans to attend the durbar. Instructions had been issued for eight leading noblemen to accompany him. Sir Afsur ul Mulk, commander in chief of the army, was to be in charge of the camp at Delhi. The party would travel in the Nizam's private train and would include the most important figures at his court, together with secretaries, messengers, valets, butlers, cooks, and an assortment of jacks-of-all-trades, as well as a complement of the Nizam's women and their attendants. Before the preparations were complete, they would involve the Cabinet Council, the army, the palace staff, myriads of craftsmen, dozens of tailors, and hundreds of food handlers and suppliers.

None of this came to pass for Mahbub Ali Pasha. In August, with preparations still in their early stages, he collapsed and died within a few days. Although he was only forty-five years old, he had been Nizam for forty-two years.

The Baby Nizam

When, in 1869, the Resident and the Dewan together led the three-year-old Mahbub to the Musnud, the action symbolized a mutual interest which over the years was not often so harmoniously expressed. From then on, Mahbub's education was primarily under the direction of two men: Sir Salar Jung, the Dewan, gentle, respectful, indirect; and Claude Clerk, the British tutor, forthright, outspoken, independent. The tutor's post had first gone, on the Resident's recommendation, to John Clerk. When after one year he was forced by illness to return to England, he was succeeded by his brother, Claude, who remained throughout

Mahbub's minority. Under the British tutor Mahbub assumed what was called *statu pupillari,* together with a few classmates selected from among the sons of the nobles. The experience was designed to give the boys the equivalent of an English schoolboy's education. To that curriculum, Indian tutors added lessons in Persian and Urdu language and poetry, calligraphy, and the Koran.

Along with his own two sons, Salar Jung chose for this class Zaffer Jung, son of Khursheed Jah, the co-regent with the Dewan; Fakhr ul Mulk II; and Kishen Pershad, grandson of the Peshkar, the second-ranking official in the state. One English boy was included, Hugh Gough, son of a major employed by the state and widely respected for his loyalty to the Nizam. There were also a few lesser noblemen's sons who acted as whipping boys. These became necessary when the Victorian educational philosophy that knowledge entered a boy's head through the seat of his pants collided head on with the sanctity of the Nizam. Since it was unthinkable to lay a hand on the Shadow of God, the theory was apparently that lesser classmates by taking the blows due him provided the young ruler with a vicarious educational experience.

Besides the school hours, fixed days were allotted each boy when he should be in attendance at the palace from morning to night. To make the boys fully aware of their position and prestige on those occasions, an honors list was prepared, and so at the Birthday Durbar of 1874 came the spectacle of an eight-year-old monarch conferring titles on his playmates.

Father-figure, lawgiver, and subject were difficult roles for one man to balance in relation to one boy, but Sir Salar Jung juggled them with grace and skill. One day when Mahbub was about ten years old, the Dewan came to visit him. When lunch time arrived, the large white cloth called a dastarkhan was spread before the Musnud and covered with an assortment of sumptuous foods. The child pitched into the feast with a healthy youngster's appetite. Seizing a marrowbone and ignoring the spoon that came with it, he pounded the bone with his palm to dislodge the marrow. Seeing this from where he sat on the carpet, arms tightly folded in respect, Salar Jung quietly dispatched an attendant to his home for the five gold coins (ashrafis) which were his standard offering of respect and fealty—the nazar.

After young Mahbub had finished his lunch, Salar Jung placed the ashrafis on a handkerchief and presented them to His Highness. The Nizam asked what this nazar was for. Sir Salar Jung replied, "No, Your Highness, this is not nazar; this is a penalty. I, who am your slave, failed to teach you the use of the marrow spoon and so it is my fault that you do not know how to use it. So this is a fine I am paying for my failure."

Not long afterward the Dewan acceded to the longing of the common people to see their young ruler. A procession was taken out with Mahbub Ali Pasha seated in a yellow amari on a richly caparisoned elephant, accompanied by the entire army. The streets were thronged with people pressing forward and calling blessings on their young Nizam, while from the amari showers of gold and silver coins rained down upon them. The two regents sat behind their ward, Sir Salar Jung's usual inscrutable expression replaced by a look of happiness never seen on his face before or afterward.

When Mahbub Ali Pasha was sixteen, the Dewan began to initiate him into the secrets of the administrative process by having the highest officials come regularly to explain the workings of their departments. Early in 1883, Sir Salar Jung and Captain Clerk accompanied him on his first official tour of his Dominions. They spent some weeks in the western divisions, where the various officers provided on-the-job training in local administration. An incident at the start of the tour shows the differences in the styles of his Eastern and Western mentors.

From Ahmednagar, where the railway line ended, the party had to proceed toward Aurangabad by carriage. Some time was lost in fording a difficult stream, and the mood of the young Nizam became petulant. On reaching the camp which had been set up on the far side, Salar Jung admonished the others to hurry with lunch so that the party could make up for the lost time and reach Aurangabad on schedule. Mahbub, however, took a different course, sending word to Salar Jung that he chose to spend the night at the camp and continue on the following day. When the message was delivered, Salar Jung sent for the tutor to take counsel. Clerk offered to carry any message the Dewan saw fit to send. "Tell him from me in the softest words and the most gentle tone," said Salar Jung thoughtfully, "that he is at liberty to stay here as long as he likes, but that a program has been fixed, that a royal command should never be countermanded, and that punctuality is the pride of kings."

Captain Clerk relayed the message, but Mahbub refused to comply. The tutor pleaded, but Mahbub was adamant. Then Clerk became angry and told the young Nizam harshly that he should not countermand his own orders. Angry in turn, Mahbub sounded like any rebellious teen-ager: "You and Salar Jung are forcing me. I will not go. Let's see how you will make me." So saying, the defiant young ruler turned on his heel and disappeared into the inner room of his tent.

When Mahbub commanded Salar Jung to present himself for the meal, the Dewan bowed low, offering his customary five ashrafis as nazar. "Your slave retracts his plea and begs forgiveness and hopes for pardon," he said. Mahbub put both his hands on Sir Salar Jung's head. "I was hasty," he admitted shamefacedly. "I did not think. Of course you are right that orders should not be changed frivolously." After lunch the royal party proceeded to Aurangabad.

Even in the informality of life in the districts, the simple surroundings of a circuit bungalow or overnight camp did not produce a relaxation of palace etiquette. From the beginning Salar Jung had insisted that the Nizam was at all times to be treated with the deference due to a sovereign of his eminence, and this tone was maintained also by the other nobles. Here is an incident reported in the words of Sarwar Jung Bahadur, another of His Highness's tutors:

One evening when the Dewan, the Amir-e-Kabir and other nobles were in attendance, a vaporous cloud ascended the sky and it began to drizzle. His Highness was then on the verandah, and the nobles were standing below under the shade of some trees. I went forward and requested the Dewan to come on the verandah, as the rain had commenced to descend. The Amir-e-Kabir stared hard at me, but the Dewan smiled and said that that was the privilege of those like myself who attended on the person of the Highness, but as for themselves, they dare not go forward without being invited. Just then Mustakim Jung called out that all were commanded to come in. Such were the nobles, who maintained at all times the dignity of the Sovereign.

It was just as well that Mahbub and his courtiers were so well versed in their roles, for only a few days after returning from this tour Sir Salar Jung was permanently removed from the scene by an attack of cholera, leaving a bereft and momentarily bewildered young man to shoulder the responsibilities of state. With this, the European tutor could not help him much, partly because of his own strained relations with the Residency. Still, in spite of the differences in their temperaments, the bond that had grown up between the young Nizam and Captain Clerk lasted a lifetime. An English visitor to Hyderabad recorded that the Resident was trying to get rid of Clerk because "he is an independent man and is honest in looking to the Nizam's interests, instead of those of the Calcutta Foreign Office."

Within a year the recall of Captain Clerk had been accomplished, against his own wishes as well as those of Mahbub. We have a glimpse of him (or possibly of his brother; the reference is not clear) at Windsor Castle in November, 1896, when a lady attending Queen Victoria noted Clerk's reiterated opinion that another guest, a British diplomat, was a scoundrel who had robbed the Nizam of £60,000. Mahbub, on his side, when it came time to appoint an English tutor for his own son, first offered the post to Clerk.

In order to mark the end of the regency, the Viceroy came to

Hyderabad in February, 1884, to invest Mahbub Ali Pasha with full powers. It was the first occasion on which Hyderabad had been host to so distinguished a guest, and the first of many such during Mahbub's reign. It was a four-day gala, with as much advancing and retreating, bowing and posturing, mincing and gesturing, as though some vast minuet were being danced by a solemn assemblage of august personages. The Viceroy in his after-dinner speech described the Nizam's dinner party, its setting and entertainment, as "one of the most beautiful sights it has ever been my good fortune to witness."

The Nizam and the Sahibs

Although he had symbolically been invested with full powers by the representative of the British Raj, Mahbub Ali Pasha wrote a letter to his Dewan shortly afterward that showed his awareness of the extent to which the British were involved in the intrigues of his court:

I wish every day for one hour to study English and Persian. For Persian, Mirza Nasr Sahib is here, but for English I do not know which person is suitable. If an Englishman is necessary, then appoint one and inform me, but it should not be an Englishman of the Resident's choosing or a resident of the Residency area. And if you think that in order to call an Englishman the Resident will say, "Without my concurrence you should not call an Englishman," or, "He should be from the Residency area," then rather than this, it is better to remain quiet. Why unnecessarily call upon trouble to follow one?

Even at that early stage in his reign, Mahbub Ali Pasha had already had several run-ins with the British, some of them even before his investiture. After Salar Jung's death the power in Hyderabad was up for grabs, and intrigues among the nobles were matched by intrigues involving the Residency. Salar Jung I, in the early part of his career, had been much honored by the British for his key support to their cause during the uprising of 1857, but their gratitude was worn thin in the last few years of his life, when he developed an annoying habit of asking for the return of the Berar districts. His death removed that embarrassment and offered an opportunity to prevent similar occurrences. To the imperial faction it appeared urgent to seize the opportunity, for they feared that the new Viceroy, Lord Ripon, might actually restore the Berars. Their scheme was to prolong Mahbub's minority for at least another two years, during which time it was hoped the moral and financial deterioration of the state would have progressed to a point that would justify a takeover. How much of this Mahbub suspected is a moot point, but knowingly or not he circumvented it by traveling to Calcutta and personally appealing to the Viceroy for investiture with full power. Fortunately for Hyderabad, Lord Ripon was sympathetic and an early date was fixed.

Having lost that round, the Resident and the Foreign Office were particularly interested in seeing appointed a Dewan on whom they could count. One likely candidate for the office was Maharajah Narinder Pershad, the Peshkar, who was senior member of the Council of Regency. According to one tradition, the British wanted to see Mahbub's friend and erstwhile classmate Salar Jung II in the post, but the Nizam, reluctant to pass over the old nobleman, had dallied over the decision. On the day of the investiture ceremony, the Viceroy resolved this ambivalence by unilateral action: he simply directed that Maharajah Narinder Pershad be seated at some distance from the throne, while young Salar Jung II was given the place reserved for the Dewan. The old maharajah was so shaken by this public affront that he retired to his palace and never came out again on an official occasion. Other, probably more reliable, sources reverse the account. According to them, the frail old Peshkar was regarded by the imperial forces as a likely puppet, for whom support could be mustered from Shums ul Umra, who had long been in opposition to Salar Jung. Salar Jung II was actually chosen by Mahbub when, to the distress of his career officers, Lord Ripon consulted the young Nizam's preference. The rest of the two versions match, and they demonstrate the manner in which decisions were often executed without regard to local sensibilities.

This event illustrates the relationships between the two sides from Mahbub's investiture in 1884 until Maharajah Kishen Pershad became Dewan in 1901: maneuvering and manipulating, jockeying for position, aligning supporters, and resenting anything that could be taken as interference. True, the same action could look rather different from two points of view, but certainly neither side was particularly interested in seeing it from the other's. In the time when the East India Company confined itself to "masked power," company officials had accorded the native rulers that show of respect which local tradition prescribed. When, however, the East India Company became the Government of India in name as well as in substantial fact, its representatives suffered from the temptation to interpret the doctrine of paramountcy personally as well as officially. In this they were the spiritual ancestors of many twentieth-century technical assistance personnel. In March, 1900, a week after taking up his new post as Resident at Hyderabad, Sir David Barr wrote petulantly to the Government of India office at Calcutta:

The etiquette of this court seems to require that until the Resident has delivered the Viceroy's Kharita [letter of appointment] and presented his credentials he cannot be visited by the Minister, except as a preliminary to the Durbar. Moreover it seems to me that the custom of leaving it to the Nizam to fix a date and an hour for the ceremony is open to some objection as it practically precludes the Resident from assuming charge of his political relations with the State until His Highness signifies his consent.

In July, he went on in the same vein:

If I may say so, I think the tendency is to treat Hyderabad with undue importance; to place the State too much on an equality with the Government of India. There is a little too much, deduced from the old Treaties, about "the two States" and the "two Governments."

39

The difference in British and Hyderabadi perceptions is thrown into relief by remarks from the opposing camps. The Resident commented in the same July letter to the Viceroy, after being in Hyderabad for five months: "I would sum up my opinion of the Nizam as follows: His Highness is by nature, and by long habit, indolent, reserved, reticent, and vain; he has an exaggerated idea of his own importance and power, fostered by the deference paid to him by all with whom he has to do."

On the other hand His Highness's tutor and adviser, Sarwar Jung Bahadur, wrote: "It is, however, clear that [the Resident's] policy and methods . . . have borne fruit disastrous to the interests of the Hyderabad State, for they have had the effect of reducing the Nizam to the position of figurehead and have depreciated his power and prestige to an extent that has emboldened certain nobles and officials to set His Highness's orders at defiance. The Nizam has exercised the most consummate forbearance." Sarwar Jung was possibly not the most disinterested witness: the Resident believed that he used his position of closeness to the Nizam for his own advantage.

Although some Residents expressed private doubts about the British policy, there was rarely any lessening of pressure on the Nizam. Even several changes of minister failed to break the pattern of factionalism and internal dissension which left him buffeted by both real and imaginary storms, uneasy about whom he could trust, and increasingly isolated. Neither the Montagues nor the Capulets of Hyderabad were willing to set aside their rivalry, and the Resident darted in and out of the fray whenever advantage could be gained for the British position. Late in 1893, when it was clear that Sir Asman Jah, who was then Dewan, could not continue in office, the faction close to the Resident pressed for the appointment of Sir Vicar ul Umra to succeed him. Sir Vicar was the brother-in-law of the Nizam, but that did not necessarily mean he enjoyed Mahbub's confidence, nor indeed even that of his own brothers, both experts at intrigue and one of whom resented being supplanted while the other resented being passed over for the office. Needing support, and finding a ready source in the Resident, Sir Vicar proceeded to act with a minimum of reference to His Highness. It was often not very easy for him to see the Nizam, and as relations between them worsened Mahbub was less and less willing to find time for him.

Mahbub Ali Pasha, apparently growing weary of the ceaseless intrigue, discouraged by his inability to protect his policies from the meddling of the Resident, and succumbing under pressure to his natural shyness, gradually withdrew more and more from activity in the affairs of state. Nobles who came to see him on official errands sometimes cooled their heels in the antechambers of the palace for several days at a time, having meals sent in from their homes and praying that His Highness would soon emerge from the zenana and receive them.

The Resident complained bitterly that the Nizam was a stumbling block to the administration, as measures sent for his signature received attention no more promptly than their bearers. The British explanation was that His Highness had surrounded himself with "intriguers" whose whispering campaigns were designed to create doubts about the legislation which the Dewan, tutored by the Resident, had maneuvered through the Cabinet Council. Maharajah Kishen Pershad was described by the Resident as always siding with Mahbub Ali Pasha out of a mistaken understanding of the meaning of loyalty. What the British found most painful was the Nizam's reluctance to accept the offer of a loan, to be guaranteed by the districts of Berar. The Cabinet Council refused the loan on the grounds that it constituted a British maneuver to annex further territory—a not unreasonable suspicion in the light of their experience. Indeed, the loss of Berar was precisely what followed when Mahbub was finally forced to accept the loan. Looking back, one can hardly escape the suspicion that by "shilly-shally and procrastination" Mahbub was snubbing his opponents in the only way he perceived as still open to him.

In the education of Osman Ali Khan, the heir apparent, the British were playing for distant stakes. The maneuvering began in 1892 when the Resident was asked by the Foreign Office in Calcutta to make a plan and secure the Nizam's acceptance of it without delay, lest "the opportunity which offers now, while the boy is quite young and the object of no great attention, may be overlooked."

Accordingly the Resident mapped out a plan which would begin with finding "a suitable native" to train the young prince in Urdu and religious studies, while the Government of India would bring out a governess to "teach him the rudiments of English, get him into the way of talking it, and break him into proper habits." After a year of such education, Osman was to be completely removed from the influence of the zenana by establishing him in a separate residence "under the control of an English Governess to whom all the teaching staff and household servants would be subordinate and by whom the expenses would be regulated."

Mahbub Ali Pasha succeeded in derailing this plan, largely by temporizing until his son was old enough to require a tutor rather than a governess. It might be added that the Viceroy openly doubted that any English governess could hold her own in the atmosphere of intrigue in Hyderabad. In the meantime, pressed to start Osman's education in Urdu and Persian, Mahbub appointed the men who had been his own tutors in those subjects. When the Resident complained that such senior men must be too old to keep up with a youngster, His Highness replied petulantly that as the Resident had been nagging him to reduce expenditures, he had rather expected that this economy move would meet with approbation. In any case, these men had the right to be supported by the palace for the rest of their lives, and appointing new tutors would merely add to the long-term burden.

Finally, Mahbub Ali Pasha ran out of answers to the Resident's reiterations that the Government of India was not satisfied with existing arrangements. The man who was being urged, not to say foisted, on him was Brian Egerton, who had, according to the Resident, "been with the Maharajah of Bikaner, of whom he has made a man and a gentleman." Like a child faced with a dose of castor oil, the Nizam dawdled over the decisive action. Eventually he laid aside his shyness and revealed his anxieties in a letter to the Resident which read in part:

My son's tutor must necessarily be in close communication with myself. In the first place, I must confess to my disinclination to introduce into my household anyone with whose character and disposition I am not personally acquainted. In the second place, a stranger to the customs and manners of the Hyderabad nobility, who is unacquainted with my Palace etiquette, is likely to do more harm than good. [Egerton] shall be considered strictly as a private servant of my household and as such he shall be subject to the restrictions which custom and my own habit has necessarily imposed on that service. He should in no way meddle with the political or administrative affairs of my State. Nor should he without my knowledge and permission visit or receive any official or nobleman whoever he may be.

In reply, the Government of India dealt with his feelings only slightly less tenderly than a computer today responds to an aggrieved customer:

The tutor would of course have nothing to do with the political or administrative affairs of Hyderabad, but it is impossible for the Government of India to entertain conditions in respect to the appointment which would be derogatory to an English gentleman.

Mahbub Ali Pasha apologized for any affront that may have been felt, saying that he had meant only to emphasize that the tutor would be paid by and responsible to the royal family rather than the state. But it is hardly surprising that matters dragged on, although eventually Egerton was appointed. On July 1, 1899, the tutor arrived and young Osman was established in King Kothi Palace, which had been purchased for the purpose, under the regimen of a boarding school. The stage was thus cleared for other preoccupations to move front and center.

While it is no more possible to say that India would be better off today if the British had never touched its shores than to say that

Britain would be better off if the Saxons had been the victors at the Battle of Hastings, one does not need much empathy to feel how galling it must have been to the descendants of the Moghuls to be alternately manipulated, coerced, and complimented like none-too-bright children. Nor were such dealings confined to the relatively minor subject of a prince's education. The annals of the British Raj are filled with examples, one of which concerned the aforementioned negotiations over the districts of Berar, whose status disturbed relations between the two sides for a hundred years.

During the time of Mahbub's father, the Viceroy insisted that the Nizam sign a new treaty transferring Berar to direct British control. The Nizam refused, declaring, "If you are determined to take districts, you can taken them without making a new Treaty." Thereupon a subordinate British official wrote to Sir Salar Jung, "I have a letter from . . . Poona mentioning that [the] troops have received orders to be in readiness to march on Hyderabad. Don't suppose military operations will be confined to the districts; and if you are a friend of His Highness, beg of him to save himself and his dignity by complying at once with what the Governor-General will most assuredly compel him to accede to."

The threat apparently achieved its purpose, for the districts of Berar were assigned to the British in lieu of payments to support the Hyderabad Contingent, which was Hyderabad's contribution to the armed forces of the British Raj. After payment of the cost of the contingent and of the administrative costs of ruling the districts, the British were obligated to remit the surplus revenue to the Hyderabad treasury. Not surprisingly, the surplus was insignificant, year after year. In fact it was inadequate to cover the cost of subsidizing food for the people during times of famine, and the Hyderabad government went into debt to the British in order to do so.

In 1902 Lord Curzon, the Viceroy, demanded that Berar be leased to the British in perpetuity and came to Hyderabad to conduct the negotiations in person. He and his staff spent two days closeted with Mahbub Ali Pasha, who was not permitted to have a

single adviser in the room with him. Mahbub capitulated only
when he was finally convinced that Berar would never, under any
circumstances, be restored.

That Mahbub undertook these negotiations is interesting. The
previous year, he had succeeded in dismissing Sir Vicar ul Umra as
Dewan and appointing his own man. The Resident had been
constrained to accept this change by recognition that intrigue had
virtually paralyzed government, while the open complicity of the
British had for all practical purposes nullified their influence.
Mahbub's choice was Maharajah Kishen Pershad, son of a Hindu
family that had for three generations held the post of Peshkar.
Ironically, his grandfather was Maharajah Narinder Pershad, who
had been publicly offended at the time of Mahbub Ali Pasha's investiture. Where Sir Vicar ul Umra exercised more independent
power than Mahbub wanted to give him, the new Dewan followed the maxim, "If in doubt, ask the boss." The Resident described Kishen Pershad as being "subservient to the Nizam to an
extent which has practically changed the whole aspect of Hyderabad politics," and added: "There are no longer the two prominent parties in the State—the Nizam's and the Minister's—
intrigues have almost disappeared; and the Nizam has taken a
keen interest in the administration and is now exercising in the
fullest sense the powers of a Ruler." Whether more comfortable in
this relationship with the Dewan or more stimulated by it, Mahbub began to come out of his withdrawal and pick up once more
the reins of government.

In doing so, he drew on what he had learned in a long struggle
with the British, which seemingly paid off to the satisfaction of
both, in the area of finance. This had been a continuing sore point
for many years. Throughout almost the whole of Mahbub's reign,
his government was considered efficient in most of its activities:
the troops were orderly, the countryside was safe, revenue was
collected without undue oppression, and justice was fairly admin-
istered. But the state was constantly in financial quicksands which
threatened the interests of the British and caused anger repeatedly

between the two sides. The difficulty in establishing a sound fiscal policy came partly from the absence of a standard form for reporting. Information came from the districts and from the various departments in all sorts of dribs and drabs which had then to be organized into some sort of whole. The shape of that whole varied from year to year, while budget headings and account headings, left to the fancy of the incumbents, lacked correspondence to each other or to the categories of previous years.

On top of all this, the fashion of conspicuous spending set by Mahbub Ali Pasha made economy seem an unworthy objective. In some years the expenditure by the palace exceeded 70 lakhs (7,000,000 rupees), and the absence of clarity in the accounting left room for genuine differences of opinion about whether the Nizam was entitled to that much from the Dewani treasury. The Government of India exerted pressure on Mahbub over the years to accept a limitation of 50 lakhs annually. When he finally agreed, there was no question about his good faith; what he said was true, and what he pledged, he performed. More than one Resident went out on a limb to the Government of India on the basis of Mahbub's word.

In 1905 Sir David Barr, turning over the Residency to his successor, made an appraisal of affairs in the state. He wrote that Mahbub Ali Pasha had entirely shed his desultory ways and become instead diligent and accurate, prudent in both public and private expenditure, actively interested in the economy of the state. He was "not only capable of controlling and directing the affairs of the State," but "most willing and anxious to do so. . . . It is not too much to say that the Nizam is *by far* the shrewdest person in the State. Since the change in Ministers, His Highness has paid the keenest attention to the administration—all orders passsed by him are remarkable for sound judgment and a ready grasp of the subject." High praise indeed from the man who five years earlier had sneered at him as indolent and vain!

Mahbub Ali Pasha's attitude toward the British did not soften correspondingly. After signing the agreement which Lord Curzon forced out of him that effectively put control of the Berar districts in the hands of the British, Mahbub was made a Knight Grand Cross of the Bath. He used to refer sarcastically to this honor, the G.C.B., as "Gave Curzon Berar."

The following year, in 1903, Mahbub Ali Pasha attended the durbar in Delhi which had been called to proclaim the accession of Edward VII. During the ceremony Lord Curzon, whom Mahbub had not forgiven for his part in the Berar negotiations, announced that at the behest of the King-Emperor he would garland every ruling prince. Instead of bowing his head to receive the flowers around his neck, Mahbub Ali Pasha, who was the first prince, held up his sword. The Viceroy drew back stiffly, saying that it was customary to garland the neck of the recipient. Mahbub replied icily that durbars were called in order that the princes should from time to time affirm their loyalty. His neck was there today but might be gone tomorrow, whereas his sword, which would be handed from father to son, was a comparatively permanent symbol of loyalty. For a few moments the two men stood like ramrods, taking each other's measure. Finally the Viceroy stepped forward again and hung the garland on Mahbub Ali Pasha's unwavering sword.

The Nizam and the Nawabs

The first years of Mahbub Ali Pasha's active reign were anything but smooth, and the British determination to drive a wedge between the Nizam and the Dewan only guaranteed the turbulence. People of both factions who had exercised power during the regency or expected to profit by internal dissension following it fanned every small spark of difference between Mahbub and Salar Jung II until it flared up in suspicion and resentment. Finally realizing that they had overshot the mark, the Foreign Office made last-ditch efforts to prevent an open breach, which succeeded only in increasing Mahbub Ali Pasha's distrust. Trained by Sir Salar Jung to be a stickler for etiquette, he found the son's insolence hard to excuse. Server ul Mulk, the man who had been tutor to both of them and who had revered Sir Salar Jung as his patron, recorded Mahbub's complaints about Salar Jung II: "He will sit on a chair with legs stretched out, while I stand; he will take out cigarettes and smoke without hesitation in my presence; and in spite of strict orders, he wears whatever dress he likes at Court functions; and will sit with his back turned towards me, laughing and joking with others. He does not consider me even equal in rank, but lower."

When the young Dewan finally provoked a break, the damage was irreparable. He had been reading aloud to the Nizam when the latter demanded, "Show me! Let me see it." Salar Jung II, who had been drinking, tossed the paper across the table. Finding this impertinence the last straw, Mahbub determined to dismiss him, although the resolve was easier to formulate than to make stick. In a letter to the Viceroy in which he resists the urging from Calcutta that he make peace with Salar Jung, Mahbub's complaints range from the unevenness of his Dewan's official work to personal difficulties—"He seldom comes to me, or brings papers, on the pretext of illness, whilst he goes to other places and gives entertainments, and so forth, wishing to show disregard for me." Eventually the dismissal was accomplished when Salar Jung II recognized that a trip abroad would be timely. Taking his family, he went to England and then returned, to Poona, whence letters of apology went out to Hyderabad. Before they elicited a reply he was dead, leaving behind his son of a few days, who as Salar Jung III was destined to become in his turn Dewan for Mahbub's son. Despite the ensuing change of dewans, the problem of factionalism eluded solution by Mahbub for many years, until the appointment of Maharajah Kishen Pershad.

Meanwhile Mahbub Ali Pasha was beginning to develop his administrative style. In March, 1884, shortly after he had assumed personal control of his realm, he wrote to the Dewan: "Send me a list of persons who are officers and such officers as are capable of sitting at my table at breakfast, that is, those who can sit in my presence." Later he directed, "Tomorrow morning at twelve

o'clock come to breakfast and bring with you some high officials
—about twenty civil officers. I will see them. And if you bring a
detailed list of their names it will be a good thing: name plus rank
plus knowledge of Persian and English, etc.; salary; where they
come from; and if they have been in service anywhere else before
they came here, where it was. I want to know all about them. And
in the same way, some other day when I tell you, you must bring
other officers, a few at a time, and introduce them to me."

These and similar letters were obviously spontaneous, written in
his own hand and sent off as the idea struck him. Several are on
bits of stationery left over from his childhood: one has a picture
of Red Riding Hood and the Wolf; another has an amusing crest
with the words "Mind Your" above crossed pea pods and billiard
cues. The informality was not allowed to become familarity, however; Mahbub was known for the respect with which he spoke to
or about the members of his court, meticulously according to each
the dignity of his proper name and title. In turn, according to a
Resident, Colonel Kenneth Mackenzie, who wrote in 1895: "He
certainly makes all his people about him 'sit up' and whether it is
due to love or fear they take no liberties with him and treat him
with respect, almost ultra-deferentially, so this implies a certain
strength of character. He is certainly not wanting in ability, and if
he chose to apply himself to public business, would, I think, do it
all much better than anyone here."

Soon after Mahbub's investiture, Nawab Imad ul Mulk wrote:

Your Majesty had given an order that the surplus for the year should
be made known. Although the correct amount cannot be known now,
the approximate estimate [is] presented for Your Majesty's perusal.
From this it appears that the balance in the District and Central treasuries will be Rs. 53,40,887 and at the end of the year, after expenditure, there will be a balance of Rs. 8,53,772.

To this the young Nizam replied with some asperity:

I have seen the estimate of income and expenditure. . . . Have another statement made and send it to me by which the expenditure for
administration, judiciary, railways, etc., can be known and what the

surplus will be. I do not want the balances in the treasuries but only want to know what the surpluses will be. When you write eight lakhs fifty-three thousand rupees, is it after deducting the amount of the loan or the account before deduction of the loan?

These exchanges point to a man intent on picking up his job of being a ruler. So far, so good. But it is not primarily his official life that interests us here. Our curiosity is to know what manner of man the young Nizam was. His inheritance was mixed, for in his veins flowed the blood both of the statesmanly Nizam ul Mulk and of the first Nizam's sybaritic descendants. Keen as Mahbub was at work, he was also passionately fond of all the current sports, including wine and women, whose acquaintance he made at an early age. As a child, he had been taught military drill and horsemanship by Mohammed Ali Baig—then a young noncommissioned officer and later, as Sir Afsur ul Mulk, commander in chief of the Hyderabad army—whom Sir Salar Jung had brought from Aurangabad. So good a pupil did Mahbub prove that he once broke a horse which had not until then allowed anyone to mount.

Tent pegging was a favorite sport with Mahbub. For this, a tent peg is fixed loosely in the earth. The sportsman rides toward the peg at full gallop and carries it off on the end of his lance; a skillful player can then swing his lance so as to dislodge the impaled peg and go on to spear another without breaking his pace. With the rifle Mahbub's marksmanship was such that he could toss a coin into the air and hit it repeatedly. A multitude of tigers met their ends by the Nizam's bullets. Wrestling also was a sport at which he excelled.

The stamina which he developed through these exercises was sometimes regarded as at best a mixed blessing by his court, inasmuch as he was unmindful of the strain he was putting on the arches of less sturdy members. Once, attending an evening party given by Sir Vicar ul Umra, then Dewan, Mahbub arrived about eleven o'clock and his attention was engaged by the dancing and then the elaborate fireworks. He was too absorbed to take notice of the chairs which were constantly being placed for him, which meant that none of the other guests might sit down. By dawn those who were still on their feet were envying those who had been carried out in a faint as the evening progressed, but the Nizam remained as lively as when the festivities began.

Although Mahbub drank heavily of alcoholic beverages, few except a small group of select companions ever saw him with a glass in his hand. One of these, who often poured his drinks, was Raja Murli Manohar, son of a Hindu family that came south with Asaf Jah I. Private secretary to His Highness from the beginning of his active reign, this young man is thought not to have trespassed on on his intimacy with the ruler to press for favors. Only one instance of such an occurrence is supposed to have taken place, and that was when some nobles who were determined to protect the state from further encroachment by the British persuaded him to fall at his master's feet and ask for a certain measure for the protection of the realm. Mahbub replied with equal consideration, "I know who has persuaded you to ask for this, and I know why. But be patient for a while longer. The time has not yet come."

Not everyone who had access to the sovereign's more private moments was so honorable. A trusted servant who looked after his personal effects was reputed to have profited hugely by them. The man had come to Mahbub Ali Pasha in a picturesque way. Some years earlier, Vicar ul Umra, a leading nobleman, had gone to Europe, taking with him as companion and general factotum a Parsi gentleman by the name of Shapurji Chenai. Being in constant attendance on Vicar ul Umra, Shapurji found no time to look after his wardrobe and therefore hired a valet, who returned to Hyderabad with him. There one day the valet came to the attention of Sir Vicar, who had come to pay a call at Shapurji's home. Intrigued by the novelty of a European servant, he requested that the valet be sent to him. This servant was still with Sir Vicar at the time that he gave Falaknuma Palace to Mahbub, a circumstance about which more will come later. While the Nizam was inspecting the palace he saw the man and, learning that he had served there for some years, asked that he be left in his post.

So the valet entered the service of Mahbub Ali Pasha. He looked after his master very well. If the Nizam were somewhat the worse for drink, it was generally the valet who undressed him and put him to bed. The morning after such an episode, the valet sometimes presented nazar to the Nizam, who inquired what it was for. The valet replied that on the previous evening His Highness had been pleased to give his servant such and such a jewel. In this position Mahbub Ali Pasha could only lose, for, extremely sensitive about his prestige, he would neither question whether the man were speaking the truth nor make the excuse of drunkenness. In this way the valet amassed a fortune which, invested in business, made him extraordinarily wealthy even for those times. Some of the nobles were said not to be above playing the same trick.

This was not the valet's only ruse. He had early in his career established the convention that his religion required him to drink only certain holy water, and so he brought his own supply daily in a long-necked pot called a surahi. On many an evening the sloshing of the water remaining in the surahi as the valet carried it home with him muffled the sound of a jewel which had been slipped into it. Socks were another source of illegitimate profit. Mahbub wore only silk ones from France and discarded them after a single wearing. The valet used to collect them, but, as Mahub's foot was unusually small, even for a man of his delicate build, the socks had little resale value. Undeterred by the limited market, the enterprising valet had them beautifully laundered, re-affixed the paper labels he had preserved from their original appearance, and after a reasonable lapse of time sold them back to his master as a new shipment just arrived from France.

On the more serious side, under Mahbub Ali Pasha the state took a number of forward steps, some positively in the direction that is today popularly known as "development" and some others paving the way for that by loosening the ties to the past. One step of the latter type was the change in the required court dress from neema jama, the old Moghul costume whose prominent feature was an overdress of muslin with yards and yards of billowing skirt. The muslin was so fine that forty yards of it could be pulled through a finger ring. In place of this picturesque costume came either the sherwani, the long, high-buttoned coat more recently made familiar to the western world by Jawaharlal Nehru, or European dress, which in the late nineteenth century included a frock coat not unlike its Eastern counterpart. Whichever apparel was worn, only two items were obligatory parts of it in the presence of the Nizam: a belt, called a bugloos, with an ornamental, often elaborately jeweled buckle, and a turban, called a dastar, of a shape indigenous to Hyderabad.

The Nizam's dastar was often, but not necessarily, royal yellow. Men whose fathers were dead wore white, and others suited their whims. Men of royal blood—the Nizam, his brothers, and his sons —wore dastars embellished with a toorah, a stiff inverted tassel of gold thread. A few nobles were permitted to wear turbans of a different shape peculiar to their families. There is a story that a young man of one of those families thought to show his respect for the Nizam by wearing a dastar. Mahbub at first failed to recognize him and, on being told his identity, responded with concern, "But what has happened that he has put aside his family turban for a dastar?"

A corollary of the change in court dress was the change in official arrangements for the durbars. For generations, when a Resident called upon the Nizam, His Highness greeted the party and then took his seat on the Musnud. The Dewan and other attending nobles, barefooted but with heads respectfully covered, sat on carpets to his left, while the Resident and his party, bareheaded and having left their shoes outside, made themselves as comfortable as they could on a carpet to his right. An earlier Resident had sent a note to Mahbub's father, Nizam Afzul ud Dowla, asking to be allowed the use of a chair for future audiences, as it was awkward to sit cross-legged in trousers. Afzul ud Dowla retorted, "Let a pit be dug to dangle his feet in!" With the adoption of the more restrictive sherwani for court functions, arrangements were modified to provide everyone with chairs.

Just as the relaxation of the rules about court dress helped to turn Hyderabad's face away from the past, so also did the change in language. Until the time of Mahbub Ali Pasha the official and court language of the state had been Persian. Even after his accession, some of the nobles clung to it as the language which demonstrated that their ancestors had come as conquerors. During Mahbub's reign, however, the official language was changed to Urdu, which in itself had an interesting evolution.

The word "urdu" is Persian for "camp" (by derivation from the same Turkish word which gave us the English "horde") and refers to the fact that its development began in the Moghul camps, as the invading army and the Hindi-speaking local people began the process of fraternization. Following the advent of peace, a third major strain was added by Arab scholars and religious men. As a result, literary Urdu has a rather high proportion of Arabian and Persian words, while the colloquial is more heavily laced with Hindi, with minor accretions from a variety of other sources. In language, as in so many ways throughout its long history, India has absorbed its conquerors.

During the early part of Mahbub Ali Pasha's reign other changes were also taking place. The Nizam and his advisers worked out a reorganization of the government, promulgated in January, 1893, which provided a system of checks and balances by separating executive and legislative functions and backed up the ministers with permanent secretaries who were career officials. For the first time, non-officials were given a voice in the formation of the laws through election by a limited franchise, based on occupational classes, to an advisory council.

During the same period the amount of money spent on education increased five times. This trend continued, leading to the formation of a Department of Public Instruction. Included in the greatly increased number of schools was the first school in India for Muslim girls (that is, it observed purdah). It was apparently well received, for by the end of the reign there were 25,000 literate women in the state, a third of whom were Muslim. Education, however, did not become generally popular. About 95 percent of the population continued to live with their illiteracy. In his Preface to the census report of 1901, Mirza Mehdy Khan complained:

It is still a very deep-rooted idea with the functional castes . . . that education is not only not necessary for their material advancement, but that, even in homeopathic doses, it interferes with one's well-being. As a general rule a man sticks to the occupation and perseveres in the illiteracy of his forefathers with a tenacity of purpose calculated to carry comfort to the hearts of the superior castes, who . . . are never tired of regretting the so-called levelling influences of education. And the rich, who have not to toil for their bread, rarely look upon education with any favor.

In the realm of higher education, a college of civil engineering had been opened with the express purpose of training young men for the Public Works Department. As early as 1888, the Nizam sanctioned annual grants to residents of his realm to assist their going abroad for higher studies. One of the first recipients of these scholarships was a young Anglo-Indian, Edith Boardman, who took an advanced degree in medicine and surgery and returned in 1890 to join the state medical service. Women doctors were much needed for practicing in the zenana. A few years later, in 1905, His Highness endowed Victoria Zenana Hospital, for which the cornerstone was laid by the Princess of Wales (later Queen Mary).

It was on that same day that Mahbub Ali Pasha's favorite daughter died after a long illness. At the request of the Prince of Wales (who returned to India a few years later as King George V), the Nizam had taken his guests to watch a demonstration of tent pegging, a sport entirely new to them, when word was brought to him that his daughter had succumbed. Mahbub Ali Pasha slipped away to take leave of the child whom he had loved above all others and returned immediately, refusing to release the news of the loss because of the shadow it would cast on the royal visit. Such an event could not really be kept secret, however, and when it became known, the state dinner was canceled.

In a letter to the Resident after the departure of the Royal Highnesses, Mahbub referred to the comfort they had given him in his grief.

An incidental result of the royal visit was the introduction of motor cars into the Nizam's Dominions. So long as Mahbub Ali Pasha disdained them, they were not available to the nobles either. To transport the Prince and Princess of Wales comfortably and quickly between Falaknuma and the city palaces, the Government of India sent in four motor cars, leased from C. B. Oakley, a firm still in business in Bangalore, at a rental of 1,500 rupees a week each. His first ride so delighted Mahbub Ali Pasha that he promptly sent off an order to Bombay for a car of his own, a lead his nobles lost no time in following.

The other form of mechanical conveyance with which Mahbub Ali Pasha was familiar was the railway. The system which crossed his Dominions by the end of his reign had a curious history.

In the time of Nizam Afzul ud Dowla, Sir Salar Jung I had discussed with the British the idea of linking Hyderabad by rail with the three Presidency towns of Bombay, Madras, and Calcutta. Afzul ud Dowla would have none of it. He feared that a railway not only would make it easier for the British to penetrate his Dominions, but also would give his relatives another means to run away. Some years later the Raja of Wanaparthy followed a similar line of reasoning when he stipulated that the railroad could cross his territory only at some distance from his capital, as he did not wish to encourage the Nizam in the habit of dropping in on him.

After Afzul ud Dowla's death, with the child Nizam still too unwary to object, Sir Salar Jung revived his plan for a railroad and the first line was laid from the western part of the Dominions to the Secunderabad cantonment. Later it was extended to the east as far as Warangal, an addition which was ceremonially opened by Mahbub himself. In time it came to afford him considerable pleasure.

Occasionally Mahbub took it into his head to go for an outing on the railroad. Word went out from the palace to get up a head of steam on the locomotive and to bring the carriages round. As often as not, something then arose to distract His Highness, delaying him sometimes for a half hour and sometimes for several days. But once a royal whim had been expressed, everything had to be kept in readiness to satisfy it. So the grapevine from the inner sanctum kept the outside informed. If His Highness were taking his lunch, the grooms knew it was safe to unhitch and water the horses, while over at the Nizam's private railway station the engine driver and firemen were able to take a little personal time off. When His Highness stood up, the alarm sounded all along the grapevine, followed by an all-clear when he decided to have a rest. This seesaw sometimes continued for several days, but for the sake of getting on with our story let us assume that he finally recollected his proposal and actually boarded the train with his party. To the salute of the guards and the tootling of the whistle, the train moved out.

Meanwhile supplies had been dispatched down the line to camps established for the purpose of providing lunch and tea during the excursion. With the train actually in motion, it was possible to estimate how far away from Hyderabad the party would be by lunch time, and the servants in charge were accordingly directed precisely where to pitch their camp, similar calculations determining the location of the party responsible for providing afternoon tea. Formidable as these arrangements sound, involving large amounts of preparation and movements of people and supplies, they were nevertheless quite simple and straightforward once they had been worked out.

Unfortunately, in Hyderabad things had a way of not remaining simple and straightforward for long. While the train was chugging along the track, His Highness might suddenly spot a mango grove or a meadow with a stream that appealed to him. Orders were issued, brakes were applied, and while the royal party alighted the outriders galloped forward to instruct the camps to be moved back down the track by some miles. But, alas, the mangoes proved unripe or the stream sluggish, and His Highness cut short his stroll. Again the riders galloped, to countermand the orders and reestablish the camps nearer their original site. Nerve-racking as all this may seem today, it was summed up by the Nawab who, as aide-de-camp, was responsible for the arrangements, as "glorious fun."

Others of Mahbub Ali Pasha's whims involved a quite opposite lack of organization. A tailoring firm from Calcutta once came to Hyderabad to take orders for Western-style suits. Mahbub Ali Pasha's fancy was caught by a particular piece of material, but in order to make sure that no one else would turn up looking exactly like him, he ordered that the entire bolt be made into suits for himself. This amounted to seventy identical suits complete with accessories, which arrived in due course. By that time, His Highness had lost interest.

What to do with that mountain of boxes from the tailor? On inspiration Mahbub started handing them out to his nobles, a box to each one whom he happened to see or think of. Unfortunately no one had thought to check what the boxes contained— not an outfit neatly assembled in each, as His Highness had apparently assumed, but trousers in some boxes and coats, waistcoats, and so on in others. Of course the nobles did the obvious thing, and for a while there was brisk trading until each had assembled a respectable outfit for himself, except for one jagirdar. His box held seventy high, starched collars. Nobody wanted to relieve him of that particular instrument of torture. The poor man spent the rest of his life—thirty years—trying to wear out the uncomfortable style which had been wished on him by the Nizam.

Some of the zest with which Mahbub Ali Pasha approached life spilled over into his relations with his nobles, and his sense of dignity occasionally had to compete with his sense of humor. When he stayed at Purani Haveli, his neighbor was Shahab Jung, whose sprawling deori was immediately adjacent. In the pecking order of the aristocracy, Shahab Jung was small potatoes, having only a revenue of 40,000 rupees. But he was also influential as a working member of the government: thorough, painstaking, and self-respecting. Because he did not like being interrupted at work, he used to sleep much of the day and work through the night. Every so often he asked the servant for a glass of water. The servant stepped outside the office door and bellowed down the corridor, "Aab khasa!" The next servant passed the shout along to the next, and so on through the rooms and across the courtyards into the pantry area. In the silence of the night these shouts not only echoed through the corridors but could be heard in the streets also. Even Purani Haveli was not out of range.

One day Mahbub Ali Pasha sent a courtier to tell Shahab Jung that his servants' shouting disturbed His Highness's sleep. Shahab Jung replied, "Please tell His Highness that his humble servant has only this one poor hut, but my sovereign has so many palaces where he can go and stay." Mahbub had the grace to burst out laughing and drop the matter.

The common people, who had no way of knowing how Nawab Shahab Jung worked at his desk throughout the night, developed a rather interesting legend to explain the shouting they could hear from inside the walls of the deori. They said that Nawab Shahab Jung was tormented by an evil spirit who came in the night. In an attempt to divert that spirit, Shahab Jung used to set a task for it which would keep it so occupied as to leave him in peace for some time. Consequently whenever the spirit approached him, he ordered it to run up and down the palmyra tree in the garden three thousand times. When the three thousand trips had been completed, the spirit returned to the Nawab and if it found him asleep it attacked him. The Nawab therefore instructed his servants to shout and make noise at intervals during the night in order to prevent him from being caught dozing off. Unfortunately the Nizam also was disturbed by the commotion and spoke to the Nawab about it. When he heard the story, Mahbub Ali Pasha exclaimed, "Ah, but Shahab Jung, this is not the correct task to set the spirit. You should order him to bring you water from the ocean in a sieve."

On another occasion, while returning from a drive, Mahbub

Ali Pasha turned in at Shahab Jung's gate on an impulse. By the time the awakened Shahab Jung could struggle into his sherwani, bugloos, and dastar, the Nizam and his accompanying nobles had made themselves comfortable in the drawing room. Their host entered, bowing. Mahbub Ali Pasha said, "I have come to pay you a visit."

Shahab Jung salaamed again and waited. The Nizam told him kindly to go and finish his rest, while he and his party relaxed in the courtyard. After they had enjoyed themselves over refreshments which Shahab Jung sent in, the Nizam again sent for the Nawab. "Shahab Jung," he asked in taking leave, "has it made you happy that I visited you?"

"It has made me happy, Sire," Shahab Jung replied, "but not in the way that you think."

"Is that so?" His Highness inquired. "What do you mean?"

"Oh, Your Highness," Shahab Jung explained, "tomorrow it will be all over the city that His Highness came here to call, but only casually as he was driving past my gate."

Several days later, Shahab Jung received a note from Mahbub Ali Pasha saying, "This afternoon I am coming especially to pay you a visit, and I have published in the newspaper that I am doing so."

In this little joke, Mahbub recognized that what was "all over the city" was important to Shahab Jung. Perhaps that is natural in a noble whose obvious status symbol, the income from the estate or jagir granted him, in no way reflected his position in the inner circles of government, including his sovereign's official life, which he attained by hard work and persistence. The big nobles maintained private armies, but Shahab Jung's jagir was too small to support such an expenditure, so he augmented his prestige by a ruse. Every morning the gates of his deori were closed, while in the courtyard just inside four men shouted military orders and tramped heavily to convey the impression that a retinue of guards was drilling. After half an hour of this exercise, the four took turns dismissing each other to their normal domestic duties and the gates were reopened. What Shahab Jung did not know was that his little game was a favorite entertainment of the neighborhood boys, who used to glue their eyes to the chinks in the gate to watch.

Although Mahbub Ali Pasha went out socially a great deal more than his ancestors had been accustomed to doing, and was the first Nizam to accept an invitation from the Resident, he rarely dined out except at the homes of his own relatives or the Paigah nobles. One lesser noble, however, yearned for the distinction of entertaining His Highness. That was Nawab Mussallum Jung, a bachelor so wealthy that he had a bridge constructed across the river and presented it to the city in commemoration of Mahbub's reign. Not only did he enjoy a large income from his jagirs and speculate in currency: he also dealt in gold and pearls. He had the reputation of being able to judge the precise value of a pearl and also its age, a skill which was occasionally tested with pearls of known history. But dearer to him than this was the ambition to entertain Mahbub Ali Pasha at a meal. One day, mustering his courage, he besought his sovereign to accept an invitation. Recognizing that it would mean a great deal to the old man, Mahbub agreed.

"Whom will you invite?" he inquired.

"Whomever Your Highness pleases," replied the Nawab.

The Nizam named fourteen people, all close associates, and fixed a date. Overjoyed, Mussallum Jung rushed home to start the preparations. He sent far and wide for the greatest delicacies, the finest decorations, the most costly carpets, the best musicians and singers. Night and day the preparations went on, until at last the auspicious moment came when the carriages could be heard in the driveway. Forehead touching the ground, Mussallum Jung received his sovereign. The Nizam looked around, observing and praising everything in detail.

In time the Nizam arose and the party moved to the dining room. Mussallum Jung had employed all the masters of the culinary art that could be found. No single delicacy had been omitted.

Countless delectable dishes had been prepared and were awaiting the choice of the sovereign.

"What have you for me to eat, Mussallum Jung?" His Highness inquired conversationally.

"Whatever Your Highness asks," replied the Nawab, barely suppressing the pride in his voice. The Nizam thought for a few seconds.

"Then give me chakna," he said.

Mussallum Jung's smile froze on his face. Chakna, made of the intestines of sheep, was considered a dish of the very poor. A deep hush fell over the company. Mahbub Ali Pasha broke the silence. He roared with laughter. "Now, Mussallum Jung, admit it; I have caught you!" he shouted. "All right, you haven't chakna? Then bring me whatever you have prepared."

But even the Nizam was occasionally at a loss. When Queen Victoria died, he sent for four nobles to convey his condolences to the Resident. Three arrived wearing black sherwanis, but the fourth, Nawab Shahab Jung, was in brocade. Mahbub Ali Pasha approached the problem cautiously. "Do you know what this occasion is?" he inquired of Shahab Jung.

"She died," Shahab Jung answered laconically.

"Then why are you wearing these brightly colored clothes?"

Shahab Jung replied earnestly, "I have to look only to the health of my sovereign. So long as he lives, I cannot wear mourning."

Sensitive to the compliment but reluctant to offend the Resident, His Highness persisted gently. "But nevertheless this is the wrong dress for this kind of occasion."

"Now I understand," Shahab Jung replied, "but let it be. The next time this happens I will be more careful."

This tact of Mahbub Ali Pasha's seems to have come from a capacity to abandon the protected place he occupied and feel with those whose lives touched his, whether simple or fortunately placed. Among the latter was Sir Afsur ul Mulk, who once suffered an accident and lay unconscious in his home for some days.

Straw had been spread on the streets all around Rahut Munzil to deaden the noise of the passing traffic. Coming to call daily, Mahbub Ali Pasha got down from his carriage well out of ear-shot of the house and proceeded the rest of the way on foot. Anxious about the lack of improvement in the patient, the Nizam arranged for additional help in the Muslim tradition.

"I am going now to ask for holy men to come and say the prayers for the sick," he said to Sir Afsur's wife. "Please arrange a room where they can intone the prayers without disturbing Sir Afsur, but from which they can have access to his room without having to speak to anyone, so that they can blow on him while the prayers are still on their breath."

Being blown upon by prayers may or may not have aided in Sir Afsur's recovery; that must be a matter of faith. But recover he did, in the end outliving Mahbub. Sir Afsur's children today remember this evidence of his sovereign's personal concern for a sick man and his family, thought through even to the room ar-rangements.

In the light of these stories it comes as no surprise that the af-fection between Mahbub Ali Pasha and his people was known to be mutual. At the durbar of 1903 the Viceroy asked Mahbub Ali Pasha why he was so plainly dressed when all the other princes were loaded with jewels. Mahbub replied that his jewels were with him. When Lord Curzon asked where, Mahbub gestured to the nobles who had accompanied him.

Occasionally, of course, someone fell from favor, and more than one nobleman had this experience. Sometimes it was obviously provoked. A case in point concerned the Sultan of Makalla.

For several generations the sultans of the small Arabian sheik-dom of Makalla had kept their primary residence in Hyderabad, in a palace opposite Mecca Masjid. From Makalla came the Arabs (so-called Chaoushes) who formed the Nizam's bodyguard and the Arab regiments; they remained a distinct group in the Hy-derabad culture, and occasionally their lord had to be reminded that he had an overlord. One day, the sultan's two children went for an elephant ride in the city. Because the elephant was obstructing traffic, the mahout was asked to move it, but he refused truculently, whereupon a policeman goaded it from behind with a pointed instrument. Taking fright, the elephant bolted, and the children almost fell out of the howdah. Eventually the party got back to the palace of the sultan and a report was made to him. Furious, he called his troops and told them of the insult to their community. Immediately 5,000 Chaoushes rushed forth with daggers drawn. Knowing that they were the target, the terrified police scurried out of the way, throwing off their uniforms and hiding wherever they could, some even crawling into large drain pipes that were lying about. The Kotwal, Nawab Akbar Jung, who was responsible for internal security in the state, took refuge in the Residency.

When word of this reached the ears of the Nizam, he sent for Afsur ul Mulk and ordered him to take out the army against the Chaoushes. The latter demurred, saying that much blood would be shed in the city as a consequence. Instead he asked Mahbub to leave the matter to him. Taking a cannon from Golconda Fort, Afsur ul Mulk had it dismantled, brought to Mecca Masjid, and reassembled atop the mosque. Then, with a troop of cavalry, he called upon the sultan and announced that there was a cannon trained on his bedroom which would be fired if he did not call off his men. The sultan saw reason, and peace was restored to the city. Mahbub Ali Pasha fined him one lakh of rupees and deported him, but after a few months he was forgiven and allowed to return.

On another occasion the Nizam was planning to miss a meeting of the Cabinet Council and sent word that his secretary, Sir Amin Jung, would preside in his stead. Nawab Shahab Jung protested that "that Madrassi" ought not to preside when "Mahbub's own nobles" were available. When after several exchanges the stubborn old nobleman still refused to agree, Mahbub Ali Pasha shot back an exasperated "Then you preside, you wretch!"

If he were sufficiently provoked or had to discipline one of his nobles, Mahbub was known to take away titles, but he never resumed the estates that went with them. Those he considered the children's inheritance, and he had no intention of visiting his displeasure on the next generation. On one such occasion, a noble was severely punished, but for the wrong transgression. The story goes that the Viceroy, having received anonymous letters complaining about Mahbub, had forwarded them to the Resident to deal with. Mahbub Ali Pasha, hearing of the investigation, got the impression that the Resident was making mischief. His resentment was cleared up when the Resident brought to him the bundle of anonymous letters, together with a signed note in handwriting which, the experts averred, matched that of the letters. The note had arrived at the Residency on Christmas Day, accompanying a gift of cake and fruit, and was signed with the name of Shoukat Jung, who was one of the Great Nobles (Umra e Uzzam).

What neither Mahbub Ali Pasha nor the Resident knew was that the note had not actually been written by Shoukat Jung, who could hardly recognize his own name in English. He had commissioned a writer whom he treated as a protégé to prepare it for him. Mahbub summoned Shoukat Jung for seven o'clock the following morning, together with the Dewan, Maharajah Kishen Pershad, and the minister of justice, Fakhr ul Mulk. Mahbub Ali Pasha went directly to the point, asking Shoukat Jung, "Do you know English?"

Leaping to the conclusion that he was to be made a high official, Shoukat Jung replied, beaming, "Oh, yes, I am well conversant with it."

"Is this your letter?" Mahbub asked, handing him one of the anonymous letters.

Shoukat Jung barely glanced at it. "Yes, it is mine," he replied without hesitation.

"Shoukat Jung," the Nizam persisted, "look at it carefully. Did you really write this letter?"

"Oh, yes," the nobleman assured him. "I read and write English very well."

Convicted by his own insistence, Shoukat Jung was stripped of his titles and deported, but his family was left in possession of the jagir.

The Nizam and the Zenana

In 1875 Albert Edward, Prince of Wales, visited India. Lord Northbrooke, who was then Viceroy, had conceived the grandiose idea of having him received on landing in Bombay by all of the Indian princes. To this end, pressure was put on Hyderabad to have the nine-year-old Nizam present. It required all of Sir Salar Jung's considerable diplomatic agility to resist, but the maneuver was finally accomplished with the aid of a letter from Mahbub's grandmother, the Dowager Begum, who said that the child was in delicate health and would not survive the rigors of such a trip.

Had they met some years later, the two monarchs would have found many interests in common, including horses and women. Both liked them spirited, but Mahbub Ali Pasha enjoyed one advantage over his European counterpart. Under Islamic law, he was entitled to four wives, although in fact he had access to any woman within the precincts of his palaces. He never went through the ceremonial parts of a marriage, and with only one did he even perform the basic ceremony, the Nikah, prescribed by his Sunni religion. It consisted of three parts: the consent of both parties, the fixing of an amount to be paid to the wife in the event that the husband died or divorced her, and a statement before two witnesses.

As a youth of seventeen, Mahbub had thrown the Government of India into a flurry of anxiety by proposing to contract a marriage in the interval before his eighteenth birthday, after which superstitious practice would make it impossible for him to do so for one full year. The British were concerned with finding a suitable match, a woman who would be a good influence on him and still be companionable over the years. They weighed the consequences of marriage to a daughter of one of the other Indian princes, with its potential political embarrassment to the Government of India, and of marriage to a daughter of a Hyderabad nobleman, with its internal political complications. They were anxious also about his continued education, since marriage, by making him unquestionably the master in his own household, would free him from their control. They debated the advisability of a simple Nikah marriage with a comely young girl of no social importance, there being several such girls already in the palace. This last was a less worthy and dignified proceeding than marriage with appropriate pomp to a noble consort, but in compensation it opened the possibility that the bride could remain with the Nizam's mother in Chow Mahalla and the bridegroom with his tutors in Purani Haveli. They feared that following any marriage at all he would upset the plans for an impending journey, finding it too difficult to be separated from his wife. On the other hand, knowing that Mahbub's female relatives had for several years been initiating an eager pupil into the delights of the zenana, they feared a pregnancy and fervently hoped that his eldest son would be "the son of a wife wedded according to law."

Sir Salar Jung was kept busy explaining the differences between Eastern and Western customs and attitudes toward marriage, and pointing out the implications of the latest version. The problem of communication was intractable because the British were agitated about questions that were irrelevant to the Indian concerns.

Eventually Mahbub decided that, since marriage was not incumbent on him, he would not bother. The Asaf Jahi tradition had never demanded that the heirs to the Musnud necessarily be sons of royal wives, nor indeed that they even be legitimate. In consequence a legal fiction had grown up which imputed legitimacy to all children of the Nizam, whatever the status of the mother.

Mahbub's wives and concubines ranged from singing girls upward and included Muslims, Hindus, and an Anglo-Indian. Estimates of their number varied wildly. A prudish Resident guessed that His Highness was supporting a "shocking" ten thousand women, adding self-righteously that his own wife had succeeded in arranging a previous engagement whenever she had been invited by Hyderabadis to a social function. A more sympathetic Resident even ventured to defend the Nizam on this score. Others have speculated that the number was as low as a hundred women, genteelly referred to as "palace ladies." Generally speaking, the Nizam got any woman he fancied, but even his score was not perfect.

One time it was the girl herself who succeeded in foiling the flirtation. The story shows some of the ambivalence in the Nizam's attitudes. On an occasion when he was thoroughly drunk, Mahbub Ali Pasha found his fancy caught by a poor girl whom he chanced to see. Sending for her mother, he inquired whether she would give him her daughter. The mother replied with dignity, "Your Highness, my daughter and even I are ready to be sacrificed for you." But when the girl appeared she proved to be tender and timid, and her innocence spoke to Mahbub through his alcoholic haze. At his first overtures she began to weep quietly. "I always regarded you as a father," she explained in her distress. Cold water could not have sobered him more thoroughly. He sent the girl home untouched and took himself off to Pahad-i-Shereef, the shrine of the saint whose disciple he was, where he remained for three days of fasting and prayer.

By no means all the women in Mahbub's zenana were of his own choosing, nor had they been objects of his attention, however fleetingly. A number, known as Bin Khawas, had been presented to him by fathers who were eager for the honor of having a daughter at the palace, or who regarded that life as preferable for their daughters to the privations which were their birthright. The Nizam's attitude was that since a child was a man's most precious treasure, the gift could not be refused. So, after the first perfunctory meeting, he sent the girl to his zenana and forgot about her. For their part, the Bin Khawas passed their days pampered and indulged in the luxury of the zenana and, like all the others there, received in addition a monthly allowance of 2,000 rupees, with which no doubt many of them supported their families.

Mahbub Ali Pasha's own choice fell on Sardar Begum, a singing-girl. From the time that he noticed her, purdah veiled her looks, about which rumors ranged from surpassing beauty to earthy allure. But there was no doubt about her charm: Mahbub fell in love with her at first sight and remained so for many years. For her, he built two palaces as well as Mahbub Mansion, which was adjacent to the racecourse, as she was fond of horse-racing. Outside it was a small boulder, hollowed out like a seat, which was a favorite perch from which His Highness watched his horses being worked out. But for a woman, this casual exposure was impossible; Sardar Begum had to watch from inside. To minimize the obstacle for her, Mahbub had the zenana screens on the side which looked out to the racecourse made of fine gold mesh, so that she could see clearly without being seen.

The zenana was that area, whether in a cottage or a palace, where the women of a household hid their attractions and resisted temptations by admitting no males over the age of twelve except the husband, sons, and other blood relatives. Houses were designed with latticed galleries and other devices which allowed women to watch unseen any festivities or other events in the mardana (the men's part of the house), which men from outside the family might attend. Of course, their presence on such occasions was not exactly a secret, and many a delightful flirtation was carried on through the purdah curtain. Even this barrier was not absolutely impermeable, for Mahbub had one lifelong friend who, as a cousin, had the right of access to his zenana. One day Mahbub appeared just in time to see this young man leading one of the palace ladies to his carriage. "My friend," His Highness exclaimed in surprise, "you don't want that girl! She's pregnant."

"But I do want her," the cousin replied. "I love her and am

going to marry her." Years later the son whom that girl was carrying at the time used to be twitted by his friends about having been born in the wrong palace.

When a girl joined the zenana, her name was entered in a record book which also showed the dates of Mahbub's dalliance with her, a precaution for validating any claims of royal paternity which might follow. If she produced a son, her status immediately shot up, and her new importance was recognized by the bestowal of a handsome increase in her allowance, a special staff of servants, and an especially beautiful apartment in the zenana.

Life in Mahbub's zenana was generally happy and comfortable, for many of the ladies far more so than they might have expected from any marriage their parents could have arranged for them. With all their daily needs supplied, they passed their time adorning themselves in silks and jewels, singing and dancing for the diversion of their lord and each other, or petting and coddling the children. Three boys and three girls lived to maturity, while a heartbreaking number failed to make it through their early years; thirteen died in infancy.

Not infrequently, some or all of the ladies formed part of the retinue on an outing. One district town today owes its beginning to such an occasion, when the Nizam took some of his ladies along on a hunting trip. A sudden storm blew down the tents, with the result among other things that the zenana was exposed to general view. Straw huts were hastily erected which, being left behind when the royal party departed, were soon occupied by squatters. This was the beginning of a village that came to be called Mahbubnagar, in reference to that memorable visit.

On another occasion a number of ladies, including some from the Nizam's zenana, were going out of Hyderabad to attend a fair. In charge of the guards for the raths in which the ladies traveled was Nawab Galib Jung. Riding alongside the rath procession, he noticed a leg sticking out from under a curtain, shod in an embroidered slipper and with gold anklets but otherwise bare past the shapely calf. One lash of the Nawab's whip and the leg was hastily withdrawn. That night its owner apologized to the Nizam, "My Lord, forgive me, for I cannot stand in your presence. My leg is too painful."

Sending for Galib Jung, Mahbub Ali Pasha gave him an opportunity to report the incident: "I understand there was some accident today."

"No," the unsuspecting Nawab replied, "nothing out of the ordinary."

"One of the ladies reports that she was lashed."

At this Galib Jung presented his sword. "Your Highness," he exclaimed, "I have done a wrong thing. Had I known it was one of your Begums, I should have cut off the leg exposed to public view. But I thought it was an ordinary lady. Therefore, Your Highness, either cut my throat or forgive me!"

The Shadow of God

Although Mahbub Ali Pasha's resumption of a more active political life after the turn of the century was welcomed by his people, his popularity had never seriously suffered during the period of withdrawal. In fact, except for the nobles who were required to wait on him in their official capacities, many were almost unaware of the change, for inertia in the political arena did not mean inactivity in other areas of his life. He was not the type to become a recluse. In his struggles with the Resident, Mahbub's trump card was the love of his people, by whom he was, in the words of one Resident, Barr, "held in reverential awe not only on account of his position, but also from their readiness to accept his eccentricities as virtues." Some of the reasons for this are not far to seek in the stories told about him. Over and over, Mahbub seemed to do a little more than was required of him.

For instance, it is a custom in Hyderabad, indeed in much of India, to feed the poor at certain times: at stated intervals after a death in the family, as an act of thanksgiving, as an act of piety toward a saint, and for an assortment of other reasons. Mahbub

Ali Pasha did this regularly, sometimes in memorable fashion.

There is on Pahad-i-Shereef (Holy Hill), just a few miles outside the city, the tomb of Baba Sherfuddin, a saint who lived some 650 years ago. Originally a disciple of Khwaja Nizamuddin, a Delhi saint, Baba Sherfuddin wandered south and on this hill near Hyderabad settled down to meditation and prayer. No solitary ascetic, he sought out people and gave them healing not only for their souls but also for their bodies, as he was skilled in the use of herbs and natural remedies. He interested himself in the daily lives of the people, their joys and sorrows, and they came to regard him as their own living saint.

One day when he was very old, he went down the hill to the village and asked some of the people to help him. A corpse, he said, was lying at the top of the hill and required burying. Glad to return his kindnesses, the villagers readily agreed and followed him at a respectful distance. Near the top of the hill he disappeared; they looked all around but could find no sign of him. They did, however, find the corpse he had asked them to bury. It was lying on the ground, its face covered with a handkerchief. In the course of performing the task for which they had come, the kerchief was disturbed and the people saw that the corpse was that of Baba Sherfuddin himself.

Mahbub Ali Pasha was a devotee of Baba Sherfuddin. This was by no means a superficial or mechanistic devotion, for one of the strains in his complex personality was piety. When in a religious mood, he used to pray for hours together, sometimes in a penitential position standing on one leg. At such times he might fast for days. Eventually the preoccupation passed and he might get drunk or do something else inconsistent with piety.

At any rate, Mahbub made an annual retreat at the saint's tomb, staying in a small house nearby for a week or so. For two days of that time, he had the poor fed continuously from dawn until dusk. Because many of the poor of that neighborhood were vegetarian Hindus, both vegetarian and meat dishes were cooked. The rule was that anyone who came was welcome to eat his fill, but no one should carry anything away. One day a young boy, fourteen or fifteen years old, sat down to the meal. He ate a small part of his serving and then furtively stowed the rest in his loin cloth. Two guards who had seen him conceal the food questioned him. Observing the stir from a little distance away, the Nizam sent to inquire what the matter was. The boy fell at his Highness's feet and begged forgiveness, saying that his sister was too far gone in pregnancy to be able to walk the five miles from their home and so had asked him to try to bring her some food.

Mahbub Ali Pasha sent for his carriage and ordered a courtier to go along home with the boy to check his story. With them he sent a silver vessel containing some of each variety of vegetarian food that had been prepared. The courtier reported that what the boy had said was true. Thereupon Mahbub gave orders that every day of his stay at the tomb, food should be sent to the girl in a silver vessel which was to be left with her and not brought back. He also sent a message that he prayed she should have a safe delivery and a bonny baby.

A story about a poor man similarly illustrates Mahbub's ability to switch from his own orientation to that of the suppliant. This man came from the outlying districts to ask the Nizam for help in marrying off seven daughters, but had the ill-luck to catch him at an off moment during a brief stop at one of the minor palaces. On hearing the appeal, Mahbub handed the man his money bag. When the poor man counted the contents, they proved to amount to less than 200 rupees. "Your Highness," he urged, "how can I marry seven children with this?"

Mahbub laughed. "It looks as though that is all that is in your luck," he replied with a shrug.

"It may be what is in my luck," the peasant pleaded, "but I came here to ask you to give me something from what is in yours."

Struck by this logic, Mahbub ordered that the suppliant be given 14,000 rupees, and that his secretary write instructions to the local official to see about arrangements for the marriages.

As with anyone, Mahbub Ali Pasha's acts of generosity often

depended upon impulse or upon someone's happening to provide the opportunity. On the other hand, some instances seemed to reflect a deliberate, if unspoken, policy. An old courtier remembers strolling in the garden with his sovereign when they were approached by a man carrying a tray of turbans worth about 400 rupees. Asked to buy them, Mahbub Ali Pasha inquired the price and agreed to take the lot for the sum that the man mentioned, 1,400 rupees. As the happy peddler went off to collect the payment, the Nizam commented to his companion: "This fellow was wiser than the last one who came. That man asked only what his goods were worth. After he paid the people whom he had to bribe to get in here, what remained for him to take home?"

Even had he not understood what the peddler was doing, Mahbub might well have bought the turbans. It is part of the graciousness of Hyderabad manners that the dignity of people is more valued than money, and pains are taken to avoid humiliating anyone in public. It sometimes happens that this consideration can be expensive. Mahbub Ali Pasha once sat in his palace examining a tray of pearls. After a while he and his attendants left the room with a solitary guard on duty. Returning unexpectedly, the Nizam caught the guard holding a string of pearls which, frozen with fear, he could neither pocket nor return to the tray. Mahbub walked quietly past him, saying sotto voce, "You had better hide it quickly or they will come back and catch you."

On another occasion Mahbub rode into his courtyard just as the sentries were belaboring a thief. The man was a barber who, after he shaved the chief cook, helped himself to a pot of ghee on his way out through the kitchen. "What!" exclaimed the Nizam. "Can any man steal from the palace of the king? Does not the property of the father also belong to the son?" With that he sent the barber on his way with what might have been called his ill-gotten gains.

This was by no means an attitude peculiar to the Nizam. It was shared by many, probably the majority, of the nobles, and many similar stories are told to demonstrate it. For instance, one Nawab held at his home a Majlis, a religious observance to which anyone might come, whether particular friend or stranger off the street. A stranger who attended took advantage of the crowd at the time of departure to slip into the private apartments and appropriate an alarm clock, presumably the handiest item he could pick up. Unfortunately for him, as he was going through the gate the alarm went off. He was, of course, seized and searched by the guards, who brought him before the Nawab. The host said to his guards, "Although you were alert to notice this, you have forgotten one thing. You see, this man came here for a religious purpose, and so he would not do a thing like stealing. I gave him the clock."

It is an article of faith in Hyderabad that Mahbub Ali Pasha had the power to heal persons bitten by snakes. Hearing that this ability was possessed by a prisoner under sentence of death, Mahbub learned it from him and rewarded the man not only with his life but with a sizable amount of money with which to start over. For the rest of his life, Mahbub was at the call of anyone who required this help, and there are elderly people today who can vouch for cures performed by him. Mahbub Ali Pasha was not alone in possessing this power, for many people apparently have it. The healing of scorpion stings is a variation of it. Certainly a vast number of people in Hyderabad, even today, educated or illiterate, believe that this power exists, though some of the more sophisticated consider its importance to be psychological. Most of them know, at least at second hand, of people who have experienced it.

That it is not now easy to produce someone on demand who has been "cured" by this power is not particularly difficult to understand. After all, who are the people who are apt to be bitten by snakes? People who walk about barefooted in the dark or who stride through undergrowth unprotected by leather boots. People who have to put their hands into plants and bushes without necessarily being able to see what may be lurking under the leaves. These are apt to be simple village people, gardeners, farmers, village women. Bitten, they come in their fear and faith to the "big people" whom they believe can help them. Once cured, they disappear again into the masses, faceless and nameless.

One victim who was not anonymous was the wife of a retired justice of the Hyderabad High Court. As a child of seven she was bitten by a cobra. Knowing that any snake-bite victim was permitted immediate access to Mahbub Ali Pasha, no matter what he might be doing, the child's father took her posthaste to the palace. They found His Highness alone in the garden, lying under a tree with a stone for a pillow. At their approach he sat up and quickly understood the problem. Taking the little girl on his lap, he said the words of a charm and some verses from the Koran. Then, making some pleasantries with the child, he felt in his pockets and produced two gold coins which he pressed her to accept. She refused them shyly and presently went skipping off with her father, quite free of either pain or aftereffects.

Some people claim that the poison was overcome also when news of the bite was sent to His Highness by telegraph. The only private messages permitted on the telegraph which existed in the cabin at almost every railway grade crossing were snake-bite messages to the palace. The victim was then bound to visit the Nizam as soon as possible afterward. Even today the charm is supposed to work if the victim immediately says "Mahbub Ali Pasha ki dohai" ("for the sake of the grace of God to Mahbub Ali Pasha") and chews two bitter neem leaves. He then visits Mahbub's tomb as soon as possible.

For some reason it seems to be easier to find people who have with their own eyes seen the scorpion charm work, possibly because the swelling of the flesh and its going down again are apparent to the naked eye. As in snakebite, the practitioners of this cure have individual routines which are for them invariable. One rather common beginning prescribes that the bearer of the news must immediately be hit hard in the face. Our retired High Court justice, whose routine included giving this slap, was upset by the report of a colleague in the districts who came a cropper on account of it. A Chaoush who reported that his child had been bitten was so enraged at this reaction that he attacked the practitioner with a knife. "I ask you for help and you strike me," he shouted. "What way is that to respond to a suppliant?"

Not willing to risk similar misunderstandings with people whom he wanted to help, the justice came to an arrangement with his servant. When there was a bite at issue, the servant stepped in front of the justice, then turned and repeated the message so that he became the informant who had to be hit.

If there is any one point on which the eighty- and ninety-year-olds in Hyderabad today are in unanimous agreement, it is that in the era of Mahbub Ali Pasha there existed a degree of communal harmony that is not likely to be achieved again soon. The harmony was not only a chance by-product of a less competitive society. It was consciously worked at: people took considerable trouble to indicate their respect for others' religious beliefs and sentiments. In many of the houses of either community, Muslim or Hindu, no beef or pork was ever cooked, in order that the sensibilities of friends from the other community might not be offended when they entered. Mutton (whether sheep or goat), poultry, and the game bagged on shikar were the generally acceptable meats. Hindu shikaris habitually included a Muslim servant in their retinues, so that the game might be prepared in a way that was acceptable to their Muslim friends.

Festivities were celebrated across communal lines. An example is the langar procession, which fell during Moharrum, although it had intrinsically nothing to do with it. In fact it was not a religious festival at all, but it might have been susceptible of a communal interpretation if a zealot had chosen to apply his mind to it. About three hundred and fifty years ago, the young Sultan Abdullah of the Qutub Shahi kingdom of Golconda, just outside Hyderabad City, was out riding on a new and barely trained elephant which suddenly bolted and, throwing off the mahout, disappeared into the jungle with its rider. The young ruler's mother prayed earnestly to Allah for her son's safe return. Some days later, on the fifth day of Moharrum, he rode into Golconda on the elephant and in thanksgiving his mother had a heavy gold chain (langar) fabricated. On foot, mother and son took the langar in procession to a spot in Hyderabad where crowds had gathered for prayers in the presence of certain sacred symbols (alams). There it was broken up and distributed to the poor.

This memorial event became an annual tradition, which under the Asaf Jahis was a festive occasion, with the langar procession routed through several of the great deoris. Hindus and Muslims alike took part. First in the procession were the Jallads, or public executioners, dressed in red and carrying naked swords before them. Behind them came the elephant of the Kotwal, beside which more Jallads walked. The elephant was richly caparisoned and around its neck was the gold chain. Next came all the regiments of the state forces, regular and irregular, the latter dancing and singing. After them came the Paigah regiments, that is, troops of the premier nobles. These were followed by some of the nobles, on foot, with their retainers. When the procession passed through the deori of the Hindu Peshkar, it was the duty of every nobleman to salute him. But Mahbub's Peshkar, Maharajah Kishen Pershad, was not comfortable with the honor. Every year when the relations of the Nizam were due to come through his deori, Maharajah took his family and retired to an inner room, so that he should not have to demean those who were tied by blood to the sovereign by taking the salaam from them.

Within a few days of the langar procession occurred the great annual procession on the tenth day of Moharrum. Despite the martial nature of many of the events memorialized in the Moharrum observances, the army did not march in this procession, although the police did. Through the reign of Mahbub Ali Pasha, the Nizam himself used to sit on the elephant and throw money to the poor, but after that the task was taken over by the Dewan. The Moharrum procession was organized by the Kotwal, who also issued the invitation to people to sit in the police office at Char Minar to watch the procession. Those honored guests were pre-

sented with bags of coins to throw to the public during the observances. A Hindu elder in Hyderabad today comments, "It is significant for those who do not believe in the communal harmony
of Hyderabad State to realize that for many years both the Kotwal
and the Dewan of the state were Hindus, and the procession was
conducted as meticulously and with as much personal participation
as if they had been Muslims."

Historically in Hyderabad, Muslims had been recruited primarily for fighting and for active executive work, while Hindus
were recruited mainly for administrative work and for any work
requiring trust and the capacity for taking pains. The accoun-
tant-general's office was staffed so predominantly by Hindus that
Hindu fast days were officially half-holidays in that department.
Somehow it was thought that the people's temperament suited
them to these different types of work.

Occasionally, as in any population, special care had to be
taken to preserve harmony between differing groups. On one
occasion the Nizam had a direct hand in this precaution. Most
Indian festivals are movable feasts, being set according to a lunar
calendar or some particular astrological conjunction. Thus it
sometimes happens that two quite opposite festivals fall on the
same day. Once the congruence was between a particularly solemn
event during Moharrum, a month of sorrow for Shia Muslims,
and Holi, a particularly rollicking Hindu festival in which
revelers take to the streets with buckets of colored water, which
they splash on anyone they happen to meet.

Riding in the Moharrum procession, Mahbub Ali Pasha happened to notice, approaching down a side street, a group of Holi
merrymakers more than a little the worse for the drink with
which they had been celebrating. Apprehensive about what might
follow if they should chance to splash color on the sacred alams,
Mahbub quietly detached himself from the procession and joined
the revelers. As soon as they recognized him they gathered
around and he, laughing and playing Holi with them, led them
away in the opposite direction.

As an everyday matter, Mahbub had great faith in astrologers, many of whom gathered about his court. One of those on whom he relied told him that he was about to enter on an unfavorable period and that to avert it he must make a gift of sheni, that is, of those things which are considered to bode evil. He must choose any Brahmin he liked and give him a set of black clothes to wear, a black elephant, and a blue sapphire ring. The blue sapphire is even today greatly feared in India and very few people will wear it without first having a skilled reading of their horoscopes to make sure that it is safe for them. Many jewelers call the blue sapphire by the name "sheni." Mahbub Ali Pasha gave these prescribed items to a Brahmin, but, just in case he might have passed the bad luck along with them, he added a gift of a thousand gold coins.

If Mahbub passed a funeral procession, he got down from his carriage and helped to carry the bier for a little way, regardless of who the dead person might have been. Even today, except in metropolitan areas, the use of a hearse is common in India only among Christians, as people prefer to carry their dear ones on their own shoulders. In many places an old person may say jokingly to a younger one, "Some day I'll ride on your shoulders," to express a sense of closeness. Consequently the pallbearers are a constantly changing group, because as many men as are able take part, wishing to perform this last service for their friend.

The characteristic attitude toward poverty in Hyderabad was that the poor deserved help. Individual cases of need that came to the attention of the wealthy were treated with generosity. Otherwise the general problem was addressed with general largess: aristocrats and officials carried brocade bags filled with coins which were thrown to the poor on the streets. This was scarcely pinpoint delivery to the target population, and many a schoolboy or thrifty housewife benefited by picking up money which had been broadcast in this fashion. One of the widely accepted niceties, however, was that the money should be left for whom it was intended. There are adults in Hyderabad today who recall the sternness of parental warnings to that effect.

Mahbub Ali Pasha helped the poor according to the accepted pattern of the time. It was a source of shame and anxiety to him that his heir apparent did not share his enthusiasm for giving. Once the heir, Osman Ali Khan, sat without participating in the lavish strewing of coins during his father's birthday celebration. "Throw money, son, that the people may celebrate with us," the Nizam urged him. When Osman still sat with his hands in his lap, Mahbub again tried to persuade him. "A man can use up only so much money," he said earnestly, "and the day will come to each one of us when we have no more use for it. So share it while it is yours to share."

Osman was unmoved. After the celebration, Mahbub Ali Pasha commented, "If that boy ever becomes the Nizam, God alone knows what will happen to my people."

A similar story, possibly apocryphal, relates that one of the tutors reported to Mahbub that Osman was ready to shed his status as a pupil and assume the responsibilities of manhood. "I have trained him well," the tutor said. "He could become a second Aurangzeb."

Mahbub Ali Pasha received this news gravely. "In that case," he said, "you are responsible for tragedy." The comparison with the last of the great rulers of the Moghul Empire was not entirely inapt. Aurangzeb had a propensity for turning good things into bad through a deficient sense of proportion, so that recognition of his statesmanship and acts of piety was clouded even during his lifetime by his reputation for craft, ruthlessness, and greed.

Such nagging doubts, at least in part, made Mahbub Ali Pasha ill tempered rather than firm in the face of family dissension. In the Moghul tradition it was not necessarily the eldest son who inherited the throne, as the ladies of the zenana well knew. Possibly sensing some of Mahbub's reservations, one of his wives began a campaign to persuade the sovereign to name her son as his successor. To do this would mean setting aside Osman Ali Khan, who for more than twenty years had been recognized as the next Nizam and trained for the position. This ambitious wife had a three-year-old son, Salabat Jah, who was twenty-one years

younger than his half-brother Osman. The pressure had been
building for a long time and finally erupted in an angry scene.
Like many a henpecked husband, Mahbub took flight. Flinging
out of Purani Haveli in a temper, he went to Falaknuma, where
he settled down to some serious drinking.

This was truly serious as he was at that time suffering from a
liver complaint and was in the care of a Hakim who had forbidden him to drink during treatment. Even people who did not
know that alcohol could damage the liver were aware that the
medicines of the Hakims' pharmacopoeia often had ill effects if
the diet that went with them was not followed. There is no doubt
that this must have been a difficult prescription for him. Mahbub
Ali Pasha had for years been drinking heavily, a consumption
reputed to have reached three bottles of whisky a day at its peak.
By steady application and the natural gift of a hard head, however, he had built up a tolerance which left most people skepti-
cal of the tales about the quantities imbibed. Even occupants of
the Residency disagreed: some said that the delays and postpone-
ments from which the government suffered were due to the Nizam's alcoholic excesses; others doubted that any man could ride,
shoot, engage in tent pegging, and show the calm nerves, physical endurance, and clear complexion that Mahbub did if his
nervous system were marinated in alcohol. On the third day of
Moharrum, the consequence of excessive indulgence caught up
with him and the golden age of Hyderabad came to an end.

For all of his enjoyment of the luxury and the glamor of his
life, Mahbub Ali Pasha had never forgotten that he was, in the
words of his illustrious ancestor, Asaf Jah I, "the trustee of the
rights of the individuals." He was many things to many people:
the Shadow of God on earth and their sovereign lord; statesman
and sportsman; diplomat and petulant child; sybarite and
pietist; poet and philanthropist. He set the tone and his people
reflected it in their various ways. Above all, he was their refuge
and their beloved; they adored him and have not ceased to
mourn him.

Chapter IV

The Paigah Nobility: Sir Vicar ul Umra

THE Imperial Durbar was in progress. The princes and chiefs had paid their respects to the king-emperor, George V, who was now taking the salute from the officers. Major Waliud Dowla felt his chest expand with emotion as he stepped forward. A Paigah nobleman, son of the late Dewan of Hyderabad, graduate of Eton, Sandhurst, and the Imperial Cadet College at Dehra Dhun, he held a king's commission. With all the pride of his birth and training, he stood before George V and raised his sword in front of his face in the traditional gesture of fealty. A few steps further on, he stopped before the Nizam and repeated the ritual.

The following day he was summoned before a board of inquiry. Waliud Dowla explained, "Certainly I am loyal to the king-emperor. But the Nizam is also my sovereign. How could I not salute him as I passed in front of him?" For this insult to the British monarch, he was stripped of his king's commission. In disgust he resigned from the army and returned to Hyderabad.

The symbolism of Waliud Dowla's gesture could hardly have been more perfect. In the harshness of the rejection of it one sees not only the arrogance which the representatives of the British Empire felt at the zenith of their power but also perhaps some fear, a dark shadow of the things to come. For Waliud Dowla in his person exemplified as complete a melding of the two cultures as one would be likely to find. He was not only the product of British environment and education from the time he was six years old, but also the scion of a family which had played no small part in the founding of Hyderabad and had since consistently provided that state with its premier noblemen and some of its finest leaders.

When Asaf Jah I set about founding a dynasty in the Deccan, he granted lands, called jagirs, to his lieutenants according to their station and service. From those grants there emerged the social hierarchy that continued until the end of the dynasty. Immediately below the Nizam came those nobles whose progenitor was Abul Khair Khan, Asaf Jah's closest intimate and constant companion in arms, whose devotion and loyalty were rewarded with vast estates and the title of Thaigh Jung, the Sword of War.

This close relationship extended into the next generation, for it was to Thaigh Jung's son that Asaf Jah II turned in 1775, when he decided to organize a second army as a counterbalance to the regular army. This was not a new idea. The Moghul emperors bestowed commands of varying numbers of troops as rewards to individuals. Receipt of a command implied both the right and the responsibility to raise an army of the designated size and to maintain it in constant readiness for service. Therefore with the commands went lands yielding sufficient revenue both to support the troops and to maintain the prestige of the commander at an appropriate level.

For the maintenance of the new force, known as Paigah or household troops, the Nizam transferred possession of large tracts, comprising 127 villages yielding an annual revenue only slightly less than the income from the Nizam's own estates. To avoid giving even his most intimate companion a block of land which might conceivably become one day a base for operations against him, however, he chose villages which were not contiguous but scattered over nine districts. These lands were given to Abul Khair Khan's son, Abul Fateh Khan, and to his inherited title of Thaigh Jung was added that of Shums ul Umra (Sun of the Nobles). This latter title became the name by which the family was known.[1]

At Abul Fateh Khan's death, in 1791, his son Fakhruddin Khan inherited the estates, dignities, and titles. To these was added "Amir e Kabir" (Chief of the Nobles), the title by which each succeeding head of the family was invested by the ruler. Asaf Jah II, having increased the already vast estates, converted them by decree into a grant in perpetuity, safe from any possibility of resumption by future Nizams—a danger which every other jagirdar could fear if he did not show himself sufficiently diligent at court or skillful in commanding the troops, or if he fell from favor for any reason. Although the estates were in theory subject only to the burden of maintaining troops, the steadily declining number of troops in the succeeding reigns was balanced by increased expenses for the civil and ceremonial responsibilities of the Amir e Kabir. In the generation of Fakhruddin Khan's grandsons, early in Mahbub's reign, the estates were divided, but the power and the prestige of the "Paigah nobles" remained, not

---

[1] There is no tradition of family names in India. A relatively small number of people today have begun to adopt some patronymic, but generally it is not possible to deduce relationship from name alone. In Hyderabad the names given to children of the nobility were changed with every title conferred on them. For instance, Sir Vicar ul Umra's successive identifications were Fazhuddin Khan, Sikander Jung, Iqbal ud Dowla, Iktidar ul Mulk, and Vicar ul Umra. Jung, Dowla, and Mulk were ascending grades of nobility. To make it easier for readers to keep track of the people who appear in this book, the authors have referred to each one only by the title by which he was most widely known and have ignored the others. This occasionally results in the anomaly of a man's being referred to by a title which came to him only some years later.

being exclusively attached to any single branch of the family.

Fakhruddin Khan also received a royal princess in marriage. From then on, the daughters of the Nizams were given only to this house, of all the nobility, thus creating a class of nobles unique in any feudal system. Tied by blood and marriage to the royal family, they were above all the great nobles of the realm, beyond the jurisdiction of the ordinary courts, answerable only to their sovereign. For almost two hundred years they maintained this enviable position, up to the end of the dynasty.

By his royal spouse, Fakhruddin Khan had three sons. The first died young; the second never married; the third married a royal princess who bore no children. Two young men claiming paternity from the third son, however, were adopted by the second, unmarried one. The younger of those two survived to become known to history as Sir Asman Jah, for six years Dewan under Mahbub Ali Pasha. He was succeeded in that post by his cousin, Sir Vicar ul Umra, son of Rashiduddin Khan (Fakhruddin Khan's fourth son, by another wife). Rashiduddin had two sons, Sir Khursheed Jah and Sir Vicar ul Umra, each of whom became head of a branch of the family. Until the generation of the three cousin-brothers, there had been only one head of the Paigah estates, the Amir e Kabir, recognized and invested by the Nizam on the death of the previous Amir. From now on, there would be an Amir e Paigah at the head of each of the Asmanjahi, the Khursheedjahi, and the Vicar ul Umrahi Paigahs. At the time that this decision became official, it was further decided that there should be no future division of the Paigah estates, lest the burden of maintaining troops become difficult of fulfillment. Instead, each shareholder should receive pay according to his entitlement from the income of the Paigah branch to which he belonged.

By 1858 the struggle of the European powers for supremacy in India was over and the English had won out. The Mutiny of 1857 had been quelled, the last of the Moghul emperors had been put out to pasture, and England had firmly established sway over the subcontinent. Despite all the polite phrases about the independent

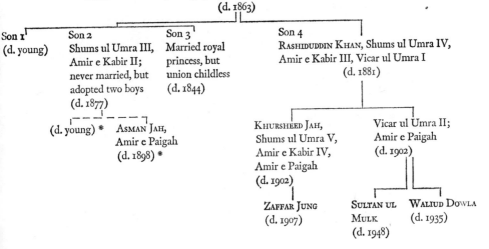

The Shums ul Umra Family

Abul Khair Khan, Thaigh Jung
(d. 1750)

Abul Fateh Khan, Thaigh Jung II, Shums ul Umra I
(d. 1791)

Fakhruddin Khan, Thaigh Jung III, Shums ul Umra II, Amir e Kabir I
(d. 1863)

Son 1
(d. young)

Son 2
Shums ul Umra III,
Amir e Kabir II;
never married, but
adopted two boys
(d. 1877)

(d. young) *   Asman Jah,
Amir e Paigah
(d. 1898) *

Son 3
Married royal
princess, but
union childless
(d. 1844)

Son 4
Rashiduddin Khan, Shums ul Umra IV,
Amir e Kabir III, Vicar ul Umra I
(d. 1881)

Khursheed Jah,
Shums ul Umra V,
Amir e Kabir IV,
Amir e Paigah
(d. 1902)

Zaffar Jung
(d. 1907)

Vicar ul Umra II;
Amir e Paigah
(d. 1902)

Sultan ul   Waliud Dowla
Mulk   (d. 1935)
(d. 1948)

* Claimed paternity of Son 3

87

sovereignty of the princes, it had become obvious, from effective interference in the internal affairs of the states, that they were intended to go the way which would best serve England's interest, irrespective of the cost to them in loss of dignity and treasure.

There had been a long struggle between Sir Salar Jung I, Dewan of Hyderabad for thirty years, and Rashiduddin Khan, Vicar ul Umra I, ending in the virtual victory of Salar Jung, who had the backing of the Resident. Long before, it was clear that Rashiduddin would have no choice but to accept the fact that the British were the heirs of the Moghuls, only much more powerful than the Moghuls had ever been. The country would never absorb the British as it had absorbed every other conquering race that had trod Indian soil, but neither could it get rid of them. The only solution was to swim with the tide. Rashiduddin felt himself too old and too set in his ways to do this, for he had in his make-up no trace of westernization. He had even refused to accept a knighthood, contemptuous of the notion that he could be either ennobled or demeaned except by his own sovereign.

Rejecting any change in his own manner of life, Rashiduddin Khan decreed that his sons must learn the new ways. They should be educated to understand the British and their ways thoroughly without losing the Moghlai culture or their own identity as premier nobles of a powerful prince. Only by this means was there any hope of being able to cope with the foreigners. Accordingly, when Vicar ul Umra II was an adolescent and Khursheed Jah somewhat older, Rashiduddin brought an English tutor into his household. The two youths were dressed in the European fashion of the day. They were taught to eat at a table with European crockery and cutlery. Special kitchens were built, and Goanese cooks, to whom the Portuguese had taught European cuisine along with the catechism, were employed to prepare the bland dishes that the sons must learn to relish. In every way, they must learn to conduct themselves, when called upon to do so, like English gentlemen. Gradually at first and then more rapidly, other noble families followed the trend. Before long, Hyderabad

became a happy hunting ground for English tutors and governesses and Goanese cooks.

The youths' initiation into Western ways was deliberate and
thorough, but they were still expected to be nobles of an oriental
court, steeped in the tradition and usage of their remote ancestors.
Along with the English language and English manners they were
taught Persian, Arabic, Urdu, and the elaborate formality of social
intercourse at a Moghlai durbar; along with tennis and billiards
they learned the skills of horsemanship, hunting, and wrestling;
along with their frock coats, cravats, and top hats they had the
gorgeous brocade sherwanis, the ceremonial dastar and bugloos,
and the splendid jewelry that went with Moghlai clothes.

When they grew old enough, Rashiduddin Khan's sons were
given brides. According to custom they would have been married
to royal princesses, thereby becoming brothers-in-law to the
Nizam, besides being grandsons of an earlier sovereign. By then,
however, court circles had begun to entertain some reservations
about the sons of the Shums ul Umra family. All three of Fakhruddin Khan's sons by his royal wife had died without legitimate offspring, and the claim that one of them had sired natural
sons was by no means universally recognized. Mahbub Ali Pasha's
father, when pressed to give Asman Jah a royal princess, threatened the proposed son-in-law with sequestration at Golconda
Fort if the question were ever raised again.

After the accession of Mahbub, Asman Jah was given the
princess he desired, one of Mahbub's sisters, and the union was
barren. Asman Jah must have been frantic for a child, not only
because children were highly valued for themselves in that society,
but also to vindicate the prolonged fuss he and his family had
made to bring about this marriage. Countless importunate prayers
must have gone up on his behalf. Finally, having turned fifty, he
went to Indore to visit a Hijra who had a reputation for helping
in cases of infertility. The degree of Sir Asman Jah's desperation
is indicated by the Hijra's gentle rebuke. "Why did you trouble
yourself to come so far? I would have come to you." Not so

gently, he stipulated: "If you have a son, you must build me a mosque here in Indore."

The noble visitor was ready to promise anything. When his son was born, Asman Jah contributed liberally to the local Hijras, but this did not satisfy the man from Indore, who came to Hyderabad and faced Sir Asman with the necessity of fulfilling the bargain. Asman Jah gave him the needed amount, despite being heavily in debt.

With regard to the sons of Rashiduddin Khan, although the royal princesses' guardians had no disposition to repeat the risk of infertile marriages, there could be no open allusion to the possibility of a deficiency in the young princes. The obvious way of saving everyone's face was to marry the boys first to girls from respectable but unimportant families. In this way Sir Vicar ul Umra took a bride when he was an adolescent. He soon became the father of a daughter. Three years later this marriage produced a son, Waliud Dowla. (At the age of six, Waliud Dowla was sent to Eton. At twelve, when he returned home for his first visit, he did not recognize his father. Introduced by the family physician who was chaperoning the youngster on his trip home, he greeted Sir Vicar with a handshake.)

When Vicar ul Umra had proved his capability, he was given Jehandarunissa Begum, Mahbub Ali Pasha's sister. She had been chosen for him by Mahbub's father, Afzul ud Dowla, who had celebrated the engagement ceremony with great pomp and then delayed the marriage until after the birth of the test baby from the first wife. When the wedding took place, Mahbub Ali Pasha, by then the Nizam, did not attend: a noble with the official title of Royal Brother-in-Law sat in for him. This royal wife assumed the title of Lady Vicar ul Umra when her husband was knighted. Her child, Vicar ul Umra's eldest son, was Sultan ul Mulk.

On one occasion Sir Vicar ul Umra and Sultan ul Mulk were out hunting. Becoming separated from their party, they found themselves by mid-afternoon exhausted and hungry. A sudden downpour capped their discomfort. Presently they came upon the mud hut where a poor peasant lived. Taking shelter there, they gladly accepted the porridge which was all the peasant could offer. By the time the rain had ceased and they were ready to leave, their retinue caught up with them. Sultan ul Mulk stripped off his gold bangles and presented them to their host. His father, determined to match the peasant's generosity in sharing what he had, pulled out the bag of money that was stowed with the supplies and gave all the 1,000 rupees in it to the poor man. On his return to Hyderabad, Sir Vicar asked Sir Asman Jah, who was then the Dewan, to make a further gift. The latter replied that he was not in the habit of refusing his young cousin-brother, and so the peasant found himself the recipient of a grant of land.

This incident tells the measure of Sir Vicar. Stories like it are legion, and most have the ring of truth. One concerns the Nawab of Tarbund, a friend who was accustomed to paying almost daily visits to Sir Vicar's home. Once when he came after an interval of ten days, Sir Vicar inquired the reason for his absence. The Nawab confessed that he was in debt to the tune of one lakh (100,000 rupees). In consequence he had recently been reluctant to leave his deori because creditors were harassing him.

Sir Vicar called to his secretary. "Tomorrow morning," he said, "deliver one lakh of rupees at the Nawab Sahib's house," and specified the number of guards that should be sent as escort, for neither paper currency nor checks had come into use in those days; only gold and silver coins were money. The secretary, however, assumed that Sir Vicar had drunk more than was good for him and would not afterward recall the incident. That was a mistake, for the next day Sir Vicar sent for him to inquire whether the money had been delivered. The secretary confessed that it had not, and, apologizing profusely, went to dispatch it.

That evening the Nawab of Tarbund presented himself at the palace. "You have sent me this money," he said to Sir Vicar, "and it was most generous and kind of you to rush to my aid as soon as you heard of my difficulties. But I cannot use it, for I cannot repay you. Have you thought of that?"

Sir Vicar answered, "Friend, did you hear me say a word about repayment?"

From his childhood Sir Vicar ul Umra had a servant, Munir Khan, who when he grew old was pensioned off at his full salary, which was several times that of most domestic servants. He went to his home to be looked after by his children, and on festival days he visited his old master. On Sir Vicar's becoming Dewan in 1893, Munir Khan went to congratulate him. When he reached the deori it was evening, and Sir Vicar was playing a game of billiards. The old servant climbed the steps to the billiard room, saw that Sir Vicar was sighting a shot along his cue, and, not wishing to disturb the shot, stood motionless in the doorway. But Sir Vicar had seen him. "Well, Munir Khan, how are you?" he called out as the cue slid through his fingers.

"By your grace I am well," Munir Khan replied, salaaming.

"How come you are here today? Anything special?" Sir Vicar asked, walking around the table and surveying the game.

"I heard that you have become Dewan and I have come to offer my humble congratulations."

"Thank you, Munir Khan. With your prayers I will succeed in the work entrusted to me."

Throughout this conversation Sir Vicar, his eye on the game, was walking around the billiard table, taking a shot here or there, looking up in between to hear what the old man said or to answer him. Then, "Anything else?"

"Yes, Master," the old servant confessed. "My granddaughter is to be married. I wanted to ask whether I could have a month's salary in advance."

Sir Vicar bent down and sighted along the cue. With one eye closed and still taking aim, he called out, "Mr. Secretary!" The secretary jumped to attention. "One month's salary for Munir Khan."

"Very good, Your Excellency," the secretary agreed.

Sir Vicar concentrated on his shot again. Straightening up as the balls ricocheted and scored, he suddenly called out, "Mr.

Secretary! Whose salary? Not his, mine! One month of my salary for Munir Khan."

The next pay day five coolies in the uniform of the state treasury jogged up to Munir Khan's house, surrounded by guards. On his head each coolie balanced a bundle containing a thousand gold coins tied up in a royal yellow cloth. The Dewan's salary was being delivered to Munir Khan in precisely the same fashion that, all over Hyderabad, officials received their salaries every month.

Sir Vicar's appointment as Dewan, on which Munir Khan had come to felicitate him, had required something of an effort to achieve. The British had backed him heavily and it looked as though the Nizam would not be able to refuse the appointment. But when his nomination became known, it provoked widespread public opposition on the grounds that Sir Vicar owed too much money to too many people. Rather than lose the honor of the post, Sir Vicar sold his fabulous heirloom jewelry and, after clearing his debts, received the appointment.

Many families today are rich because their forebears who were involved in those jewelry sales invested their substantial commissions wisely. One such is the Parsi family of Shapurji Chenai, whose name indicates that his family were once engaged in trading with China. On one of his trips to Europe, Sir Vicar took Shapurji Chenai along as a kind of aide and secretary. On that trip Shapurji acquired the Christian valet who eventually wound up in Mahbub Ali Pasha's employ. Sometime after he became Dewan, Sir Vicar had a falling out with Shapurji. We do not know what it was about, but some contemporary notes indicate that, although hardworking and honorable, Sir Vicar had a strong need to be liked which led him to be peevish when forced to defend himself against criticism. This time Sir Vicar was downright vindictive, for he sent people to loot Shapurwadi, his erstwhile friend's home. Fortunately, his elder brother, Sir Khursheed Jah, heard about it in time to intervene.

Rather than fight, Shapurji switched; he spent the remainder of his career in Khursheed Jah's service. It seems to have been a most profitable change, for a story exists that at one time in their association Khursheed Jah entrusted a crore of rupees to Shapurji, specifying only that it should be available on demand. Like the Biblical steward with the ten talents, Shapurji invested the money and, in the space of ten years, nearly doubled the original sum. When Khursheed Jah sent for the money, Shapurji brought the total amount, but the Amir e Kabir rejected it, saying, "I gave you one crore to keep for me and I want one crore back. It is against my religion to take interest. You may do what you wish with the rest, but give me my crore." The excess amount became the foundation of the Shapurji fortune.

A descendant of Khursheed Jah doubts this tale on the grounds that the Amir e Kabir, although generous with lands, was stingy with money. That reputation persists despite the fact that he once advanced money for a gem which Mahbub fancied but could not afford. The story of the crore of rupees may be wholly or partly true. It does not say why this money should have been given, but it would surely not be the first time that someone had found it convenient to make a small fortune disappear for a period of time. The practice of giving large sums of money to someone to hold for an indefinite period, often during a journey the owner was undertaking (Khursheed Jah, an inveterate traveler, was said to be the first prominent Muslim to visit the places of Hindu pilgrimage in India), was so common as to figure in a number of folk stories, many of them dating to the seventeenth and early eighteenth centuries.

Neither debts nor official responsibilities could long divert Sir Vicar ul Umra from his first love, the building of palaces. In the early 1890s, Razak Ali Baig, secretary to Sir Vicar ul Umra, wondered whether his employer's grandiose ideas had rubbed off on him. He was in debt to his eyebrows over a house he had built on top of a hill. The house was proving too expensive for him to maintain, quite aside from the initial investment. Merely supplying water to the hilltop was costly. The house was small enough, by the standards of the Paigah nobleman for whom he worked, but it commanded a beautiful view over the lake and lay just off the main road between the city and the cantonment. Being a clever man, Razak Ali Baig began to develop a plan to recoup his position. He invited Sir Vicar ul Umra to a lavish entertainment which showed off the house and location to best advantage. When the property received from the chief guest the admiration that the host expected, it was presented as nazar. Sir Vicar ul Umra protested that he could not accept such an expensive gift. His host begged him to take it as "more suitable to your taste than to mine." Eventually Sir Vicar bought and enlarged the house, re-naming it Vicar Munzil.

When he took on this project he was already an experienced builder and man of property. He had inherited a huge deori which he enlarged and modernized. He had built Begumpet Palace in a sixty-two-acre compound which included, in addition to the main palace, separate mansions for his sons and grandson. In each case the upper floors were occupied by the zenana, the lower by the mardana, which were apartments used only by the men. Also within the compound was a mosque, a copy of one in Spain.

At Vicarabad, in his jagir, he had built a summer home where he could stay in comfort while seeing to the development of roads and schools there. Vicarabad was a place of large orchards and good water, both of which helped to give an impression of cool-ness in the summer heat. Following Sir Vicar's lead, it became fashionable for the nobles to build themselves summer places there. To increase further the comfort of his trips by avoiding the inconvenience of going some miles into town to Nampalli Station, Sir Vicar had built Begumpet Station, a new stop on the railway line near his property.

But the crowning achievement of Sir Vicar's career as a builder of palaces was Falaknuma, "Mirror of the Sky," begun in 1884. One of the four roads radiating from Char Minar runs out to a hill atop which is a spring called Bibi ka Chashma, in honor of the daughter of the Prophet. Somehow this spring had acquired a reputation for making barren women fertile, and as a result an annual fair came to be held at the place. Attending the fair, Vicar ul Umra was struck by the beauty of the hilltop, with its view over the city for miles, and he determined to erect a palace there. When it was finished, even the sophisticates of Hyderabad marveled. One of them, Sir Asman Jah, also worried about his cousin-brother's expenditure. "Chota bhai [younger brother] is bankrupting himself over this," he said prophetically.

The palace was a lavish display of international skill and products. Marble came from Italy to create a foyer chaste in its simplicity. Workmen from Florence tooled the leather ceiling of the great banquet hall, while nuns from France worked the camel-hide upholstery. According to the fashion of the day, which had been set so prominently by Sir Vicar ul Umra's father, everything in the mardana apartments was in Western style. The furniture and ornaments were imported from Europe. French brocades covered chairs and sofas which were carved and curved in the Empire style. Ruched and ruffled valances stretched across the doorways and French windows, where the light picked out the sheen of the draperies cascading from them. Pedestals held marble statuary, and Victorian whatnots displayed delicate English, French, and German figurines. Tables were laid with elaborate, crested gold and silver cutlery for a succession of courses served on monogrammed china. Gone were the local liquor and the golden goblets; in their place, crystal glasses and stemware held Scotch whisky and French champagne.

This luxurious setting represented the apogee of the double life that men had begun to lead in Mahbub's Hyderabad, for side by side with the new culture, the old culture remained as it had been for the past two hundred years. Western ways did not invade the zenana for almost another half-century. So the Western beverages and crystal, the cutlery and china, together with the frock coats and trousers, were left behind in the mardana when the men joined their ladies. When they ate in the zenana, silver sailabchis and jugs of warm water were brought for washing fingers and rinsing mouths before meals. The men sat down at the dastarkhan in pyjamas and elaborately embroidered kurtas of sheerest muslin, to a meal of twenty different dishes, fragrant with spices, pungent with chilies, garnished with gold and silver leaf and served in great platters and bowls of ancient red, blue, and green pottery.

Both modes were observed at Falaknuma, but it was for Western ways that the palace was famous. Here Sir Vicar lived in the grand manner, entertaining at hunt breakfasts, formal dinners, and houseparties for visiting European royalty and nobility, and holding receptions for the Viceroy. Smart equipages, teams of beautifully matched horses, and liveried coachmen and postillions were daily at the door. It was such hospitality that led to Sir Vicar's leaving Falaknuma.

In the spring of 1895, Mahbub Ali Pasha attended the fair at Bibi ka Chashma and, with a small retinue which included a few of his favorite ladies, stayed at Falaknuma. Obviously pleased with the site and palace, he kept on extending his stay—ten days, two weeks, twenty days. When he eventually confessed the extent of his admiration, his host replied according to the time-honored tradition: "Sire, I built it for you."

The following day, taking only their clothes, all three generations of the Vicar ul Umra family left Falaknuma for good and moved to the deori in the city. By November a settlement had been agreed upon. Mahbub Ali Pasha declined to accept the whole of the palace and its contents as nazar; he accepted a part and for the balance paid a substantial amount. Despite his wealth, Mahbub found it necessary to pay for his new home in several installments, a rather endearing detail that makes him seem like the rest of us.

One gets the impression that Sir Vicar ul Umra did not really mind parting with his exquisite palace and rather felt some relief. Although his annual personal income was eleven lakhs, he was almost constantly in debt. To unload that much money—and run up debts besides, which stood at more than eighteen lakhs at the time of his death—one might assume he gambled heavily. Horse racing was a favorite sport and, like all the nobility, when the Nizam was present at Malakpet Racecourse, Sir Vicar ul Umra was also expected to attend, arriving in a four-in-hand preceded by buglers. But there was no betting in the royal boxes; that was an indulgence of the common people.

Like his contemporaries in England who bankrupted themselves entertaining Edward VII, Sir Vicar found that his palaces and all that went on in them, including the hospitality, were enough to eat up several fortunes. In his turn, moreover, he was not a niggardly guest. When on one of his European trips he visited Edward VII, with whom he carried on a personal correspondence for some years, he took as the gift to his host a coat sewn all over with pearls. Such stately travel is no longer possible. A few years ago, the Indian government's tightened restrictions on foreign exchange caused a present-day Paigah nobleman to complain: "When my father went to Europe he took with him three lakhs. Now I am allowed to take seventy-five rupees."

Helping Sir Vicar, Khursheed Jah, and Asman Jah to attain this staggering level of expenditure were all the dependents who had a claim on the Paigah estate. One young relative, sowing his wild oats, exceeded the bounds of discretion even for that permissive society. After an all-night party he presented a wonderful sarapa to a singing girl in appreciation of her many skills. This sarapa, a set of jewelry "from head to toe," had come to the Shums ul Umras through an alliance with the Asaf Jahs. Hearing of the gift, the angry Nizam sent an emissary to negotiate the return of the jewelry. The terrified girl could scarcely hand it back fast enough and had to be repeatedly assured that the Nizam really wanted her to have the large sum of money that was being offered in exchange. Having thus secured possession of the sarapa, Mahbub Ali Pasha arranged it on a tray and sent it off to the rash young nobleman with a curt note saying that this jewelry had been given in the dowry of a princess and was not intended for singing girls.

Animals represented another expensive taste. Sir Vicar's son

Waliud Dowla had a female tiger cub which he eventually presented to the municipal zoo. He had brought the cub home for a pet when he had gone into a cave and found her after shooting the mother. He and the children used to play with the young tigress, naming her Suraiya, after the queen of Afghanistan, and she had the run of the house. One day Colonel Azmathullah, a solidly built man, entered the drawing room to call on Waliud Dowla. Suraiya, who had been lying behind a bookcase, sprang on the visitor and knocked him down just as Waliud Dowla entered the room. Shouting her name, he beat her with the crop he always carried and sent her off in disgrace, but the colonel convinced him that Suraiya had become too big to be safe with children, especially as she was being fed on raw meat. Accordingly, she was confined in one room until a cage could be built for her, and when Waliud Dowla went on Haj, the pilgrimage to Mecca and Medina which is enjoined on the Muslim faithful, she was sent to the Public Gardens.

It was customary for a noble family to keep a stable of race horses along with the riding and carriage horses and children's ponies. The Shums ul Umras were no exception, but their personal tastes ran to more exotic animals. Sir Vicar's brother, Khursheed Jah, kept a herd of ostriches which had been trained to be ridden, although that message had not always got through to the birds. Ostrich races added hilarious entertainment to his parties.

Beyond all this expenditure for pleasure, Sir Vicar ul Umra was a generous man who gave money and gifts unstintingly. That some of the giving was extravagant, not to say foolish, marked him as a product of the feudal society that Hyderabad was, rather than of the industrial society that it was to become. One of the surviving figures of that earlier period describes himself as a remnant of feudalism and recognizes as one of the stigmata of that order an inability to understand the value of money. Although the simple circumstances in which this man now lives bear few reminders of his former luxury, he still has no comprehension of the relation between money and himself except in the most distant, intellectualized fashion. A hundred rupees given him today, either as payment or as windfall, might well go toward staving off one or more of his creditors. But some needy person, happening along while the sum was still intact, might find himself the recipient of all of it. Our anachronism says matter-of-factly: "My children would not do that, and my grandchildren even understand a budget. But for my generation money was not something to think about; it was the merchants' business to look after that."

Even so, and in this respect also differing from present practice, the giving of money in those days was by no means an impersonal way to salve one's conscience or discharge one's social obligations without getting involved. Like his peers, Vicar ul Umra was generous also with his energy and attention. On one of his trips to Bombay word soon spread that a prince from Hyderabad was staying with his retinue in the Taj Mahal Hotel. One of his callers was a Hindu who said that he had four daughters to provide for and no money for their marriages. Sir Vicar inquired how much was needed and was told that 200 rupees for each would do nicely. Sir Vicar thereupon ordered his secretary to give the man 6,000 rupees and to secure his name, address, and the date for the weddings. When the marriages took place, Sir Vicar returned to Bombay to attend, bringing gifts for the brides and grooms.

Once after he had ceased to be Dewan and was being pressed hard by his creditors, Sir Vicar was sitting on the verandah at Vicar Munzil when he was accosted by an elderly woman who said that she had lost her husband and her only son. As she had nothing more to live for, her only desire was to go on Haj, hoping that she might die in the Holy City of Mecca. Moved by her despair, Sir Vicar summoned his secretary and asked him how he could help her. The secretary replied, "Your Excellency, there is no more money. You have only debts." Then, concluded the nobleman, it would be necessary to pawn something, for the woman must go. With the pawnbroker's money, Sir Vicar not only paid for her trip but also sent a man to escort her to Bombay and make sure that she was placed in reliable hands for the journey.

Although he was soft-hearted toward anyone in need, Sir Vicar could be stern when he felt punishment was justified, as a servant once discovered. In one of his palaces Sir Vicar had decided to shift to another suite of rooms, and a platoon of servants was engaged in moving his personal effects. During the process, the secretary came in a state of agitation to report the disappearance of a pearl thasbi, a Muslim rosary containing a hundred beads for the hundred names of God. Legend says God actually has a hundred and one names, but the last is known only to the camel, which explains why the animal looks down so superciliously on the rest of us. Few Muslims can recite the whole hundred, and most generally tell the beads by repeating "There is no God but Allah, and Mohammad is His Prophet," or some verse from the Koran. A silk tassel marks the beginning of the circle. Joining the search, Sir Vicar noticed the tassel dangling from the pocket of one of the servants. Not the flickering of a facial muscle betrayed the discovery. Presently the secretary also noticed the tassel and, pouncing on it, pulled the thasbi triumphantly into view. "Oh, is that what you were looking for?" Sir Vicar said negligently. "I gave him that."

But when evening came, he called the offender before him and discharged him. "Let there be no misunderstanding," the contemptuous employer said. "I am not sending you away because you stole the thasbi but because you are a fool! When you put your hand to anything, whatever it may be, you should do it properly."

Even the servant who had been fired continued to receive his wages for the rest of his days. The punishment was the dismissal from service, not the deprivation of livelihood. A Paigah descendant today remembers seeing his mother dismiss one of her women servants in anger. "You may send the woman away if you like, but one thing you may not do," her husband warned her firmly. "You have children; she also has children. You may never withhold the money by which she buys the food for her children."

In spite of all the splendor of his surroundings, the glamor of his habits, and the abundance of his largess, Sir Vicar ul Umra was not immune to tragedy. Fabulous jewels, fairy-tale palaces, and a real princess as wife no more guaranteed happiness-ever-after in Hyderabad than in Hollywood. Among the Paigah nobility, gracious manners often masked severe conflicts, at times amounting to such open enmity that the Resident felt called upon to intervene. No one can run up debts amounting to double his income, as Sir Vicar ul Umra did, without collecting some enemies along the way. Intrigue was mounting against him at the court, and it was not clear how long even his alliance with the British could hold out against it. To top it off, his first son was in trouble. Sultan ul Mulk was young, handsome, intelligent, vigorous, the descendant of two great houses. How could his world come tumbling down about his ears? Sir Vicar ul Umra found his son's situation difficult to understand, possibly because he was himself a thoroughly feudal man while Sultan ul Mulk was probably as close to a modern man as Hyderabad had yet produced.

In a burst of drive for personal achievement, the young man had declared that he was going to earn by his own wits as much of a fortune as his father had inherited. This determination alone was enough to mark him as eccentric. But more than that, he set out to achieve his objective. He engaged in foreign trade, including the opium trade; he speculated in currency; he got involved in all sorts of schemes which put him well on the way to his fortune. Behind his back, he was known by a nickname which indicated the derision in which people were held who were overly concerned with money making.

Suddenly the blow fell. Whether success went to his head and he overestimated his capacity, or ambition pushed him into illegal activities, or he had an attack of insanity, as was whispered, or whether enemies simply succeeded in discrediting him, the cause of his downfall is a secret still closely guarded in Hyderabad. At any rate, the Nizam was led to believe that his young kinsman was dangerous, and banishment followed. Justly or unjustly, in mercy or vindictiveness, Sultan ul Mulk was sent to England. Through financial control it was possible to keep him living with people who could be trusted to direct his activities and send back regular reports on him. It was given out that he had been sent abroad for medical treatment, which may even have been true, though if he was ill there was no indication that his mother had noticed, even to the extent of inquiring about his health.

Lady Vicar ul Umra was said to be a beauty, and charming enough to captivate the European ladies who met her. What they rarely had the opportunity to see was that she was also a descendant of princes who had not stopped at waging war against brothers who stood in the way of their grasp of power, or at poisoning or stabbing them. Lady Vicar ul Umra could be imperious when she wanted something and ruthless when displeased. Dark tales were whispered of the fate of servant women unlucky enough to draw her anger. Daughter of one Nizam, sister of another, wife of a premier nobleman, beautiful and wealthy, her position was nearly impregnable.

Then suddenly, in the face of all this, Sir Vicar ul Umra did something that was the epitome of his attempts to live in two cultures at once. After two arranged marriages, to women he had never seen and about whom he was not even consulted, he married for love. There was in Hyderabad a Parsi lady of the Viccajee family, Gulbai, as delicate and lovely as the rose for which she was named. As a practicing physician she had a substantial income of her own, in addition to what she had inherited from her prosperous family. It was at a party in Bombay that these two met and fell almost immediately in love. The measure of their feeling is what it ultimately cost them.

With the service of the dead read for her when she married outside her Parsi religion, Gulbai became a Muslim, taking the

name of Nur Jehan. Giving up her medical practice, she entered
purdah and, although the marriage was only a brief idyl, remained true to that secluded mode of life for the almost thirty
years of her widowhood. As Lady Vicar ul Umra lived for the
most part at Begumpet Palace, Sir Vicar installed his new bride
at Vicar Munzil, which he also used for his office while he was
Dewan. Built on the crest of a hill, this palace had at a lower
level an inconspicuous apartment with its own concealed courtyard. Whenever Lady Vicar ul Umra came to Vicar Munzil, Nur
Jehan lived in that apartment. The wooden shutters on the windows still bear designs which she once painted to amuse herself
while she was hidden there.

This marriage lasted less than two years, for Sir Vicar died in
1902 at the age of forty-eight. He was on shikar when an urgent
message came asking his return to Hyderabad. Calling for food
before starting on his journey, he ate some curry puffs and, before
he could even set out, died. During her husband's absence Nur
Jehan had gone to stay at her own house. Immediately she heard
the news of his death and its circumstances, she knew that she
was in peril. Disguised as a servant woman, she fled to a relative
in the Secunderabad cantonment, where she would be under the
protection of the British Raj. Lady Vicar padlocked Nur Jehan's
house. Only after ten years, by which time Mahbub too was dead,
was Nur Jehan able to return there, armed with a court order.
When the house was unlocked, she took one look and fainted
dead away. The tropics had done their work. Damask curtains
hung in shreds. Costly Persian carpets were reduced to odd tufts
that the moths had disdained. Beautiful inlaid furniture had
furnished picnics for the termites. The jungly garden showed almost no trace of its former charm. Impoverished but still gallant,
Nur Jehan took a small apartment, where she lived quietly until
she died of plague in 1931.

Widow of a man whose name lives chiefly in the palaces he
built, Lady Vicar ul Umra, with unconscious irony, built herself
a new palace in which to pass the remainder of her life. She died
on the day India received its independence.

Scion of the first family of nobility, brother-in-law of Mahbub Ali Pasha and pledged to serve him in the most important post in the government, Sir Vicar ul Umra was in a position to influence both the events and the tone of the 1890s in Hyderabad. Some of the results of that influence were the opposite of what he wanted, both for others and for himself; the culmination was his dismissal from the Dewani. Educated to be at home in both the British and the Moghlai cultures, Sir Vicar's preferences kept him close to the former politically and to the latter in his personal life. Honorable, diligent, unimaginative, eager to be liked by everyone and to deserve the liking, he could not really understand that good intentions were not enough. He failed to perceive how he had put himself into a position to be used, or to conceive how that posture might appear to the Nizam. The harder he worked, the more surely doomed he was, for his choice of the Resident as his political mentor had put him on a collision course with the Nizam. Mahbub Ali Pasha attended Sir Vicar's parties, accepted Falaknuma when it was presented, responding with a handsome settlement, and treated Sir Vicar with every courtesy. But there was no warmth between them. Mahbub did not trust him, and eventually this brought about his downfall.

Chapter V

Maharajah Kishen Pershad

SINCE he was Dewan, there had been no question but that Maharajah Kishen Pershad would be in the royal party traveling to Delhi in December, 1911, for the Imperial Durbar. There he performed his duties with the charm and smooth efficiency that were his special gifts. None who did not know him would have guessed that when he was alone, he wept. Tears were as natural to an Indian man as to a woman, and when Maharajah remembered his late sovereign, tears watered his memory of Mahbub Ali Pasha, as though to keep it fresh. His feelings found expression in verse:

> But when without you came the time to live,
> Ah, what a plight my weeping eyes were in!
> Before you went, life had so much to give.
> Yet still continues this sad world to spin.

For a full half-century, the title "Maharajah" indicated only one person to every man, woman, and child in Hyderabad: Maharajah

Sir Kishen Pershad Bahadur, G.C.I.E., Yamin us Sultanath. Tracing his ancestry from Todar Mull, the Vizier of Akbar the Great, through Rai Mull Chand, who accompanied Asaf Jah I from Delhi, and Maharajah Chandulal, Peshkar from 1809 to 1842, Kishen Pershad was the grandson of Chandulal's grandson, Maharajah Narinder Pershad. The latter had been Peshkar and, briefly, Dewan during the minority of Mahbub Ali Pasha.

Kishen Pershad was born in 1864. Being so nearly of an age with his sovereign, he was occasionally asked in later years whether he was the older. Because in Urdu the word for "older" is the same as for "bigger" (and therefore colloquially for "more important"), Kishen Pershad would never answer the question as it was put to him. Instead he always used to reply, "I was born two years before His Highness."

In the closing decades of the nineteenth century, democracy in Hyderabad was still a long way off; government posts were largely hereditary and the Nizams chose their ministers from among the nobles. It was necessary, therefore, that the scions of the nobility be groomed from an early age for future responsibility. Kishen Pershad's education was both broader and deeper than that of most. English education and British administration had so impressed Sir Salar Jung that around Mahbub's educational program he built a Western-type school to which Kishen Pershad was sent, along with a select few of his contemporaries. Academic education, however, was by no means the most important of the qualifications required of these young men. The elaborate court etiquette had to be mastered, and they were carefully brought up by both precept and example to the great traditions of the Moghul court, its manners and courtesy, its minute consideration for the feelings of others, its noblesse oblige, and, indeed, its humility. In the words of the poet Fani which Maharajah was fond of quoting:

> A paradox: stoop to elevate;
> Humility marks the truly great.

Beyond all these lessons, on account of his Hindu birth Kishen Pershad studied Sanskrit, the language of the sacred writings; on account of his hereditary charge of the Royal Treasury he learned accountancy; to satisfy his artistic interests he took instruction in poetry, music, calligraphy, painting, and photography. Because of his interest in humanity, he studied medicine and astrology. His philosophic bent sent him to esoteric works on religion. In later manhood, he took to ceramics and produced beautiful objects at the potter's wheel. While he was still a young man, an accident of travel was responsible for his exploring the art of cookery.

Although in later life he lost his orthodox ways, at the age of nineteen, on a tour of the Dominions with the Nizam and Sir Salar Jung, he was still a strict vegetarian, eating only food prepared by his own Brahmin cooks. During the journey, an accident separated the carriage containing his staff from the royal retinue, and as time for the evening meal approached, Sir Salar Jung became concerned about what his young protégé could eat. He offered Kishen Pershad raw supplies if he could prepare them himself, but the young man only had a vague notion of how to boil rice. Cooking his rice as best he could, he sent to a nearby village for some pickles from a Brahmin household to complete his simple meal. He had already learned to turn adversity to advantage by extracting a lesson from it, however, and he determined then never to allow himself to fall into another such predicament, causing anxiety to others as well as discomfort to himself. As soon as he returned home, he set about learning cookery. His interest deepened with every lesson and in time he became a superb cook, able to prepare dishes from one type of lentil in fifty-two ways.

In addition to various skills, Kishen Pershad was developing the attitudes that would mark his entire life. King worship had, from time immemorial, been the foundation of Indian society. Just as to Muslims the king was the Shadow of God, so to Hindus he was a divine incarnation. This belief served through the centuries to hold people of different faiths together in fidelity and

obedience to their sovereign, who in all walks of life was regarded to some degree as more than human. An incident in
Kishen Pershad's family, years later, illustrates this.

While Kishen Pershad was Dewan, Mahbub Ali Pasha paid a
ceremonial visit to his home, and the ladies of the household
were instructed by his father to present nazar to their ruler. One
of Kishen Pershad's sisters demurred, saying that in the absence
of her husband, who was out of the state on a business trip, she
wished to be excused. Yielding to her father's insistence, however, she offered nazar, but only after wrapping herself in a shawl
so closely that only her hands and a fraction of her face were
visible. As this was the manner in which Hindu widows effaced
themselves, Mahbub turned to Kishen Pershad and asked, "Is this
sister of yours a widow?"

As soon as he heard his own words, Mahbub was appalled at
the faux pas. He apologized nervously for the question and departed in precipitous haste, leaving his perturbed hosts to wonder
how came this evil omen, that such a question fell from the lips
of the sovereign. It was no doubt pure coincidence that the sister's
husband died in a distant city on that very day, of a heart attack.
From that moment on, no lady of the family ever again appeared
before the Nizam.

In Hyderabad each generation fostered in the next this feeling
of awe of the Nizam. As Kishen Pershad grew up, his reverence
for and personal devotion to his sovereign increased until it became the very breath of life to him. Something of how that
devotion should be expressed was taught him by Sir Salar Jung in
1883, during the aforementioned tour. After Mahbub Ali Pasha
had refused to keep to the schedule and Salar Jung had coaxed
him back to it, the Dewan summoned his two sons and Kishen
Pershad to his tent to teach them the lesson they should learn from
the incident:

If the welfare of the sovereign or the state or the people be at stake or
the right of any man be imperiled by an order which the sovereign
uttered in anger, then it is the duty of a subject to tell him so, but

with refinement and tact. For the sovereign's anger is like a storm at sea; when the storm has abated he should be told that his orders will be carried out, but that, the circumstances being what they are, the matter should perhaps be reconsidered. And this is the practical thing to do, for if harm should result from obedience to an order given in anger, then the sovereign will say, "With full knowledge and for his own advantage the ingrate did not warn me of the danger."

Familiarity between sovereign and subject is most dangerous and should be avoided at any cost, for it is impossible to maintain due respect and honor under such circumstances.

By the time their father's precept and example could have been of any practical use to him, the elder of Salar Jung's sons lay dead. The younger disregarded the father's wisdom, forgot himself, and paid the penalty. Only in the case of Kishen Pershad did the advice fall on ground which was receptive and bear fruit.

Although the nineteen-year-old Kishen Pershad went on the tour as deputy Peshkar, other recognition was slow in coming to him. He saw his companions, Salar Jung II and Fakhr ul Mulk, attain the status of Dewan and minister long before he himself was honored with official position. A serious setback occurred in 1888, when Maharajah Narinder Pershad died after a two-day illness. Immediately claimants arose on all sides to dispute his grandson Kishen Pershad's title to the Peshkari, the jagirs attached to it, and the personal jagirs and property of the late Peshkar.

The opposition was led by the revenue secretary, who was the real power behind Asman Jah, the Dewan. He argued that the Peshkar was in effect the deputy Dewan, and that, since he was himself performing the deputy's function, the title too should be his; further, the Peshkari should be abolished and the jagirs attached to it should revert to the state. He also advocated a policy called the doctrine of lapse, under which, as practiced in British India, adoptions were not recognized and estates were turned over to the crown in the event of the holder's dying without a male heir. This could be considered applicable to Kishen Pershad, as he was the son of the old Peshkar's daughter and had been adopted by his grandfather, who had no sons. The question sent a wave of consternation through the Hindu jagirdars and samasthan chiefs. For them, adoption in the event of a sonless marriage was a religious duty and many families had carried on their lines in this way for generations. Mahbub Ali Pasha remarked, "During the administration of Asman Jah, the personal government of his assistant has become so autocratic as to need my immediate attention."

In matters affecting his nobles, the ruler had always reserved the right to make personal decisions. Mahbub was away shooting when Narinder Pershad died. On his return, he sent for Kishen Pershad and placed around his shoulders the shawl of condolence, the sign of royal recognition of the heir. In view of the dissension, however, this only created difficulties, for Kishen Pershad then became responsible for the maintenance of the vast family of dependents of the dead Peshkar without the income of the post or the jagirs attached to it. The debts mounted while Kishen Pershad kept his counsel, approaching no one in his difficulties except his sovereign, to whom, as a Great Noble, he had the right of direct access. Mahbub took his time to decide, and it was not until three years later, in 1891, that he made up his mind to his "immediate action." It was announced with Oriental indirectness.

The langar procession traditionally passed through the Peshkar's deori for him to take the salaams, but since Narinder Pershad's death it had not done so. In 1891 Mahbub Ali Pasha ordered Afsur ul Mulk to send the procession along its traditional route. The next day he issued an order in favor of the retention of the Peshkari and declared Kishen Pershad to be the incumbent with all the properties, honors, and allowances attaching to the position.

During the ten years between his succession to the Peshkari and his appointment as Dewan, Kishen Pershad played little part in the government of the state, except for taking his seat in the Cabinet Council as military minister. He fulfilled the duties of the Peshkar, which required constant personal attendance on the sovereign, and remained on hand for state formalities.

Otherwise he spent his time looking after his personal estates

and continuing his absorption in intellectual pursuits. In spite of
the feudal structure of society, in which the most fortunate had
almost no contact with those who were humbly placed, Kishen Pershad's associates during that period comprised people of every
class, from the nobility to the beggars in the street. His family
became accustomed to the sight of him sitting beside a ragged,
louse-ridden mendicant on a sofa in his drawing room, pouring
tea for his guest. "Do not despise anyone," he advised them when
they remonstrated with him. "You never know; it may be God
Himself who visits you in the guise of a beggar."

Through contacts such as these, Maharajah had his finger
firmly on the pulse of the common people and came to know
their sorrows and joys, their ambitions and frustrations, their difficulties and dilemmas. Even after he had become a great public
figure he kept up his habit of contact with all levels of society,
often through attending public functions, from laying a foundation stone to presiding over a schoolgirls' concert, inaugurating a
veterinary clinic, or being chief guest at a traveling circus. During
the marriage season, many marriages took place every day. Maharajah rarely failed to attend any to which he was invited,
especially if the house were a poor one, and he never went empty-
handed.

All this varied activity kept him away from his own large
household of wives and children. He kept those fences mended
by reserving one full hour each day, however pressed he might be,
when he called them all together. It was a jolly, playful hour, a
time for joking with his children and teasing his wives, but he
managed to combine playfulness with lessons in the virtues he
cherished. By means of stories, he taught them compassion and the
necessity to distinguish between a man's true nature and the evil
he might commit. "Avert your eyes from evil," he told them, "and
look for the good that is surely hidden somewhere."

That belief in the hidden good was the basis of his method for
enforcing discipline. Servants who were found to be dishonest,
indolent, or disrespectful were not dismissed or punished, but

Khursheed Jah, the Amir e Kabir
or premier noble of the realm

Courtesy of Nawab Rashid Jung Bahadur

Waliud Dowla in the uniform
of the Imperial Cadet Corps

From A. Claude Campbell,
GLIMPSES OF THE NIZAM'S DOMINIONS,
Bombay and London: C. B. Burrows, 1898.

Rameshwar Rao I, Raja of Wanaparthy

From A. Claude Campbell,
GLIMPSES OF THE NIZAM'S DOMINIONS,
Bombay and London: C. B. Burrows, 1898.

Nizam ul Mulk, 1724–1748

Nasir ud Dowla, 1829–1857

Afzul ud Dowla, 1857–1869

Nizam Ali, 1762–1803

Sikander Jah, 1803–1829

Mahbub Ali Pasha, 1869–1911

Osman Ali Khan, 1911–1948

Left. Maharajah Kishen Pershad wearing the jewels and robes of office presented to him by Mahbub Ali Pasha when he was appointed Dewan

Photograph by Amichand Deen Dayal, Secunderabad, from a painting in the possession of Raja Rattan Gopal Saincher.

Below. A durbar at Chow Mahalla

Courtesy of Amichand Deen Dayal, Secunderabad

Water jug of Bidri ware

*Photograph by Tarachand, from the
collection of Mr. Nowzer Chenoy, Secunderabad.*

Char Minar

*Courtesy of Achimand Deen Dayal,
Secunderabad.*

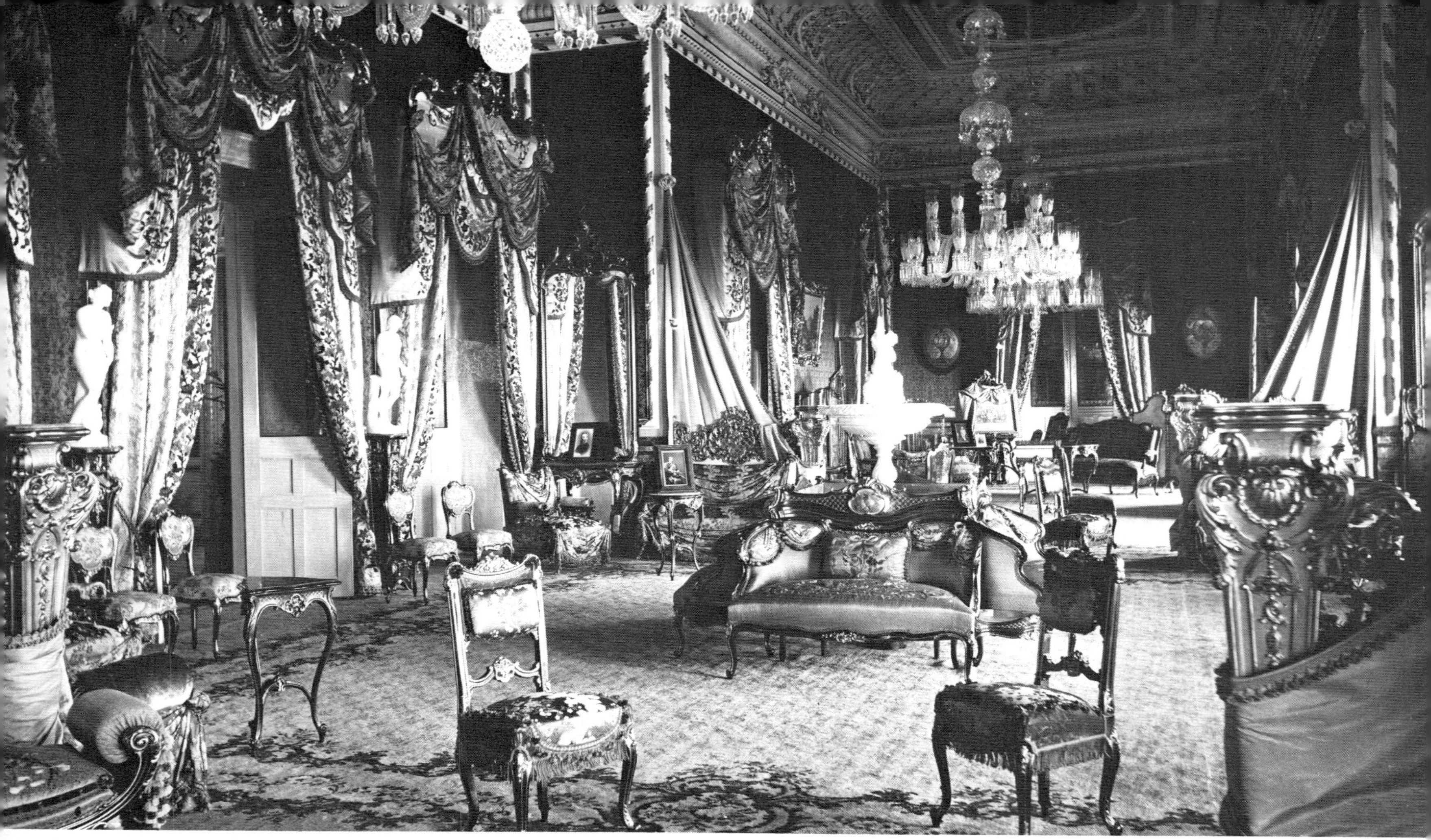

Courtesy of Amichand Deen Dayal, Secunderabad

Zenana servants: All that glitters is gold

From *A. Claude Campbell,*
GLIMPSES OF THE NIZAM'S DOMINIONS,
Bombay and London: C. B. Burrows, 1898.

Hunt breakfast with Sir Vicar ul Umra on the steps of Falaknuma

Courtesy of Amichand Deen Dayal, Secunderabad

Sir Asman Jah's grave with the mark
of a male in green marble

Photograph by S. M. Rajan

The grave of Shums ul Umra I
with an ostrich egg suspended over i

Photograph by S. M. Rajan

Details of the plaster work
from the Shums ul Umra tombs

Photograph by S. M. Rajan

Group of Hijras at a traditional ceremony in their graveyard

Photograph by Krishna Reddy

instead were quietly transferred to the service of the wife whom Maharajah judged able to deal with the particular failing.

Family members were disciplined with equal discretion. Anyone he wished to correct received a gently-worded letter, beautifully written in his own hand on monogrammed note paper. One cause for such correction was violation of the unfailing respect for seniority which his own traditional upbringing had instilled in him. He would not tolerate disrespect, however unintentional, toward his first and eldest spouse. One of his letters to a wife reproved her for sitting during the family hour with a foot exposed in the direction of the Senior Rani, a position of disrespect which even the lady who was supposedly aggrieved had not noticed. Whether it were one consort guilty of disrespect to another, a child who did not pay enough attention to his studies, or a son whom he thought had behaved condescendingly to a poor man, the offender received a letter delivered in a sealed envelope by Maharajah's personal attendant.

But his sister once stung Maharajah to public reproach. Conscious of her own noble birth, she refused to acknowledge the position of any of the junior wives; she addressed or referred to only the senior wife as "Bhabi," that is, sister-in-law. One day in a conversation which included several of the wives, the sister referred to the senior wife as "Bhabi" and to another as "she." Maharajah's face darkened. "Why do you speak so disrespectfully?" he demanded. "When I accord equal respect to all my wives, what right have you to behave differently?"

Despite these brave words, the Senior Rani was unquestionably the first among the equals. Every morning all the other wives and their children presented themselves in her apartments to salaam her before breakfast. Sometimes Maharajah took the entire household on a picnic to a garden property outside the city, where he cooked for them himself. The Senior Rani's cooks, however, went along to prepare her food separately; being very orthodox, she ate only vegetarian food cooked by Brahmins. When Maharajah dined with her, he ate only her food, although she knew that outside the palace he ate meat. But on the occasions when Maharajah required his family to undertake menial tasks in the palace, the Senior Rani was not excused. "After all, God's will may change and I may become a pauper," he would say. "What will you do then?" He felt that only personal experience could teach them the dignity of labor.

The entire family lived in one great, rambling palace, each wife with her own children in a separate apartment where, with a separate staff, she could live and eat according to her tastes. Wherever he went, they all went with him. He maintained a palace at Maula Ali, about twelve miles from the city, where there was an annual pilgrimage to a hill-top shrine dedicated to the son-in-law of the Prophet. The Nizam and his court repaired to Maula Ali every year and Maharajah went, too, taking with him everybody in his palace, down to the four little maids who attended on each daughter. The city deori was left empty except for the guards.

When he went to Simla, in northern India, to be invested as Knight Grand Commander of the Indian Empire, G.C.I.E., the family traveled in a number of private cars attached to the train. The Senior Rani, together with Maharajah and her children, occupied one car, which had a separate compartment for her own servants. The other wives and children all traveled together, and their servants shared a car which also carried an enormous quantity of the most unlikely luggage. Every night, all of Maharajah's cars were detached from the train and shunted onto a siding. Tents were set up, meals were cooked over open fires, and the family slept in airy stillness. In the morning, after the ritual of salaam and breakfast, the cars were attached to the next northbound train. Despite these interruptions, it took only a week to make the journey.

Although Maharajah maintained the palatial splendor of his deori and conformed in dress and ornaments to the elaborate richness customary at an Oriental court, his private and unofficial life was one of great simplicity. His abiding interests were the things of the mind and spirit: wealth was chiefly of use to maintain dependents and to relieve distress, and the true worship of God lay in the service of man. His sympathy for his fellow man moved him to acts of generosity which became legend and which over-shadowed the memory of his valuable and lasting contribution to the administration when he was finally called to office. The call came in 1901.

The Nizam, during the intervening seventeen years since his nominal assumption of power in 1884, had been driven by British pressure into near apathy toward the administration of the state, and the resulting vacuum came close to creating havoc. In 1901, Mahbub Ali Pasha exerted himself sufficiently to insist upon the retirement of Sir Vicar ul Umra from the Dewani and to appoint instead his childhood companion and lifelong friend and devotee, Kishen Pershad. Almost immediately the atmosphere in the state was changed, with Mahbub resuming his rightful place as head of the state. Maharajah had the Nizam's and his people's interest primarily at heart; he had never sought or wielded power for its own sake, since he was capable of finding personal fulfillment without it. Instead of hobnobbing privately with the British Resident, he acted as a buffer between that power and the Musnud.

From 1901 until Mahbub's death, Kishen Pershad's intellectual pursuits, which had absorbed almost his entire energy until then, took second place. He was determined to set the house in order, maintaining the old traditions as far as possible but adopting new ideas and methods wherever the old ways were inadequate. In keeping with his quiet, unassuming nature, his deep sympathy with distress, and the balance and perspective acquired from his habit of reflecting on his experience, he directed his energies to remedying the defects in the administration; to engendering a sense of security in all cadres of government service; to stimulating the desire for education and professional advancement in that section of the people who had no other hope of benefiting from their abilities, and to regenerating the finances of the state.

For centuries, officialdom had been a closed shop. Old government posts were mainly hereditary and were the preserve of "good families," a rating compounded of blood lines and economic standing. So long as the pace of advancement toward modernity was equally slow in the rest of India, this system had its advantages. Fathers tended to train sons to take their places; economic independence rendered a man less susceptible to the temptations of graft. The tradition of liberal learning gave balance and maturity of judgment, while inherent courtesy and good manners made for smooth public relations. But these qualities were not sufficient to cope with the changing times and the complications of a sophisticated structure of government. Lower-paid government posts which were not hereditary were handed out haphazardly under pressure of influence. The Hyderabad Civil Service, inaugurated many years previously, had become virtually defunct because there was no retiring age, and therefore few vacancies occurred. Many incumbents held their posts into their dotage, the younger generation doing the actual work while the ancients rejoiced in the titles of office and collected the salaries.

One of the reasons for the disinclination to retire was the fact that there was no legal provision for the dependents of persons who died while in receipt of pension. The state provided for the destitute dependents of those who had served it, but the assistance was given at the discretion of the head of the department where the pensioner had worked. Its granting therefore tended to become a personal favor, often bestowed only after long delays and the use of influence and power.

Finally, the low morale of the administrative services could be attributed also to the number of outsiders who were occupying executive positions. Sir Salar Jung had systematically imported Indians from other states, trained by the British administrators, to carry out his innovations. They in turn distributed the appointments within their jurisdictions to relatives and friends. In addition to this Indian influx from outside of Hyderabad, the administrative service was flooded with Englishmen during the years from 1884 until 1901, when the Nizam succeeded in naming his own man as Dewan. Stemming this tide was one of Maharajah's goals.

The Resident had long wanted to see an Englishman, Casson Walker, in charge of the finances of the state, and his appointment figured in the bargaining whereby the Viceroy's agreement to a change of Dewans was obtained. Walker was appointed finance secretary in 1901 and promoted to finance minister several years later. Since he held that post until 1911, his tenure coincided with that of Kishen Pershad, who occupied the Dewani from 1901 to 1912. During that time the cash reserves and securities of the state quadrupled. For this improvement British historians have usually given credit solely to Walker. Hyderabad tradition, on the other hand, assigns it entirely to Kishen Pershad, lumping Casson Walker with the outsiders who were considered a threat. Being quite willing to cooperate wherever he saw the possibility of advantage to the state, Maharajah might well have been the first to admit it was a mutual endeavor. He consistently maintained friendly relations with the Residency, but he was an astute negotiator and a master of the art of employing delaying tactics until, unobtrusively, he got his own way.

In one particular area, however, there was continual friction, although no open breach was allowed to develop. As might be expected, both sides sought the power to make political appointments. Walker, indeed, set about installing his countrymen in administrative posts with a determination which alarmed the public. The Mulkis, or local citizens, feared that no posts of even moderate importance would presently be left open to them, and they resented the fact that the foreigners were paid much higher salaries on account of their supposed superiority. The polite tussle between Maharajah and Casson Walker over this issue was a long and continuous one, and almost every department was affected by it.

Support for Maharajah came from an unlikely source: a young Hyderabadi who was a mere superintendent in the Home Office, drawing a monthly salary of 200 rupees, joined battle with Walker by means of a bit of doggerel which served to crystallize public opinion. Most of the poem, "Walker," consisted of comment on the great figures of the day and their subservience to the British designs in the person of the finance minister. A few of the lines set the public aflame; translated they read:

> You have taken all the responsible posts from us poor
>   nationals and given them to Englishmen.
> If your policy prevails, no Mulki will ever earn more
>   than five or six hundred.
> Whether you fear the Viceroy or not is his lookout
>   and yours,
> But you should fear the agony of us miserable people.
> Have mercy on our plight, for you too must one day
>   take your last journey.

The versifier was deported, but the aroused public feeling was a support to Maharajah, who henceforth no longer had to battle over every appointment. On the other hand, when he deemed it fitting to employ an outsider, whether Indian or English, he did not hesitate to do so. He brought them for help and guidance into many departments, paid them handsomely for their temporary services, and made sure their services were temporary.

In anticipation of the resuscitation of the Hyderabad Civil Service, bright graduates from the Nizam College were sent on stipends to British India for training in revenue administration. Appointments to the lower cadres of government service were based on entrance examinations, and successful candidates were required to serve a six months' probationary period. Every promotion depended upon qualification by further examination. This created an impetus to study and qualify for government service and to continue studies with some assurance that effort would bring its reward. As opportunities opened up, education with a view to government service became a goal in almost every middle-class family; many sons and even daughters were sent abroad to learn new methods and technologies. The effects were not apparent immediately, and indeed were not seen during Maharajah's first term as Dewan, but by the end of the next two decades the only top posts held by Englishmen were in the railways, in education, and, at the insistence of the British Government, in the revenue and district police departments. This was in startling contrast to the situation in British India where, from the grade of district collector to governor, superintendent to inspector general of police, district magistrate to high court judge, almost all posts were reserved for Englishmen, at salaries roughly twice those of the rare Indians who managed to wangle any of the coveted appointments.

Maharajah Kishen Pershad's general policy was that no appointment should go to an outsider if a qualified Mulki were available; that family background was reduced to secondary importance, while academic and professional qualifications became the first essential; and that openings for the promising younger men should be assured by fixing fifty-five years as the age of retirement, as it continues to be in most of India today.

With retirement made obligatory, a family pension scheme was started on the lines of an insurance policy, to which all government employees were free to contribute. Dependents of pensioners who died could claim half the pension as a right, whatever their circumstances. Meanwhile, government servants who continued to work, then as now, felt the pinch of fixed salaries in the face of rising costs of living. Accordingly Maharajah instituted a reorganization of the salary scales. For instance, the range for accounts officers had been 100 to 700 rupees. Now that they were required to be qualified, payment of 400 to 900 rupees was provided. The minimum salary for the lowest-paid civil servant was raised from 15 rupees to 25. The latter sum, in purchasing power, compares favorably with the salary of the same grade today. Wheat and rice were then available at thirty kilograms for a rupee.

These increases, however, made it necessary to take a closer look at other areas of expenditure, for the finances of the state were generally precarious and had worsened in the reign of Mahbub

Ali Pasha because of the fashion of conspicuous spending. Resources were being further eroded by the thousands of munificent mansabs, or royal grants, which each successive Nizam from the foundation of the state had made, and which descended from generation to generation. By the time of Mahbub, the state was burdened to the extent of seven or eight lakhs per year for such grants, which by obviating the need to work had begun to create a class of parasites living on the rewards given to their ancestors for services to a former Nizam. These generally were educated persons who had no incentive to employ their talents for the public weal and therefore diverted their intelligence and energy to dilettantism in the arts and literature. In a country where literacy was confined to a small fraction of the population, it was a great waste of potential.

British advisers had for some years been urging the wisdom of reducing the mansabs, but then as now those responsible for official policy were reluctant to reduce the handouts to people who were actually or potentially influential. It was only when Kishen Pershad and Casson Walker discovered economy as a mutual interest that effective steps were taken. Because a sudden stoppage would have caused hardship in many cases, the mansabs were reduced by 25 percent in each succeeding generation, to give the families time to orient themselves to the changed times by educating their young according to modern standards and fitting them for employment of some sort. Mansabs to persons who had sufficient income from other sources, however, were stopped at once. For example, the wealthy Nawab Behram ud Dowla was given, as miscellaneous minister, a mansab of 1,500 rupees a month; when Asman Jah retired him the mansab was kept going. Because Sultan ul Mulk and Zaffer Jung had been born to royal princesses, they were given special mansabs of 1,000 rupees a month each in Sir Vicar ul Umra's time. Many other such mansabs were being carried on, unnecessary for the recipient and a burden on the state. They were all stopped forthwith. Other large special mansabs granted during Mahbub Ali Pasha's time, such as that to his tutor, were made terminable on the death of the recipient. Wherever possible, mansabdars were required to take up some service which would save a fresh appointment. Mansabs to religious foundations were continued unabated.

An earlier attempt at economizing had been made by imposing a limit on the monthly total of mansabs for the state, with predictable though curious results. When the holder of a non-hereditary grant died, the mansab came to be regarded as "vacant," much as a position or office might be. A new form of petty intrigue grew up as small men curried favor with greater ones whom they imagined could secure their nomination to a vacant mansab. This system was now abolished.

With communal peace and a sense of security among all classes of people, trade flourished and the state revenues from excise, customs, railways, and agriculture steadily increased. Part of the surplus was invested in Government of India securities or in company and railway shares; part was accumulated for use in time of famine or of abnormal rise in prices, when grain might have to be made available at subsidized prices. Cash deposits and securities, which amounted to 13 million rupees in 1901, were increased to more than 50 million in 1910, although many capital works had been financed from revenue.

One part of the reorganization of governmental structure associated with Maharajah Kishen Pershad grew directly out of his personal concerns. So long as Hyderabad remained a backwater, its culture and its tradition of communal amity were inviolate. Many religious observances, particularly the festivals, had come to be observed to some extent by both communities. Sir Asman Jah celebrated the lovely Hindu festival of lights known as Diwali, while his cousin who succeeded him as Dewan, Sir Vicar ul Umra, even had a special set of crockery painted in the gay yellows and reds that were particularly associated with another Hindu festival. In the same way, large numbers of Hindus joined in the observances of Moharrum, following the processions in which banners symbolizing the martyrs of Kerbala were carried around the city. The drummers who accompanied these processions were invariably Hindus. Attending the Majlis, the religious meetings where the stories of martyrdom were read aloud to the accompaniment of tears and breastbeating by the Shias, Maharajah wept also for the dissension and the tragedy that had resulted, in the name of religion, centuries ago.

Maharajah was determined to prevent such dissensions from occurring in Hyderabad, where friction between the major communities was unheard of. By contrast, it was common in British India, where the government found it advantageous to play one group off against the other. Maharajah was deeply disturbed by the reports of communal trouble across the borders, and he took early steps to prevent the importation of such discord by outsiders. Separating religious affairs from the Judiciary Department, he organized a new department which supervised grants to religious institutions, including the ancient mansabs, all of which were continued. As, in the experience of other states, religious processions were frequently the starting point of communal conflagrations, the granting of permission for processions was an important function of the new department. Each application had to be scrutinized by an official of the Department of Religious Affairs in consultation with representatives of the localities through which the procession intended to pass.

Such respect for everyone's point of view was an integral part of Maharajah Kishen Pershad's own life. Although he had been born a Hindu, he was forever in search of truth and forever finding it enshrined in every religion. He was as familiar with the Koran, the Bible, and the Granth Sahib (the sacred text of the Sikhs) as he was with the Hindu scriptures, to all of which his knowledge of languages gave him direct access.

His personal life followed his beliefs. He married Hindu as well as Muslim wives, the children of each union adopting the mother's religion. Indeed, it is difficult to distinguish merely by their names which were Hindu and which Muslim, for his Hindu wives were often called by the Muslim names given to the apartments they occupied, and their children were given Hindu or Muslim names quite indiscriminately.

Maharajah's readiness to ignore communal barriers to marriage once got him into trouble and even threatened to cost him his official position. It began lightheartedly enough, on an outing when Mahbub and his zenana, together with the inner circle of the court, were encamped in the Public Garden. Perhaps in the holiday atmosphere the servants became negligent or the surveillance was relaxed. Or perhaps it was a well-intentioned breeze or a mischievous fate that provided a chink in the blinds just at the moment when Maharajah strolled past the zenana tents. At any rate he caught sight of a very pretty girl who was visiting His Highness's ladies and knew at once he must see her again. When a few discreet inquiries uncovered her identity, Maharajah impulsively sent for her father and made an offer of marriage. A jagirdar and no stranger to the ways of the court, the father persuaded Kishen Pershad to put into writing the settlement he was willing to make on the Muslim girl. With this paper as evidence, the father secured the ear of the dowager Begum, who reproached her son for keeping so susceptible a man in his service. Confronted with his own handwriting, Kishen Pershad had to admit his actions. He was in disgrace, and rumors that Mahbub Ali Pasha was about to dismiss him from the Dewani flew about Hyderabad. Nothing came of them, as the Resident predicted, "for the simple reason that there is no one to replace him, and that the Nizam knows that in all official matters he serves him loyally, to the best of his ability."

This was not the only time that Maharajah's heart tripped him up. The love of his life was Ghousia Begum, a girl from an orthodox Muslim family. The story of their courtship was an exciting one of disguises and escapades, contrived in spite of the strict purdah in which the girl was kept. As in all true romances, the lovers' path was strewn with thorns. Since marriage between a Muslim and a person "not of the Book" was not lawful, Maharajah was willing to declare himself a Muslim; but Mahbub Ali

Pasha forbade it, saying that he could not have a Muslim Peshkar and that he would abolish the post if necessary. Eventually the girl ran away from her father's house to Kishen Pershad, and her uncle, disinclined to fight a battle that was already lost, produced a Kazi (Muslim judge) who was willing to marry them.

Maharajah had even before this involvement admitted to his belief in Sufism, an Islamic sect whose emphasis was not on theology but on the personal union of the soul with God. To him, labels had no meaning: God was the same for every man; only His name differed:

> Some lips form one name and some lips another.
> By the names for our God we are kept from each other.
> But a man is to other men surely a brother:
> There is only one Master for all.

Like his peers, Maharajah was undiscriminating in his generosity, never leaving his deori without throwing money to the poor on his return journey, in gratitude to God for his safety. While both the compassion and the religious expression implicit in this largess were undoubtedly genuine, probably something of vanity was also involved. When British authorities at the hill station of Ootacamund, who had banned the custom, forbade him to practice it at the resort, Kishen Pershad remained in his house for several days and then decided to return to Hyderabad. "How can I go out," he asked rhetorically, "without throwing money to the poor?"

The marriage of daughters, then as now, posed a sometimes insoluble problem for the poor because of the necessity to provide a dowry. Whenever an appeal of this nature came before Maharajah, he replied, "She is now my daughter," and the marriage was performed at his expense, according to the religious tradition of the family but in a manner the family could never have afforded. In one instance, when he was traveling by train, an old Muslim begged at his car for help to marry off a last daughter. Maharajah enquired the man's name and address and the proposed date of the wedding, noting the information in his pocket diary. Three months later, on the appointed day, Maharajah arrived in the old man's village with a trousseau for the bride, complete with jewelry and household utensils. There appeared to be no sign in the village of an impending marriage: no music, no crowd of gaily dressed peasants. He sent for the old man and asked him what had happened. "The groom's people came yesterday," he replied, "but they have gone back since I have not the means to perform the ceremony."

"Send for them at once," commanded Maharajah. "Tell them that I have come to perform the marriage of my daughter and it must take place today as arranged." It was almost precisely the story that has been told of Sir Vicar ul Umra at a village on the way to Vicarabad.

On a visit to Delhi, Maharajah was approached by a ragged beggar on the street. Something about the suppliant struck a responsive chord in Kishen Pershad, who began to talk with him. When he realized that the beggar was in fact a son of the last Moghul emperor, whom the British had turned out when they sent the old Shah into exile in Burma, Kishen Pershad felt covered with shame that a prince should be reduced to such a state. Taking the man along with him, he returned to his hotel and emptied the contents of his strongbox into a bag, which he handed over, saying, "I kept it for you."

Afterward Maharajah exclaimed, "How God has blessed me! Even a prince has asked me for help and I was able to give it." His associate, Nawab Mehdi Nawaz Jung, a Muslim who later went on to a distinguished career of his own, did not immediately regard the event as a blessing, however, for the generous Maharajah had just dispersed every last rupee that they had with them in a strange city. Not even the price of their return tickets had been held back. Commercial practice had evolved a system for making payments across long distances, but this depended on prior establishment of credit links, a need which Maharajah had not anticipated. With no quick means of ascertaining a man's identity in a city where he was a stranger, no bank would lend money on the basis of reputed assets nearly a thousand miles away. Fortunately for the Maharajah, who was serenely unconscious of the problem he had created, Mehdi Nawaz Jung happened to meet a wealthy merchant who knew him and was willing to stand guarantee.

Maharajah's generosity was equally lavish toward poets, painters, writers, and musicians. Whatever the quality of their work, Maharajah gave them his attention and sent each away with a gift, a word of encouragement, and his thanks for their troubling to come to him. In the early hours of the morning, his durbar was crowded with writers and artists from various parts of India and even from Persia and Arabia—for he was famed for his patronage, a characteristic he had in common with his ancestor, Maharajah Chandulal, who also held his durbar from midnight onward.

Under the pen name of "Shad" (meaning "happy"), which adorned his personal stationery, Maharajah was, like Mahbub, a poet of distinction in both Persian and Urdu. Among his many literary activities was the publication of an Urdu magazine, *Mahbub al Kalam* ("Mahbub's Poetry"), in which the first poem was a ghazal, or lyric, by Mahbub, beautifully ornamented with scrollwork and followed by the ghazals of other poets, Kishen Pershad himself heading the list. The ghazal originated as a dialogue in the form of questions and answers between lover and beloved. The final word of each couplet was the same and the meter of the whole poem uniform. In time the aspect of dialogue was omitted and a ghazal became a poem about love, but the form otherwise was unchanged. In *Mahbub al Kalam* all the poems were written in the same measure and with the same rhyme scheme as Mahbub's "leader," a feat of no mean order in Urdu poetry.

This poetic relation with his sovereign was a particularly appropriate expression of much else that was important to Maharajah. He took more pride in his hereditary Peshkari than in his Dewani. The first nazar to be offered at the durbar was the

Peshkar's, and in verse Maharajah declared that this distinction was given to him as the most humble of Mahbub's slaves. Whatever good fortune came his way he attributed to his beloved sovereign, for whose greater glory it was to be held in trust. For himself it was enough to be Mahbub Ali Pasha's slave:

> By this you know, O Shad, God's love sublime:
> That He created you in Asaf's time.

Chapter VI

The Great Nobles:
Fakhr ul Mulk Bahadur

As ONE of the foremost nobles of the realm, Fakhr ul Mulk accompanied his new sovereign, Osman Ali Kahn, to Delhi for the Imperial Durbar. Steadfast in his allegiance though he was, his heart was not with the seventh Nizam as it had been with the sixth. To Mahbub Ali Pasha he had been devotedly loyal and had served him all his life. "To serve him was a joy," he said of Mahbub. But apart from his special duties Fakhr ul Mulk had been drawn, even as a very young man, to the activities of the Westerners whom he met, and they eventually absorbed almost the whole of his social life.

This preference for living with a foot in each world was perhaps influenced by the fact that his father, Fakhr ul Mulk I, was known for his service to the British during the war of 1857, when he and his troops had the special duty of assuring the security of Englishmen in the Nizam's Dominions and in carrying out that duty escorted many of them across the frontiers to safety in British territory. When Fakhr ul Mulk I died at an early age, responsibility for administering his vast estate and for bringing up his two small sons was assumed by Sir Salar Jung, who was married to their sister.

Fakhr ul Mulk II and his elder brother, Khan Khanan II, were numbered among the Umra e Uzzam, the Great Nobles of the Realm, who ranked next to the Paigah nobles. They traced their ancestry to nobles and high officials of the Moghul court who had either accompanied Asaf Jah I to the Deccan or followed shortly afterward, sometimes at his summons. There they were given vast estates. Privileged only slightly less than the Paigah nobility, they maintained their own household troops and administered justice in their jagirs. The Umra e Uzzam in Mahbub Ali Pasha's time were Salar Jung and his brother; Maharajah Kishen Pershad; Fakhr ul Mulk II and Khan Khanan II; Behram ud Dowla, whose daughter married Fakhr ul Mulk's eldest son; the heads of the Shiv Raj and Sham Raj families; and five or six others. The criterion for inclusion among the Umra e Uzzam was not wealth but the honor and prestige accorded by the sovereign to those not tied to him by blood or marriage. From among this group the Nizams had always chosen their ministers and high administrators; many of the posts had become hereditary, like the Peshkari of Kishen Pershad.

In contrast to the Nizam, who was a Sunni, the Muslims among the Umra e Uzzam were all of the Shia sect. Their ancestral deoris were grouped in a single area of the city, near to the shrines where the alams, or religious symbols revered by them, were housed. This site, near the river, was chosen for them: when Mohammad-Quli Qutub Shah decided to build himself a new capital away from the walled fort of Golconda, he proceeded according to a carefully designed city plan. The first building to be constructed was Char Minar and the second one, completed in 1593, was the Ashurkhana to house the sacred alams.

As Fakhr ul Mulk II and his elder brother grew up, they de-

veloped very different temperaments. Khan Khanan was intro-
spective, scholarly, conservative; his chief personal achievement
was as a calligraphist. Of the two, only Khan Khanan ever went
abroad, visiting Europe in Sir Salar Jung's party in 1876—a curious detail since he was so rigidly orthodox as to be interested
only in things Muslim.

Fakhr ul Mulk, by contrast, was outgoing, devoted to sports,
and trained in judicial and revenue work. As a young man he received from Khan Khanan, who wished to live only in the city,
full title to a palace called Asad Bagh which they had inherited
together. Asad Bagh, today the site of Nizam College, was several
miles outside the city, across the river in the direction of the British Cantonment. This was symbolic of the direction Fakhr ul
Mulk would take, for he was the first of the nobles to mingle
freely with the British officers. The association began in sports and
spread until it absorbed most of his social life, virtually to the ex-
clusion of his countrymen from the circle of his intimate friends.

Not surprisingly, many British fashions were adopted in his domestic life. He began the education of his children early with
tutors, so that while they were still very young they spoke Urdu,
Persian, and English as though each was their mother tongue. In
1894 the first three sons, Ghazi Jung, Shah Nawaz Jung, and Rais
Jung, were sent to England under the supervision of an English
tutor, who was a Cambridge graduate. After three years at a small
preparatory school, they were entered in Eton College as day
boys. Since there was no room for them in the boarding houses,
they lived in a house taken for them by their tutor at 21 High
Street, Eton.

They were living there when the Duchess of Battenburg, who
had been a guest of Fakhr ul Mulk in Hyderabad, mentioned
them to her mother, Queen Victoria. That durable monarch expressed a wish to see them, but specified that they should come as
Etonians and not as Indians. The boys were taken to Windsor
Castle and instructed to bow but not to speak. The queen appeared, erect, stout, leaning on the arms of two Indian servants in

gold livery. The boys bowed. Five words rolled off the royal tongue: "Hum bhi Hindustani bolthai hain" ("We also can speak Hindustani"). The boys bowed again and she retired. When, shortly after that, two scholars were expelled from Eton, the queen herself arranged that Fakhr ul Mulk's three sons should be taken in as boarders. They brought the number of Indian students at Eton to five, the two earlier ones being the Maharajah of Cooch Behar and Nawab Waliud Dowla, son of Sir Vicar ul Umra. On the occasion of Victoria's jubilee, a pageant was held at Eton. A photograph of one of the scenes shows the five Indian boys in national dress flanked by schoolmates costumed as heralds representing England, Scotland, Ireland, and Wales.

When Nawab Ghazi Jung returned from England in 1900, he found the family established in a new palace, Iram Munzil, which Fakhr ul Mulk had built on a hilltop several miles further out. The first he knew of it was when the carriage bringing him from the station turned in the "wrong" direction. The story goes that Fakhr ul Mulk, who "had a habit of building palaces," had a wager with Sir Vicar ul Umra as to who would build the higher palace. The product of the competition on the one hand was Vicar Munzil and, on the other, Iram Munzil; as each was on a small hilltop, the wager ended in a draw.

Whatever the motivation for constructing it, Iram Munzil was one of Hyderabad's great palaces, set in spacious grounds enclosed by miles and miles of compound wall. Inside was nearly everything needed for a pleasant life, including formal gardens, bridle paths, picnic grounds beside a pleasant pond for boating, tennis courts, and two full-sized polo grounds. Near the dairy, which had twenty or thirty animals, lived the dairymen and their families, while grooms and troops had quarters not far from the stables. There were riding horses, carriage horses, and polo ponies, and vehicles in great variety. The lofts held enormous quantities of fodder for the animals, while huge stacks of hay from the jagir rose yearly between dairy and stables.

Whole families were employed on particular jobs: for instance, dozens of gardeners were assisted by their wives in keeping the garden sparkling and the gravel paths swept and smooth. Some of the wives were employed as sweepers inside the palace. As flush toilets had not beeen introduced, scavengers and their families had quarters at some distance from the others.

The washermen had their quarters near the dhobi ghat (steps leading into a tank where clothes were washed). All palace laundry was done there, except that Fakhr ul Mulk's European wardrobe was sent to Paris for laundering or cleaning, aside from his socks and handkerchiefs, which were discarded after being used once. Happily the Nawab was not inconvenienced by the length of time required for shipment to and fro: the Nizam once observed that Fakhr ul Mulk possessed a change of clothing for every degree marked on the thermometer, surely an underestimation.

With the exception of one courtier who had a house across the road, the entire indoor staff also lived within the compound. A small army of servants did the menial tasks of sweeping and scrubbing, scouring vessels and grinding spices, cleaning rice and lentils, lifting and carrying. A permanent cadre of masons and carpenters constituted the maintenance staff. A labor force of thirty devoted themselves exclusively to cleaning and filling the lamps, trimming wicks, fitting candles into candelabra and chandeliers, and seeing that every room in the palace was brightly lit after dark.

The more skilled part of the indoor staff consisted of clerks for estate work, clerks and accountants for palace work, two Goanese cooks and their helpers who prepared European food, six women to prepare Indian dishes, two butlers for the dining room, and two telephone orderlies. Fakhr ul Mulk's personal servants were three butlers and three valets. Assisting all these persons and receiving training from them were a number of small boys who were being brought up in the palace.

In addition to these five-hundred-odd retainers of varying degrees of importance, the staff included seven Musahibs or courtiers —men from respectable middle-class families who had been put on the Nawab's payroll. For the most part their job was to hang about the Nawab, ready to pass the time of day with him according to his whim and to take on errands or negotiations for which a gentleman rather than a servant was required. Four of the seven also had special jobs: one was in charge of the treasury, one taught Arabic and the Koran to the children or grandchildren, a third was in charge of the billiard room, and the fourth was in charge of protocol, deciding on seating arrangements for banquets and on the appropriate plate, crockery, and linen.

Providing occupation for this army was a palace of more than six hundred rooms. Fakhr ul Mulk had his set of rooms in the mardana, and his Begum had hers in the zenana. Each of the five sons had his own spacious set of rooms, which he occupied with his wives and family. There were offices for estate work, and rooms for those of the Musahibs who lived in the palace proper. There were two large drawing rooms, a banqueting hall, a large dining room, a smaller dining room and a breakfast room. There were two billiard rooms and two card rooms. Another room was filled with silver trophy cups and the skins and mounted heads of game animals. Yet another was the repository for the swords, guns, and other arms that had come down in the family through generations, as well as the guns used for shikar. A beautiful large room, opening on a courtyard and used for family parties and informal entertainments, was called the baradari, meaning "twelve doors"; the name suggests both its airiness and its accessibility from other parts of the palace.

In a separate building, two kitchens with their storerooms were set apart for European cooking, and two with their storerooms for Indian cooking. The latter included a couch kept covered with a white sheet, where the ladies of the household could sit should they choose to come to the kitchen personally to give instructions or supervise the preparation of some delicacy. All the cooking was done in silver pots or pans. As one woman of that time explained, "Brass, steel, and aluminium may be all right, but what do we know about them? We *know* that silver is safe." Innumerable pantries contained the plate, crockery, cutlery, glassware, and linen that was needed for the elaborate entertainment that went on.

Three permanent employees of the palace lived outside the grounds in their own homes: the doctor, the Anglo-Indian housekeeper, and the compounder. The doctor's duty was to give every new servant a thorough medical examination and to attend on the staff when they were ill. He was also consulted for minor ailments of family members, but specialists were called in for any serious illnesses. Servants who became ill were isolated in rooms at a distance from the main part of the palace grounds. Those who died were buried in a plot of land which Fakhr ul Mulk had bought for that purpose, but, as was frequent in Muslim tradition, funerals were not permitted to go through the gate of the palace. The wall at one side was broken to allow the funeral through and immediately afterward was repaired by the palace masons.

The housekeeper's particular domain was the kitchens and pantries. Not a speck of dust should be anywhere, food should be protected from flies and dust both during preparation and after, and the kitchen staff should be in perfect health. The compounder's work was to supervise the sweeping and swabbing of the entire palace twice a day, see that the drains were clean and disinfected morning and evening, and have prescriptions made up at the chemist's when required. The zenana staff was completely separate and had no connection with the staff in the mardana except for a few mamas, women servants who were old and steady enough to be able to walk both worlds without danger and who carried messages between them.

Fakhr ul Mulk's day began early and actively. At four in the morning he rose and spent an hour at a vigorous workout with Indian clubs. To refresh him afterward, two quarts of milk all frothy and warm from the buffalo were brought in a silver bowl. With the milk he took two pills of opium, a practice he shared with Maharajah Kishen Pershad among many others. A large number of people past forty took opium to soothe their aches from old wounds or from rheumatism and other infirmities of age; it was the "aspirin" of the 1890s. Abuse of the drug was virtually unknown; those who took it did so for years on end without varying the dose. An old saying goes that opium is honey for the infant, death for the youth, and longevity for the old man. Fakhr ul Mulk's opium was prepared by one special servant. It was ground with sugar candy, almonds, and ghee, shaped into pills, wrapped in silver foil, and placed in a small gold box which had a matching pair of gold tongs.

A few minutes after taking his opium, Fakhr ul Mulk donned riding clothes and went for his morning canter, preceded and followed by four cavalrymen from his own troops. Returning by seven, he was bathed and dressed for the day. Then he took his first meal in the breakfast room in the mardana. As at all regular meals except tea, which was served in the separate apartments, the entire personnel of the mardana was expected to be present. The menu was largely British: hot or cold cereal with cream; eggs to order; liver, kidneys, or fish; toast, butter, marmalade, jam; and tea with milk or coffee with cream. The Nawab always ate six poached eggs, often only the yolks, and sometimes meat or fish, but no starchy items.

Following the ceremonial salaams, the morning was spent in his office, largely dealing with his work as an administrator of the state. Fakhr ul Mulk had held various state offices. For some time he rejoiced in the title of Miscellaneous Minister, to the distress of the Resident, who considered it undignified. When the Cabinet Council was formed, Fakhr ul Mulk added the judicial portfolio; after Maharajah Kishen Pershad became Dewan, he was made vice-president of the Council. Much of the work for these posts he did in his office at Iram Munzil, where streams of messengers came and went, laden with files, reports, and petitions. While he was minister for police and public works, he often went in person to inspect trouble spots. During that period he had a silver casket made in the shape of a prison, which he presented to Queen Victoria's son, the Duke of Saxe-Coburg, on the occasion of his visit.

Most of the estate work Fakhr ul Mulk passed along to his sons, who sat together to hear appeals from the jagir. This was sometimes referred to as the "Committee of Brothers," and the office where they held the hearings was the "Committee Room." Typical appeals concerned land disputes, questions of payment of debts, or restitution for injury. In such cases, testimony and evidence had already been presented before a local taluqdar, or magistrate, who made a decision, but an appeal was always possible to the jagirdar on any question, civil or criminal. In addition, petitions for schools, hospitals, or other amenities which the jagir administrators considered beyond their authority were dealt with by the Committee of Brothers. Occasionally the question was one of remission of land revenue. In good or average years the ryots (tenant farmers) were expected to pay a fixed land revenue, but this amount was remitted in whole or in part when there was crop failure. In times of famine, the revenue flowed from the jagirdar to the ryots so that they could purchase food grains in the market.

The origins of this system lay less in tender feelings for the ryots than in the officials' passion for their own solvency and consequent refusal to destroy the means by which their wealth was produced. The lesson had been learned when, early in the nineteenth century, the hand of the tax collector had squeezed the ryots until many of them found farming more precarious than brigandage. At that time a system had been introduced into the Dewani lands whereby revenues were collected by "revenue farmers" who bid against one another for the right to collect the taxes in a given area. Collections in excess of the contracted amount constituted their profit. Whatever the evils of this system, it made the obvious apparent: peasants who died of starvation or were wiped out during famine did not raise revenue-producing crops after the next monsoon. The result of disaster to the ryots was instant bankruptcy for the tax farmers, who had to recover the contracted revenues. It was in their interest, therefore, to protect their investments by seeing that at times of famine the ryots were assured of the means of survival, not only for themselves and their families but also for their work animals.

By the time of Mahbub Ali Pasha's birth, the idea of a famine reserve by which starvation deaths were prevented had become a routine part of the state administration. When in 1865/66 the British Raj proved itself philosophically and administratively unequal to the disastrous sequence of flood and famine in Orissa, Sir Salar Jung, Dewan of Hyderabad, had written to suggest that "if the authorities at Orissa are unable to cope with the situation, the Government of India would be well advised to hand over the province of Orissa to the management of the Government of Hyderabad, who would administer the province in the interests of the people and remit to the British Exchequer the balance of the revenue receipts." Sir Salar Jung's black eyes must have sparkled as he administered to the cocksure foreigners this dose of their own medicine.

The jagirdars also had recognized the profitability of preserving the ryots and absorbed this approach into their own philosophy and conduct. As absentee landlords, most jagirdars were far more interested in the revenues than in the properties or the shadowy people who inhabited them, but when their turn came to give, they gave handsomely. The right of appeal to them was not only theoretical—it was actually exercised, and it frequently prevented extremes of injustice.

On the other hand, such occasional contact was not sufficient to arouse much loyalty. In contrast to the city people, who knew and loved the aristocrats in whose shadow they lived, the villagers were more apt to consider them at best an impersonal court of last resort. What the villagers probably did not realize was that they hardly existed for most of the jagirdars. Many knew only vaguely where their lands were or the condition of the people who lived on them. They did not even know the amount of income which their jagirs yielded. That it was ample was enough to keep in mind, though keeping it so got many of them into trouble. Not knowing one's income is a great way to live beyond it, and many of them did, steadily or occasionally.

Fakhr ul Mulk was no exception. If the Viceroy was coming and he wanted to buy a new car for the occasion, or to travel or entertain lavishly at a season when the revenues were low, there were always the moneylenders ready and eager to oblige. Not that they received any respect for so doing. Even the most prominent moneylenders, receiving a summons to Iram Munzil, had to get down from the jutka (horse-drawn taxi) on the road in front of the main gate. There they donned bugloos and dastar and walked up the path to the palace where, meeting Fakhr ul Mulk, they stood with arms folded respectfully, awaiting his command. There was no question of notes or security: told that he required three lakhs of rupees, they immediately went and brought the money. So long as the interest kept mounting, neither they nor he worried about speedy repayment.

To the state, Nawab Fakhr ul Mulk Bahadur gave honest and competent service; if not brilliant, at least unquestionably devoted. His own affairs got scant attention from him, except when they involved an appeal to him. Then, for others as well as for his own pleasures, his attitude was, "Money is there to be spent. Let it be enjoyed." Every morning, coins amounting to about a hundred rupees were washed with scented soap, put into bags of new cloth, and kept at hand for Fakhr ul Mulk to distribute to the poor when he went out. Once a month he sent a man to each of his jagirs in turn to buy up the entire bazaar on market day and distribute the goods to the poor. In times of scarcity, food was cooked in his kitchens all day long and sent to the gate for the poor to eat their fill.

Perhaps he was helped to an awareness of the hunger of the poor by his own unstinting pleasure in food. As the morning wore on, his poached eggs apparently wore off, for he had frequent snacks. At ten o'clock daily an enormous spoon was brought to him containing a paste made by grinding 75 almonds together with sugar candy. This he nibbled at with a teaspoon while looking over files or conversing with his colleagues or subordinates. At eleven he had the broth of three chickens, concentrated to two cups.

At one o'clock, lunch was served, in the zenana unless there were guests. It consisted of soup, two European courses, six or seven Indian dishes, a European and an Indian dessert, and fruit. Afterward everyone rested until tea time. Fakhr ul Mulk took his afternoon rest in the mardana, while a Musahib read the newspaper to him. For this exercise the two men were separated by a silken curtain, so that each could sprawl in comfort without regard to formal etiquette. At three-thirty, refreshed by a cup of tea, Fakhr ul Mulk went out once more, often on inspection visits or to call on someone.

About six he returned to find his almond paste waiting for him. For two hours he received callers, chatted with his Musahibs and sons, or played billiards or snooker, and again sipped his chicken soup. Then he went to be bathed and changed into comfortable Indian clothes in time for eight-thirty dinner, which, unless there were guests, followed the same general pattern as the noon meal. If no function claimed his attention, the time after dinner was a family hour when he and his Begum held court for their sons and daughters, daughters-in-law, and grandchildren, each of whom had his appropriate place according to his position in the family; if one were absent his place was left vacant. Conversation was general; grandchildren were sufficiently in awe of their elders to remain subdued and orderly but were encouraged to participate. Jokes, gossip, news, tales from the latest shikar were all exchanged, hopes shared and triumphs celebrated, until ten o'clock arrived. That was bedtime.

With Fakhr ul Mulk, bedtime itself was something of an interesting routine. Unlike many nobles, he generally slept in the zenana with his wife. There, four female servants were on duty all night long. Two took turns massaging his legs until he fell asleep, but they had to remain awake so that they could resume if he woke up or was restless. A third sat with a fly swatter, ready to attack any fly or mosquito that came along. She was a relic of the days before electricity, before the two ceiling fans with which the room was fitted had supplanted a punkah worked by punkah-wallahs; but she remained at her nearly nonexistent duty until the end of **Fakhr ul Mulk**'s life. If by chance any wildlife escaped her and he had a bite to be scratched, she complied with a piece of cotton moistened with perfume.

The fourth woman on night duty was a storyteller. (A sample of her tales is given in Appendix II.) It was her task to sit at the head of the bed and tell stories. She stopped when the Nawab fell asleep, but had to remain alert so that if he woke and said "Hmm?" she could pick up the tale where she had left off. During the day she read storybooks to increase or refresh her stock in trade. In continuing this practice throughout his adult life, Fakhr ul Mulk was unusual but by no means unique. Almost every prosperous household included an ayah whose duty was to tell stories after dinner to the children who assembled around her, on their beds, on the floor, in any spot or attitude they found comfortable. Every child was expected to say, "Hmm" whenever the ayah paused, a trick which enabled her to keep track of how many had dropped off to sleep and who was still wakeful. When her pause was greeted only by silence, she began the process of distributing the children to their beds.

Major breaks in this regular routine arose mainly when a dinner party was scheduled. Nawab Fakhr ul Mulk met a great many of the British officers through the sports which they shared —polo, riding, hunting, shikar—and it was these friends whom he entertained. His parties were so famous in the Cantonment that newly arrived officers were routinely advised by their friends to go and sign the Nawab's guest book, which was kept at the main gate. Every few weeks he sent for the guest book to see who had come to pay respects. From that list plus old friends, the commandant, and the family, the guest list was composed. The Dewan, one or two ministers, and some of the Paigah nobles were among the few Hyderabadis likely to be invited. About once every six months, the Resident was invited.

A formal dinner for eighty was not exactly a spontaneous undertaking. Once the guest list had been drawn up, invitations were printed and sent out about three weeks ahead; the replies came promptly, and few were "regrets." The next step was to make up the table plan, a task at first assigned to a Musahib but later taken over by a grandson. This was done with the aid of a long board which had an elastic tape down its middle, fastened with tacks at regular intervals. The spaces thus created represented place settings. Cards containing the names of guests could thus be moved around until a proper distribution of guests in accordance with strict protocol had been achieved and recorded. At the dinner, a printed copy was put beside each place setting.

Parties were scheduled for eight o'clock. The Resident, who of course came last, was met at the main gate by a general salute from Fakhr ul Mulk's troops. Ranged on the main steps were the guard of honor. Ordinary guests were met by the sons, who were stationed along the steps in order of seniority; when the Resident arrived, Fakhr ul Mulk himself descended the stairs to receive him as he alighted from his carriage or car. Mixed drinks, served in the downstairs reception room, chiefly provided an interval in which each gentleman could pick up the small envelope containing the name of the lady he was expected to take in to dinner and check the seating plan to see where at the table to look for their place cards. The main drinking was expected to take place only after dinner.

By eight-thirty the military band in the garden struck up the "Roast Beef"—the British army mess call—and the party proceeded up the staircase and down the broad passage to the banqueting room, which was a sight to remember, glittering with the reflections from the great crystal chandeliers, gleaming with white napery, silver, and a forbidding array of wine glasses, and alive with bearers, one for each two guests, in their white uniforms and gloves and made taller by starched turbans. In front of every place card lay a printed menu and table plan, bearing the Nawab's crest. By each lady's place was a gift: French perfume was a favorite, or perhaps a manicure set or compact.

Scanning the menu, a guest might well remind himself that "England expects every man . . ." (A sample is printed here.)

MENU
Dinner, Wednesday, 27th October 1910

———

Hors d'Oeuvres Royans a la Bordelaise

SOUP
White Asparagus; Turtle Soup

FISH
Fillets of Fish fried, Prawn Sauce

SIDE DISHES
Chicken Cream cold with Cucumber
Wild Duck with green Peas
Mushrooms

ROAST
Roast Turkey
Roast Saddle of Venison
Wine Sauce

SECOND COURSE
Cheese Biscuits with Caviar
Pilau and Curries

PUDDING
Cabinet Pudding, Sauce Madeira
Badam Kheer

ICE
Strawberry Ice with Strawberries in Syrup
Coffee and Liqueurs

When everyone had finished, Fakhr ul Mulk nodded to a servant standing in one of the windows, who in turn signaled to the bandmaster in the garden below. Immediately everyone stood for the Nawab's toast, "His Majesty, the King!" and "God Save the King," followed by the senior British guest's response of "His Highness, the Nizam!" and the Hyderabad anthem.

After dinner the men adjourned to the drawing room for whisky and brandy. The ladies, guided by one of the men belonging to the family, detoured to another room, where Begum Fakhr ul Mulk received them for a short visit before they rejoined the men. Everyone left about eleven o'clock, except for a few of the younger intimates, who remained to drink and play snooker with the sons while Fakhr ul Mulk went to bed.

With this kind of lavish entertainment by the nobility, it is not surprising that Hyderabad became a predictable stop on the itineraries of distinguished visitors and touring European royalty. During Mahbub's reign, he and his court played host to the Prince and Princess of Wales, the Duke and Duchess of Connaught, the Duchess of Battenberg, the Duke of Saxe-Coburg, the Duke of Hesse, the Archduke Franz Ferdinand and Count Toren of Austria, the Czar and the Grand Duke Alexander of Russia, and a whole bevy of other European royalty, governors, commanders in chief from the Government of India, and other dignitaries. No other Indian state had such a constant procession of Very Important Personages. Even the Viceroys, based in distant Calcutta, found their visits sufficiently habit-forming to look for frequent justifications for a return engagement; every Viceroy during Mahbub's active reign paid him a visit.

There was one instance in which the Resident did not receive the customary lavish hospitality from Fakhr ul Mulk, who believed that respect should be mutual and was not afraid to tell the Resident so. By established usage, when a new Resident arrived, five of the Great Nobles called upon him: Maharajah Sir Kishen Pershad, the Dewan; Nawab Salar Jung III; Nawab Fakhr ul Mulk; Nawab Khan Khanan, his brother; and the Amir e Paigah. Although each was preceded by buglers and outriders, the retinue was minimal compared with that of an ancestor of whom it was said that the first marchers in his procession were knocking at the Residency gates while the Nawab was still mounting his elephant at his deori. When these five nobles alighted from their carriages, a guard of honor of British

troops saluted them. This was part of a strict protocol which regulated every detail of the visit. They were received at the foot of
the stairs by an attaché, at the top of the stairs by an officer of
the staff above the grade of attaché, and "by the Resident at the
carpet of the hall outside the drawing room." On leaving, each
was presented with a memento: a pandan and some bottles of
attar, which might range in number from two to five according
to the Resident's estimate of his importance. After the ceremonial
visit, each of these noblemen gave a dinner in honor of the new
Resident.

One new Resident, however, ordered the guard of honor stopped
except for the Dewan, whereupon Nawab Fakhr ul Mulk retali-
ated by refusing to give a dinner. Some time later, the Nawab
fell ill and the Resident called to see him. Still smarting over the
guard of honor, the Nawab refrained from offering so much as
a cup of tea. When the Resident said something about being sorry
to see him ill, Fakhr ul Mulk replied, "Well, sir, it is good to be
ill sometimes. It can even bring the Resident to you."

Pride of this sort was not confined to the head of the family:
it was imbibed by every generation along with the mother's milk,
and the servants strictly upheld the assumption that members of
the family were important personages. When Nawab Ghazi Jung
returned from school in England he naturally accompanied his
father for the first morning's ride. Mounted and waiting for the
others to assemble, he was approached by a groom who respectfully reminded him to carry the crop in his left hand along with
the reins. Eyeing his crop, whose gold handle was in the shape
of a parrot's head with a ruby and an emerald for eyes, the young
man replied curtly that it belonged in the right hand. "Yes,
sahib," the groom persisted, "that is no doubt correct in England,
but here you must always keep your right hand free to take the
salaams."

The servants' support of the dignity of the family was a blade
that cut two ways. By the time servants had been with the family
long enough to achieve the status of an "old retainer," some of

the aura of the head of the house had rubbed off on them. Even Begum Fakhr ul Mulk spoke very circumspectly to those of the staff who had been with her husband since his youth. One of the younger generation recalls running afoul of this attitude when he was a child. KhatijaBi was a hefty old African woman who had spent her life guarding the zenana gate. This child and his brother one day teased KhatijaBi by calling her "fatty." Without a word the woman strode after the boys and caught them in a spot where they were out of sight of anyone who might have intervened. Seizing a small throat in either hand, she left them in no doubt that she would not stand for such disrespect.

Released, the boys fled cying to their grandmother, who complained indignantly to her husband, "Just look how boldly KhatijaBi spoke to those boys. Surely this time she has gone too far!" Nodding, he sent for the boys. "It is God's mercy," he told them sternly, "that she didn't kill you both. The next time you will speak more respectfully to KhatijaBi."

Once even Mahbub Ali Pasha paid his respects. Shortly after Fakhr ul Mulk's eldest son, Ghazi Jung, had returned from England and became an officer in the Hyderabad army, he had to have an appendectomy. The operation was performed in Iram Munzil by Nawab Arustu Yar Jung, who was the Nizam's surgeon and medical adviser to most of the nobility. Hearing of this emergency, Mahbub Ali Pasha came in person just as the patient was beginning to waken from the anesthetic. Nawab Fakhr ul Mulk wanted his son's bugloos and dastar to be put on him in order to receive the royal visitor, but the surgeon refused to allow it. The Nizam paid his call on the patient and immediately on returning to Purani Haveli sent him six gold ashrafis. Ghazi Jung Bahadur still recalls this happily as probably the only time nazar was given by the Nizam to a subject.

Just as Fakhr ul Mulk was meticulous about offering the proper respect to anyone, particularly to his sovereign, so he expected it to be offered to him in appropriate measure, even by the royal family. On the occasion of one durbar, the nobles were standing on the steps leading up to the Durbar Hall waiting for the Heir Apparent, Osman Ali Khan, to come and take his place before they took theirs. Osman finally arrived, having had more than he should have to drink. As he passed them, each noble gave him the required royal salaam, which was a very low bow incorporating seven salaams by the time they straightened up. Instead of going slowly up the stairs, accepting each salaam, Osman perfunctorily raised his hand to his forehead as he rushed by. Incensed, Fakhr ul Mulk said loudly to the nobleman standing beside him, "Just look at that! The Heir Apparent is brushing flies with our salaams!"

Osman overheard the remark, as he was meant to, and ever after he was careful to return a salaam properly. In this he was merely observing the minimum rules of etiquette. Whatever one felt, it was considered bad form to show ill feeling of any sort, and the slightest hint of it caused a great deal of gossip. Courtesy demanded that even a salaam be received as though one had enough time for the greeter, and that all the smallest formalities be observed. Even if a host simply passed a plate of sweets or pan to a friend, for instance, the recipient first salaamed and then took it. This is still observed in families, whether rich or poor, who were brought up in the old way. There was no question of extenuating circumstances as an excuse for rudeness. The niceties had to be observed. They were what kept the heavens up and the sounds of the earth sweet.

Protocol, courtesy, family name took pride of place even over a question of law and order. On one occasion a brother-in-law of Fakhr ul Mulk got into trouble over a woman, and the Kotwal, Nawab Akbar Jung, gave orders for his arrest. In disguise, the brother-in-law fled to Iram Munzil for protection. Fakhr ul Mulk ordered the gates shut and had his soldiers post themselves with guns on the roof of the palace. He himself sat on the verandah with a loaded six-chamber revolver on the table in front of him. When the Kotwal arrived, Fakhr ul Mulk ordered that he should be admitted only if he dismounted and entered through the postern gate. In terms which allowed for no misunderstanding, he expressed to Akbar Jung his indignation at the very idea that orders should have been given for the arrest of any member of his family. He explained that the Kotwal should have made the complaint to him in full confidence that it would be properly attended to. Fearing lest any show of persistence might precipitate violence, the Kotwal withdrew with whatever grace he could muster under the circumstances.

Another of the things which upset Fakhr ul Mulk was lack of punctuality. Tardiness brought swift reproof to his children, but from a servant it was not to be borne. "Since you cannot come on time," he would thunder at a laggard, "go sit in your house and do not come before me again." The disgraced servant, banished from service, knew that he would still be given his wages regularly and that when he was in real need—in case of illness or death in his family or even the marriage of a daughter—he could come back to the Nawab with assurance of being helped. If Fakhr ul Mulk reprimanded a servant in the morning for a lesser offense, he forgave him by evening and gave him some money.

Backbiting brought immediate censure, with the curt instruction that if one had something to say about another person, it should be said to his face. Children or grandchildren who were heard swearing felt the full weight of the Nawab's disapproval, in the form of banishment from his presence for a specified number of days. In later years he was greatly distressed by a rumor that a grandson studying in England was running around with girls. When eventually the young man returned and presented himself to pay his respects, Fakhr ul Mulk did not return the salaam. Averting his face, he asked sarcastically, "Haven't you brought a lady with you?"

Although he was an exceedingly moral man, Nawab Fakhr ul Mulk was not a particularly religious one, at least with regard to organized observances. He insisted that all his children and grandchildren should study Arabic and know the Koran, and be able to read and understand their prayers, as well as the words of the Prophet. It never, of course, occurred to any of them to eat pork or pork products. Beyond that, not much was required of them. As a Shia family, they observed the month of Moharrum with evening readings from the Koran and from the stories of the death of the Prophet's grandsons, Hasan and Husain. Devotees then, as now, worked themselves to a fever pitch of emotion over these stories, weeping and beating their breasts in sorrow for the events at Kerbela. As Mohammad-Quli Qutub Shah wrote, "Even the angel Gabriel threw dust on his face for his intense sorrow at the martyrdom of Husain." Fakhr ul Mulk, probably out of deference to the wishes of his wife, attended these sessions regularly but never exhibited the slightest emotion during them. On the other hand, he was not known ever to express criticism of what he obviously regarded as a superstitious practice.

During Ramadan, when for a month orthodox Muslims did not permit even a drop of water to pass their lips from sunup to sundown, Fakhr ul Mulk appeased his conscience and placated his Begum by observing the fast on any three days which happened to suit him. For the staff, having Nawab Sahib fast was more trouble than having him eat. Waking up long before anyone else in the pre-dawn hours, he announced to those on night duty that he intended to fast that day. The news was sped down the stairs and shouted out through the courtyards and servants' quarters to the kitchens: "His Excellency is fasting!" Within minutes a crew was bustling about, long before they otherwise would have been, for Fakhr ul Mulk's fasting diet included special dishes which took extra time to prepare: various delicacies made with ground almonds and pistachios, and ripe guavas cut into cup shapes, their seeds scooped out and the hollow filled with figs that had been mashed with powdered sugar. Juices of several kinds of fruits were squeezed and big jugs filled so that he would have a choice. These foods were required to help him keep up his strength during a day without the accustomed almond paste and soup.

One of the two biggest festivals of the Muslim year was the popular Bakr Id. It commemorated Abraham's willingness to sacrifice his son Isaac to what he believed was God's will, and the Lord's substitution of a sacrifical animal. In memory of this redemption every householder who can afford it is enjoined to slaughter a goat and distribute some of the meat to the poor. Fakhr ul Mulk used to have a herd of goats driven in from the jagir for this festival. In order to cover the distance in time, they had to set out about a month before the festival! On the day before, he distributed four or five of the animals to each of his sons and sons-in-law. His own share of the sacrifice was cooked for the midday meal.

On this day everyone ate the same. Otherwise the hundred or so indoor servants who regularly received three meals a day from the palace kitchens had menus far simpler than those of the family. Even so, if a servant wanted some particular chutney or other accompaniment to his meal, he had only to ask the servant in charge of that section of the stores: supplies were freely available to the staff.

On festival days the entire establishment came in order of precedence for the holiday salaam, bowing until their heads were on a level with the Nawab's stomach. First came the family members in order of seniority, in holiday finery and jewelry; to them Fakhr ul Mulk presented gifts of ashrafis. Next were the Musahibs and their families, offering nazar which the Nawab touched in token of acceptance and remitted. They received gifts —a length of silk, a fountain pen, or something of comparable value. Lastly came the employees of all degrees and their families in pecking order. Each of them was given a tip of some rupees and in addition new clothes and bangles. In their turn, the guard of honor in full dress and carrying spears saluted while the captain presented his sword. Everyone passing through the line was given the ceremonial attar and pan (perfume and savory). Through all this the naubat sounded special holiday tunes. From every deori the naubat players, whether Hindu or Muslim, made the rounds of all the other deoris collecting tips.

Id (festival) prayers were said at the Idgah, a place specially built for such occasions. It was essentially a wall with a minaret at either end and was erected in a field or equally open place that allowed large numbers of worshipers to congregate. Although the prayers at the Idgah in the Public Garden were said according to the Sunni rites, Shia nobles such as Fakhr ul Mulk also attended.

With the religious obligations and household rituals taken care of, there remained only to enjoy the holiday. Attached to the household were Meerasni, girls whose hereditary work was singing. As Saul had his David, so Iram Munzil had its Meerasni, so that anyone who felt bored, had the blues, or wanted to make merry could call on them. On Bakr Id their number was augmented by dancing girls called from Mahbub ki Mehndi, the quarter where the Muslim nautch girls lived.

Although these girls formed a recognized part of the social structure of Hyderabad, Nawab Fakhr ul Mulk was not very likely to have called them for himself. He was most unfashionably in love with his wife. This made another wall of distinction between himself and his peers, for he married only once and remained faithful to his Begum all her life.

Fakhr ul Mulk was no man to be taken lightly. If his appetite was mighty, so was his strength. Trying one of those machines used at county fairs to measure the force of a hand grip, he sent the needle completely round the dial. The grandsons who watched this performance found it somewhat easier to believe that in his prime the Nawab had been able to lift with one hand a cot on which three men sat, without upsetting their balance.

Legendary in his own strength, he was also a patron of athletes and strong men. Once he heard of an African called Mabrouk Siddi, who was reputed to be a veritable Hercules. Fakhr ul Mulk invited him to the palace, where he gave him a room and, in addition to the plentiful palace food, special rations of milk, eggs, and meat. One day he and a friend, who was also a patron of muscle, were discussing the merits of their protégés when the friend boasted that his man could break a horseshoe. Thus challenged, Fakhr ul Mulk sent for Mabrouk. "Can you break a horseshoe?" he asked him.

"Of course, Your Excellency," Mabrouk replied. A new horseshoe was sent for. Mabrouk flexed his muscles, but try as he might, he could only twist the metal. "There must be something wrong with that horseshoe," Fakhr ul Mulk said, sending for another, but again Mabrouk failed to break it. Irritated, Fakhr ul Mulk snatched it out of his hand and broke it himself. The high priest of muscle was unfrocked. "You are a hoax," Fakhr ul Mulk thundered at him. "Fancy not being able to break a horseshoe!" The Nawab sent the discredited strong man to live in a room outside the gate of the city deori, on an allowance, warning him never to appear before him again.

Fakhr ul Mulk was as strong in his loyalties as in his muscles. He and Mahbub Ali Pasha were two men of very different make-up, yet both were devoted to the service of the same state and held similar visions of its future. Differing in temperament and in most of their personal preferences, they shared the same basic values. Each in his own way exemplified the appetite for life and relish for experience that seems to have been a characteristic of the era of Mahbub Ali Pasha.

Chapter VII

Begum Fakhr ul Mulk

DESPITE the people that surrounded her and the activities that filled her day, Begum Fakhr ul Mulk was lonely while her husband was in Delhi for the Imperial Durbar. In their entire marriage he had rarely been absent from her for such an extended period, and in the past few months, since the accession of Mir Osman Ali Khan, he had spent more time than usual with her. But in his absence there was consolation in having their grandchildren with her.

One of these had been brought up almost as her own child. She had only just finished her prayers, with head covered as was required, when a servant brought word that her daughter-in-law was about to deliver. She went straight to the room and arrived just in time to hear her new grandson's first wail. "Send the child to me," she said, and so, before even the umbilical cord had been tied, the new baby took up residence in his grandmother's rooms, where he continued to live for the next ten years, until he was old enough to be sent to boarding school. Her recollections would bring to mind the daily round of secluded lavishness.

They slept in an enormous bed, the grandfather on one side, the grandmother next, and then the little boy and a girl cousin six years older. Grandmother got up at seven, but it seemed as though no matter what time the children woke, grandfather had already gone. Begum Fakhr ul Mulk washed her face and hands while the ayahs did the same for the children. Water was brought in large covered basins called sailabchis, made of silver, with wide rims to prevent spilling and filigree covers to reduce splashing. Face washing required the assistance of four servants: one to hold the sailabchi, another to pour warm water from a silver jug, a third to hold the silver soap dish, and a fourth to stand ready with the towel.

While they were thus occupied, other serving girls spread the white dastarkhan and laid it with big plates. Covered serving dishes kept the warmth in parathas (a ghee-rich unleavened bread much the size and thickness of a French pancake), eggs, kitcheri (rice cooked with dal and herbs), and keema (finely ground spiced meat). Every morning at daybreak a goat was slaughtered for the breakfast meats. The butchering was done by a Muslim servant in a manner which, except for the difference in prayers, duplicated the kosher technique.

Chilled fruits and melons in their season added color for the eye and lightness for the palate: trays of mangoes in shades of yellow and gold; papayas in their green skins, the yellow of their meat enhanced by the round black seeds; pale peaches from Kashmir; apples from Simla; grapes packed in cotton wool, fifteen to eighteen to a tiny box made of wood shavings and shipped at vast expense from Afghanistan; and delicate lichees. All year round there were bananas—fat and red, slim and green, yellow and stout, or the Nanjangud, the size of a woman's finger. Adults and children alike drank sweet hot tea, thick with milk, that had been simmering for an hour or more.

They sat cross-legged on the carpets, at the edge of the dastar-khan, and ate with their fingers. Children were expected to observe the precise rules of etiquette. Only the right hand might be used, even for breaking the paratha into bite-sized pieces to wrap around a bit of other food. Fingers dexterously twirled the rice so that a few grains at a time became fully coated with gravy. Only babies were allowed to smear their fingers above the second knuckle. Immediately after the meal, hands were washed and mouths thoroughly rinsed.

After breakfast the Begum was dressed for the day by her personal maids. Her clothing was elaborate. The skin-tight trousers were of silk; a silk midriff blouse called a choli was tied in front; the short sleeves were edged with large solid-gold beads. (In such a household there was full-time work for a seamstress just taking the decorations off the ladies' clothing and sewing them on again after laundering.) Over the choli went a sleeveless overblouse of net, embroidered or sequined.

Then she was ready for her jewelry: earrings, five on each ear, starting with single stones at the top and ending in elaborate drops at the lobes. Around her neck, besides a string of black beads interspersed with pearls or gold which she always wore as a symbol of marriage, hung a string of pearls, a jeweled necklace, and two golden chains reaching to her waist, to which the circles holding her keys were attached. On each arm, above the elbow, were two gold bands studded with diamonds. At her wrists, a pair of heavy gold bracelets was separated by an inch of glass bangles of a color to match her clothes. Elaborate rings on her fingers and plain circlets of gold on her middle toes completed the ornaments.

Last of all came the dupatta. This was a piece of sheer cotton, three yards long and a yard wide, which had been dipped into a thin starch containing powdered mica to make it sparkle. While still wet, it had then been gathered into a narrow strip and twisted until it coiled like a skein of yarn; dried, and thus "permanently pleated," it was worn draped across the bosom, with the ends over the shoulder and down the back. One end, like the decorative end of a sari, became an all-purpose garment in itself. In the presence of elders or men of the family, it was draped modestly over the head. Out of doors, it went over the head as a protection against sun or breeze. In the presence of the Nizam, from whom no woman was purdah, it formed a partial screen for her silhouette as she pulled the edge forward and turned her head slightly to avoid meeting his gaze.

In the winter she wore also a long-sleeved, collarless brocade jacket reaching to her waist. In other seasons the jacket was always at hand to slip on quickly if visitors who were not relatives should come to call, for the overblouse was transparent.

On Fridays and Mondays the ceremony of the bath took place. Seated on a low stool, she was first massaged all over with oil and rubbed with ground gram (a lentil) mixed with a little water to form a paste. Its slightly grainy texture stimulated the circulation and left the body glowing. Next her hair was washed; liquid made by soaking rheta nuts, called in English soap nuts because of the rich lather they produce, was used for the shampoo. After this beauty treatment, she emerged from rinsing cascades of warm water with skin like silk. Toweled dry, her hair was carefully oiled and done in a tight braid, with a ribbon twisted round and round the end and tied in a bow.

By the time she was presentable and seated on the musnud in her drawing room, it was eight o'clock and Nawab Fakhr ul Mulk had returned to the zenana. The mamas, those women servants who were permitted to move freely back and forth between the zenana and the mardana, had gone through the apartments summoning the household to "come for the salaam." This was a review of every soul on the palace premises, filing past in order of precedence. First came the married sons with their wives, then the unmarried sons; then any married daughters and sons-in-law who were at Iram Munzil, followed by the unmarried daughters; the grandsons followed by the granddaughters; then the Musahibs, clerical staff, servants, and laborers down to the smallest boys and girls in training. As they filed past, each bowed low in salaam to the Nawab and Begum, who knew every member of their staff and noticed immediately if any were missing, so that enquiries could reveal whether the doctor ought to be sent.

In about an hour the groups had disbanded. The men of the family went to their offices or other commitments as necessary, the children to their lessons, and the daughters-in-law to their own apartments, except the eldest, who stayed long enough to give the day's menus to the mama who would relay them to the cooks. Perhaps a favorite daughter-in-law or two might remain to chat with the Begum or to help her select designs if a jeweler or silk merchant had brought his wares. Occasionally the Begum looked in on the lessons being conducted by the English governesses for the girls and youngest boys. Although it was fashionable to have English tutors and governesses, their presence was not merely for the sake of fashion in this house; the youngsters were expected to study. In his memoirs, Lord Dufferin, who had been Viceroy of India, commented on the beautiful diction of the eldest Fakhr ul Mulk daughter.

At one o'clock, lunch was served on the dastarkhan in the zenana, with all sixty-odd family members present unless there were guests. From the beginning of the fly season until the first rains had fallen, a mosquito net fifteen yards long and three yards wide was suspended from the ceiling over the dastarkhan and the family sat within its protection. Meals were eaten in pin-drop silence, except for the voice of the Nawab and the subdued reply to an occasional question. Only the grandson who shared his bed dared to initiate conversations or to ask for favors, and he rarely met with a rebuff. This made him predictably popular with the other youngsters, who channeled through him their requests for cuff links, microscopes, shikar expeditions or whatever it might be. Afterward, while Fakhr ul Mulk enjoyed a pan (the savory concoction wrapped in a betel leaf), everyone relaxed as he chatted with his children and joked with his grandchildren, for whom he had private names like Firecracker or Butterball. He was formal with his sons, tender with his daughters, playful with his grandchildren. Soon after two o'clock, everybody went to rest, the Begum with her two special grandchildren in the huge bed.

Unless there were guests, the Begum enjoyed sitting on the balcony after tea to watch the children and grandchildren at their games in the garden and fields beyond. For team sports, visiting relatives, clerks, servants and their children, even younger sisters were co-opted. Girls over twelve who continued to ride did so in the uniform of a cavalry officer, their hair covered by a turban. One of Begum Fakhr ul Mulk's daughters was a devoted horse-woman. Although she rode only on her father's property, she was accompanied by a bodyguard of thirty mounted Africans.

The zenana over which the Begum held sway was a dominion in itself. Her subjects were the women of the family and some two hundred employees, ranging from the ancient crones who had been with Nawab Sahib since his childhood to small children, of whom the boys would be transferred to the mardana when they reached the dangerous age of ten. Among the servants, too, there was a pecking order. At the top were the old ladies from the city deori, who were treated with respect and given purely sedentary occupations, if any at all. Next in rank came the servants drawn from the jagirs, who had been many years in service, well dressed and decked in gold according to their mistress's resources and generosity. Many of them were mamas who had special responsibilities and whom even the daughters-in-law had to placate. They attended on the women of the family, looked after their wardrobes and jewels, protected food and water from any attempt at poisoning, and performed other tasks reserved only for the most trusted retainers. Other elevated women were those who could read and write, to whom books were given so that they might memorize stories and relate them at night to the Nawab Sahib. These received tea during their hours of night duty and a special ration of a cup of milk with some special flavoring every day.

Next in the hierarchy were six women known as Booas, who did the Moghlai cooking; each was a specialist in several dishes which she alone was allowed to prepare. Under each were four girls to stir the pots and blow the fires while learning the culinary secrets of their Booa. Kitchen personnel were required to bathe and don clean clothes before starting the day's work. Each head was covered with a clean white cloth tied to form a cap. If, however, a hair should by dreadful mischance fall into the food, it was easy to tell by the dish which cooking group it had come from. The offending hair was matched against the heads of the girls in the group and the one considered guilty had her head shaved.

On the next rung of the service ladder stood the rest of the boys and girls being brought up in Iram Munzil, together with the sweepers and scullery maids.

In a separate echelon were twelve "Guardans," the word being pidgin for female guard. Drawn from the Harijan community, they were possibly a relic of the time when female soldiers, who had been drilled and trained to arms by the French, were employed by the second Nizam and his nobles to guard the zenanas, instead of the eunuchs used by the Moghuls and other Muslim and Hindu dynasties. In Begum Fakhr ul Mulk's dominion, their occupation was purely domestic and muscular: pounding chilies into powder or the husks off the various lentils which came unhusked from the jagirs, or washing the enormous quantities of rice that had to be cooked every day. On their heads went the trays of food and fruit dispatched frequently to friends and relations and to the mosques, to the gate for the poor in times of distress, and to the mardana servants every day. These women, under a leader called a Vazir Guardan, were distinguished by their yellow saris with red borders, their red blouses and red sandals, and the red sticks with silver knobs which they carried, the Vazir Guardan's stick being very elaborate.

Scores of children of both sexes were brought up in Iram Munzil. They labored in return for their maintenance and the security of a permanent home, either at the palace or with a male worthy to be married off to. They were by no means slaves, for when they were old enough to exercise their choice, they were free to leave. Once a year, a drummer went round the jagirs calling upon those who wished to do so to give their children to be

brought up at Iram Munzil. The little ones came to Hyderabad
by the cart-load. Once arrived, they were deloused and bathed
and put into new clothes, their old ones being burned. Then they
were given into the care of a group of mamas who gradually got
their stomachs used to palace food and their habits of cleanliness
and their manners in line with palace requirements. They came,
naturally, from the very dregs of society in the jagirs, from the
poorest families, who could not afford to feed them properly.
Most were girls, for in Indian families a girl was a liability and
the parents were often grateful to have her taken off their hands.
A boy, on the other hand, would rarely be sent, for he was his
parents' old-age insurance. Not only would he grow up to earn,
but he would also bring money into the family with his wife's
dowry.

In the zenana, the girls were distributed about to work under
various older women servants. They were kept in the palace for
as long as they wished; when they left, possibly to accompany a
daughter of the family to her new husband's home, or to work
for someone who had asked the Begum to find a servant for her,
a gift of clothes and money went with them. When their parents
came to see them, the children were asked whether they wished
to return home and the parents whether they wished to have
their children back. There is no instance of an affirmative answer.
But there were instances of girls who, perhaps out of pique at
being scolded or punished, decided to leave. When this decision
was taken, the girl was told to hold out the end of her dupatta
and into it were put some money and some salt, signifying that
her salt from the palace was finished. This little ceremony termi-
nated the relationship between mistress and servant with no
lingering obligation on either side. A guardan escorted her to
the gate and she was free. Many of those girls regretted their
decision and returned to throw themselves at the Begum's feet.
Unless they had married during their sojourn outside, they were
always taken back. When they grew up they were married off,
either to a man in the mardana who had petitioned the Begum

for a wife, or to a man outside the palace who was known to the family. The marriages were performed in the palace.

All the Muslim women servants lived in strict purdah and dared not go beyond the purdah gate, where KhatijaBi sat like a gorgon. Nevertheless, as will happen in the most strictly regulated institutions, occasionally the supervision was eluded. A few managed to meet a man from the mardana side, to fall in love, and to elope. When this happened, the existence of the couple was ignored. No attempt was made to trace their whereabouts. Nawab Sahib was stern about it. "Should I advertise this thing and spoil the reputation of my house?" he demanded when once a plea went to him that a girl should be traced. Even marriage to a man of the palace scarcely freed a woman from these restrictions. Once a week, a husband sent his greetings to the Begum through the purdah mama. That night, his wife donned a burqa and joined him outside the purdah gate, from where they went to his quarters. Next morning, he brought her back.

With this number of women of all ages and temperaments, together with little boys of mischievous ages, populating a single household, some disputes were inevitable. The Begum would not tolerate any quarreling or disruption of the peace of the zenana. When her fiery temper flared up, she used a cane on recalcitrant girls, but she was so delicately made that her strokes were described as "hitting with a dupatta." More heinous offenses, such as stealing, were punished elsewhere. The offending woman was taken to a tree outside the zenana gate and tied to it for a caning. If she was married, her husband was sent for from the mardana and instructed to give her a certain number of strokes.

The zenana gate, where fat old KhatijaBi held sway and had her room, was closed during the day by a broad red felt curtain which was lifted only to admit visitors to the zenana. The burly bhois on whose shoulders the feminine visitors' painted and tasseled palanquins were carried through the streets set down their burden inside the zenana gate and went back to the main gate to join the rest of their party—the boys who ran ahead to clear the way and the armed guards who paced alongside the palanquin.

Any other caller was first appraised by the formidable Khati-jaBi, who then bestirred her mountainous flesh and waddled slowly to the zenana apartments to announce the caller or give the message and bring a reply. When the doctor came, however, she got up and lumbered along in front of him, calling out, "Doctor Sahib has come! Veil yourselves! Veil yourselves!" Following closely behind her, the doctor used to burlesque her gait, to the delight of the children, who could scarcely contain their laughter until they were safely out of earshot. None of the other servants dared to report this caricature to KhatijaBi, though many saw it, for they were not purdah from the doctor. Of course, the adult women of the family retired to other rooms at Khati-jaBi's warning.

If his call was to treat the Begum, the doctor had to do so through a cloth held stretched in front of her by two women. Putting his hand under it to feel her pulse, he asked her symptoms through an older woman, knowing it would embarrass the Begum to give the answers directly to a man. That completed the permissible examination. When the dentist came to do his work, a small square was cut in the purdah cloth so that only her mouth was visible.

Providing change in Begum Fakhr ul Mulk's orderly routine were both social and religious events. The head of the zenana was responsible for the spiritual welfare of her household. To this end she marshaled her women for all-night prayers on Shab e Meraj, a Muslim vigil. Religious observances dominated two months of the year: Moharrum and Ramadan. During the former the evening Majlis were almost daily occurrences, and although they were occasions of sorrow they were also enjoyed for the social gatherings they entailed. During Ramadan, the Begum reorganized affairs so that everyone could have food after sunset and again during the hour before sunrise, for not so much as a swallow of water should be taken during daylight. When Ramadan fell during the hot season, the prohibition on water worked a real hardship and the pace of life was slackened in order to reduce the physical demands on the servants.

The social ceremonies of Ramadan Id were much like those of Bakr Id. This festival, also called Id ul Fitr, was the occasion for paying fitra, a kind of voluntary tax or alms that went to the mosque or religious institution of one's choice. It varied according to the number of servants in the donor's employ and also according to whether his family were Syeds (descendants of the Prophet). This money was used for the feeding of the poor on holy days.

On festival days the women busied themselves with arranging trays of sweets or other delicacies appropriate to the occasion and sending them out to the homes of friends and relatives, one tray or a whole procession of them to a household. The dishes were covered with a white cotton cloth and over this was placed a dome of gold, silver, or wood, designed to protect the food from the weight of the outer wrappings of elaborately embroidered velvet or heavy brocade. The whole package was then tied up in ordinary cotton cloth and sent out balanced on the heads of Guardans or bhois, who jogged through the streets with their loads, chanting to keep in step. Because many Hindu friends were forbidden by their religion to eat food cooked by persons outside their community, their trays were piled with fruits.

Women from friendly households visited back and forth on social schedules quite independent of those of the men. What brought these sheltered women together was often and most excitingly the preparations for a wedding. A bride, of course, took with her a complete trousseau, accumulated over the years. Its glory was the jewelry, which kept the women of the family busy almost from the time of the girl's birth. Like any prudent mother of her station, Begum Fakhr ul Mulk began while her daughters were still small to commission the making of jewelry which was put away against the day of their marriage. For this purpose pearls and gem stones had to be collected and pored over, and their qualities and possibilities discussed. Designs had to be considered, modified, and approved. For the making, twenty-two-carat gold from the family treasury was weighed and entrusted to the goldsmith.

Nor were the ornaments few. On the head were golden hair ornaments, which sometimes acted as anchor for the jewels on the forehead. Earrings came in three parts: slim strings of gems, hooked into the hair, outlined the edge of the ear, and studs decorated the lobes, from which swayed enameled or jeweled pendants. Arm bands, bracelets, and bangles came in so many traditional shapes and forms that there were names for the different styles. Decorated with all this jewelry and bedecked in clothes bordered and ornamented with gold beads, many a noble bride found her wedding finery so heavy she could not stand up in it without help. The saying that a girl was "sent from her father's house covered in gold from head to foot" was literally true.

There still exists in the Fakhr ul Mulk family the inventory of the dowry brought by the bride of their son Ghazi Jung. It is written in Persian script on red hand-laid paper flecked with gold. Today one sheet is indecipherable and several sheets must have been lost, for the inventory now contains no record of the jewelry that the bride assuredly brought with her from her father's house.

THE LIST OF THE DOWRY OF SULTAN JEHAN BEGUM, ELDEST DAUGHTER OF NAWAB BEHRAM UD DOWLA, BAHADUR, FILLER OF THE HOUSE WITH THE JOY AND DIGNITY OF VIRGINITY, NOBLE, MAGNANIMOUS, THE ONE WHO ENSNARES GOOD FORTUNE.

REQUISITES FOR THE PANDAN

For the Bridegroom	*For the Bride*
Pandan, silver, of ganga-jumni design,[1] one	Pandan, silver, of ganga-jumni design, one

With the following items for each: silver tray; silver under-tray; large silver center box; smaller silver pandan with chain and tray;

---

[1] Ornate gold decorations on silver.

silver box for slaked lime; silver box for unslacked lime; 8 small silver boxes for spices; thandan; 20 silver pan leaves, with designs; lime spoons; 20 silver betel nuts; 4 egg-shaped boxes, silver; small mirror with carved silver frame; silver betel leaf box, ganga-jumni design; spittoon, silver, ganga-jumni design; carved silver stool for pandan.
Pandans, plain silver, 2
Brocade wrapping cloths for pandans, 6
Plain silver tables for pandans, 2

LIST OF KITCHEN UTENSILS, SILVER, SIMPLY CARVED

Large and small vessels, 4

Large ladles, assorted, 4

Frying vessel, large, 1

Baking vessel, large, 1

Thali, large, for kneading, 1

Trays for materials, 2

Plates for materials, 2

Griddles, 2

Rolling pins, large and small, 2

Puri cutters, 2

Tongs for puris, 2

Milk bowls, 2

Plates for covering vessels, 6

LIST OF REQUIREMENTS FOR DRINKING WATER

Carved silver stand for water pots, 1

Embroidered net cover for stand, 1

Brocade covers, 6

Damask or gold embroidered covers, 4

Water ladle, silver, 1

Large pots, silver, 2

Goblet, silver, decorated, with cover, 2

Plate and bowl with cover, silver, 2 sets

LIST OF REQUIREMENTS FOR BATHING

Large and small mugs, silver, carved, 2 each

Pumice stone, 1

Clogs for groom, silver, 1 pair

Clogs for bride, silver, studded, 1 pair

Soap dish, silver, carved, 2

Vessels for herbs and gram flour, silver, 2

Incense box, silver, carved, 1

Towels, 12

Bathing cloths, 2

Head cloths, 2

Bath mats, 2

CLOTHING

Dupattas, tissue, different colors, embroidered gold and silver, 11

Dupattas, silk or mullmull, dif-

ferent colors, plain or embroidered, 13

Handkerchiefs, silk, colored, for hand, 4

Handkerchiefs, Indian or Chinese silk, for shoulder, 39

Saris, silk, brocade, or gold embroidered, 8

Cholis, colored, net or brocade, embroidered with gold and silver or plain, with or without sleeves, 71

Kurtas, sleeveless, colored, plain or embroidered in gold and silver, 60

Pyjamas, various materials, qualities, and designs, 95

Pyjama cords, silk, cotton, brocade, or woven silken net, 56

Waistcoats, brocade, damask, silk, or cashmere, plain or with silken or gold or silver embroidery, 30

Ribbons, colored silk or brocade, 64

Burqa, silk or brocade, 2

Night dupattas, red or white cotton or silk, 9

Brocade cloth, 1 roll

Velvet cloth, 1 roll

Damask cloth, 1 roll

ARTICLES FOR COMFORT AND DECORATION

Bridal bed, silver, ganga-jumni design, 1

Silver poles, ganga-jumni, and canopy, 1 set

Canopy pole cases, plain or brocade, 8

Wrapping cloth for canopy, brocade, 1

Mosquito poles, silver, 4

Mosquito net, red, embroidered with sequins, 1

Floor coverings and items pertaining to formalities for bedroom, 1 set

Footstool, carved silver, 1

Footstool, carved silver, for applying henna to the feet, 1

Carpet for footstool, 1

Carpets, 2

Floor sheets, 4

Silk cords, 3

Brocaded bed cover, 1

Counterpanes, cotton, silk, brocade or silver embroidered, 9

Quilts, brocade or damask, 4

Sheets, colored, silk or cotton, 15

Pillow cases, silk, embroidered or plain, 22

Pillows, round, walled, or embroidered silk or brocade, 9

Wrapping cloth for bed linen, brocade or plain, 8

Musnud, red velvet, embroidered gold with pillows, 1 set

Carpet under musnud, 1

Wrapping cloth for musnud, brocade and plain, 1 each

Divans, carved silver, ganga-jumni design, 2

Mattresses, 2

Stools, carved silver, ganga-jumni design, 2

Divan covers, brocade, 2

Back-rest pillows, embroidered gold and silver, 2

Small bolsters, embroidered gold and silver, 4

Flower holders, silver, carved, ganga-jumni, 2

Garland holders, silver, carved, ganga-jumni, 2

Rose water sprinklers, silver, carved, ganga-jumni, 2

Scent bottle holders, silver, carved, ganga-jumni, 2

Incense bowl, silver, carved, ganga-jumni, 1

Fly whisk, silver handle, ganga-jumni, 1

Large mirrors, silver carved frames, 2

Dastar box, silver, carved ganga-jumni, 1

Wrapping cloth for dastar box, brocade and plain, 3

Dastar cloth, 1 roll

Collyrium boxes, silver, carved, ganga-jumni, 2

Kajal boxes, silver, carved, ganga-jumni, 2

Sailabchi, jug, and soap dish, silver, carved, ganga-jumni, 1 set

Sheet for under basin, brocade, 1

Sheet for under basin, canvas, 1

Jewel trays, carved and studded silver, 3

Jewel trays, carved and studded silver, himroo lined, 3

Large tea trays, silver, 12

Small tea trays, silver, 2

Tray cloths, lace, several sizes, 16

Tray cover, gold dome, 1

Tray cover, silver dome, 1

Tray cover, painted wooden dome, 12

Large felt-lined trays, painted wood, 12

Food-covering cloths, cotton, 25

Red cotton cloths for wrapping food trays sent out on special occasions, 50

Cloths for wrapping food trays, damask, velvet, or brocade, embroidered with gold, silver, or sequins, assorted sizes, 21

Gold and silver sequins, cutorees, and flowers, 1 large box

ARTICLES FOR PRAYERS

Prayer mat, 1

Carpet under prayer mat, silk, 1

Wrapping for prayer mat, damask, brocade, felt, and velvet, 1 each

Wrappings for Koran, brocade, 2

EQUIPMENT FOR HORSE FOR GROOM

Riding crop with silver handle, 2

Halter, silver, carved, 1

Stirrups, silver, carved, 1 pair

Bridle and saddle, studded silver, 1 set

Fodder vessel, silver, carved, 1

Fan, brocade, silver handle, ganga-jumni, 1

Fly whisk, silver handle, ganga-jumni, 1

Processional fly whisks, long, silver, with ivory hair tassels, 2

Cases for processional fly whisks, brocade or embroidered net, 8

Wrapping cloth for fly whisks, brocade or red cotton, 4

Boxes for storing wrapping cloths, Egyptian coffin design, painted wood, 12

Sewing machine with lock and seven keys, 1

The dowry was sent with the bride when she was taken away by the bridegroom. This ceremony, known as the julwa, was one of the major events of the marriage festivities, which all together sometimes stretched over as much as two weeks. At the julwa the bride sat in all her finery, head demurely bowed and eyes closed. Women guests put their hands under her chin and lifted up her face to see it and to look closely at the jewels, the traditional cosmetics, the gold dust beneath her eyes and in the parting of her hair. In a dramatic ceremony peculiar to the Deccan, the pair were called from their respective apartments—by seven elderly women who were happily married—to come and take their first glimpse of each other. Although they were, by this point in the ceremonies, legally married, neither had yet seen the other's face. The julwa was no doubt originated to help alleviate the embarrassment of that first moment. The couple were made to sit on a platform, separated by a curtain stretched between them, where, supported by the encouragement and laughter of friends, they took their first look at each other in a small mirror.

Then the bhois arrived to pick up their burdens, and the moment of departure was at hand. Bhois, of the fishermen caste, had the additional hereditary duty of bearing palanquins on their shoulders or bundles on their heads. Each great palace and deori had a complement of bhois and a space near the main gate, rather like the guard room, where they waited to be called for an errand. Leading the julwa procession was the band, followed by the dowry borne on the heads of the bhois. Then came the bridal couple in a palanquin, and after them the groom's family and guests on horseback or in carriages. At Ghazi Jung's wedding this procession included Rais Jung, who had been brought home from England to perform a brother's duties in the wedding ceremonies. The entire procession was flanked by bhois who in the old days carried flaming torches but by this time balanced gas mantle lamps on their heads.

To mitigate the strangeness of her new home, a bride of this station was accompanied by female servants from her father's home, and these would remain with her. Familiar with her habits and preferences, they could also share her memories of childhood and guide her in the adjustment to her new life. They included the ayah who had taken the most care of her during her childhood, other personal maids, and seamstresses.

Like other women of the Umra e Uzzam, Begum Fakhr ul Mulk occasionally had social contact with the Nizam's zenana. There follows an exchange of notes between Osman, Mahbub Ali Pasha's heir, and Begum Fakhr ul Mulk. Both the style and the content of the exchange, which took place in 1924, would have been very similar in the time of Mahbub. The letter bearing the royal crest was brought by a messenger, who waited for the Begum's reply. The note read:

MUNIRUNISSA BEGUM SAHIBA, WIFE OF NAWAB FAKHR UL MULK BAHADUR:

Since my ladies have for a long time been anxious to see your house, if it is possible on the twenty-first Moharrum I will bring them at three or four o'clock. It will be a private visit so there will be no need for formality.

OSMAN

For her reply, Begum Fakhr ul Mulk selected a piece of stationery on which the family crest was placed in the lower left-hand corner, rather than in its usual place at the top of the sheet, a nicety observed in writing to His Highness. On it a secretary or a daughter wrote at the Begum's dictation, in the courtly Persian phrases:

I have the honor to beg that this message will be received by his great and sacred Majesty. This slave of the exalted one will be present and await His Majesty with folded hands on the twenty-first Moharrum. The presence of His Highness will be a mark of honor, according to the desire of the Holy Master who is King of the World. I pray to God that my king and his family members should prosper and that He will give them peace and prosperity and long life. I pray God that the sun of prosperity and good fortune should shine forever in the sky of your honor and glory.

Your hereditary slave,
MUNIRUNISSA BEGUM
Fourteenth Moharrum

Another type of social contact—and one that ran counter to Begum Fakhr ul Mulk's preference—was the receiving of the European women who attended her husband's dinner parties. She no more admired these women than she understood them; she disliked the bold way they looked men directly in the eye,

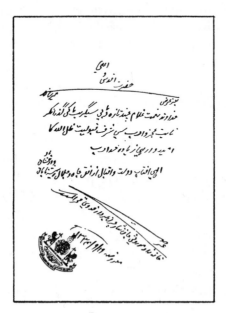

their uncomfortable-looking clothing, their strident voices, and their breath sour with the wines and liquors they had consumed at the table. After they had gone back to the party, Fakhr ul Mulk used to come to the gold and white sitting room, where his wife had briefly met with the female guests. It was his habit to spend a few moments of quiet companionship with her before rejoining the party. Once he arrived on the heels of the departing women, to find the serving girls bringing the sailabchi and jug. "What's happening?" he inquired curiously.

His wife replied somewhat sheepishly, "You see, these drunken women kiss me on the cheeks, so I like to wash my face before you come."

He stroked her cheek fondly. "Never mind about your face, darling," he told her; "your heart is pure."

Even so, the Nawab was not above taking advantage of that pure heart on occasion. Once he wanted to have a dinner party during Moharrum, but the Begum objected to having a party at that time of sorrow. "Don't worry, my dear," her husband assured her. "It will be quite appropriate. All the ladies will wear mourning." So the invitations went out specifying black dress, and the military band was dispensed with.

For all her deference to her husband's wishes, the Begum did not lack for spirit. Perhaps that was one of the qualities which kept her husband infatuated with her for a lifetime. His faithfulness was the subject of some good-natured jokes among his contemporaries. Even Osman, the Heir Apparent, was aware of the sport and participated. He once twitted Begum Munirunissa, "What nonsense this is that your husband should never be interested in another woman! He persists in this attitude even when I tell him that a man needs a change of face. How boring it must be to have to look at the same face every day of one's life."

The Begum replied demurely, "Yes, sire. A woman has also to look at the same face every day of her life. Should she also have more than one husband?"

But after the first time he saw her, Osman must have understood Fakhr ul Mulk's attachment. So struck by her beauty was the Heir Apparent that he forgot his manners and stared at her. "What!" he exclaimed. "Is it possible that there are such in this world?"

A beauty she was, with alabaster complexion and jet-black hair. Two years her husband's senior, she had been married late for those times, when she was almost twenty. An intelligent and spirited woman, she not only brought the zenana under her control but devised ways of knowing everything that went on in the mardana as well. As she had her spy system there, so Nawab Sahib had his in the zenana, with the result that husband and wife knew the secrets of each other's worlds. The two investigation departments became a standing joke in the family, although no one ever discovered the true sources of information. In any event they were accurate, for the couple often surprised one another with remarks which betrayed knowledge that was not intended for them. Sometimes, after Fakhr ul Mulk had attended a mixed party outside the palace, he was astonished to hear a description of some European lady with whom he had chatted at length. Betraying her jealousy, the Begum Sahiba went into a huff until he pleaded his innocence and placated her.

Their tiffs were generally over family affairs. A sample, which took place much later, arose over the fact that one of their sons had eighteen children. Fakhr ul Mulk considered this excessive and one day, after a few whiskies, launched into a tirade on the subject. "What does our son think he is doing?" Nawab Sahib demanded. "Where are all these children going to find employment or suitable husbands?"

Begum Sahiba tried to calm him down: "Didn't you enjoy yourself when you were young?" But when he was not to be diverted, she changed her tactics. "Having many children is a comfort to me," she declared. "Why do you want to interfere in these zenana matters?" Before they could come to an exchange of angry words, the Begum simply turned her face away and sulked. When he came round to sit on that side of her, she tossed her head and whisked round again. After some minutes of this game, Fakhr ul Mulk got up with a sigh and left the zenana. Later he would persuade Begum Sahiba's sister, who lived with them, or a daughter-in-law, to reconcile them.

The Umra e Uzzam married among themselves and most of them were interrelated. Both Fakhr ul Mulk and his wife were of the Umra e Uzzam. First cousin of the Salar Jungs, the Begum brought to Iram Munzil the pride and dignity of her birth and traditions, which were similar to those of Fakhr ul Mulk's family. Mahbub was no stranger to either her father's or her husband's house. Except for her beauty, which would have set her apart in any age, Begum Fakhr ul Mulk was representative of the way of life of the most privileged women in Mahbub Ali Pasha's Hyderabad, a society in which privilege had been developed to a fine art.

Chapter VIII

The Samasthans:
The Raja of Wanaparthy

RAJA RAMESHWAR RAO II OF WANAPARTHY was not one of the nobles attending the Delhi Durbar, nor had he often formed part of a royal retinue. As a feudatory of the Nizam, however, he had personal as well as official ties with the Asaf Jahis. When Mahbub Ali Pasha was stricken, the Raja hastened to Hyderabad, impelled both by concern for the Nizam and by anxiety for the state, should a question of succession arise. Normally, however, his visits to the court were infrequent and by command rather than on his own initiative. As the ruler of an indigenous Hindu population of about a hundred thousand people, together with a small minority of Muslims, Christians, and Sikhs who lived together in amity, he considered his place to be in his principality, Wanaparthy Samasthan. A typical visit would be as follows.

Getting down from his carriage in front of the durbar hall at Chow Mahalla, the Raja of Wanaparthy signaled to his servant to go on to the guard room. Long legs encased in tight white pyjamas, the severity of his black shewani broken only by his bugloos, he climbed the steps and joined the throng of nobles waiting for the birthday durbar to begin. Wanaparthy did not often attend these functions. Living almost entirely in his samas-than, more than a hundred miles from Hyderabad, he was generally excused from attendance at court. But some days previously he had received a letter from the private secretary to Mahbub Ali Pasha saying, "His Highness is thinking of you."

Recognizing this as tantamount to a summons, he had driven by carriage for three days. About every ten miles along the route he had a small house and stable where he stopped to change horses or to spend the night. Arriving several days in advance of the durbar, he sent greetings to His Highness to announce his arrival and settled in his house at Hyderabad to wait until he was bidden to the palace. Meanwhile, attendance at the durbar was not only compulsory but would serve to remind Mahbub Ali Pasha of his presence in the city.

Entering the hall just before eight o'clock in the evening, the hour for which the durbar was scheduled, Wanaparthy made his way among the guests, greeting friends, salaaming acquaintances, seeing and making sure he was seen by the maximum number of persons there. It was a Mulki affair; no Britishers had been invited and no one was a stranger to the others. After more than an hour of this concentrated social exercise, Raja Rameshwar Rao slipped quietly out of the door. He knew that the others would remain, their courtesy becoming an increasingly thin veneer over their impatience as hour followed hour with no sign that Mahbub Ali Pasha had recollected his appointment with them. Having no intention of being caught in that web, he turned his footsteps toward the guard room, where his servant, by a judicious distribution of tips, had established a claim to a corner. There the Raja's bedroll had been spread out and he was soon asleep on it.

Just after one o'clock, his servant wakened him, for Mahbub Ali Pasha's retine had been heard approaching. Even as the servant buckled the bugloos around him and gave his shoulders a final brushing, he felt his pulse quicken at the prospect of being again in the presence of Mahbub Ali Pasha. He shared the excitement of the nobles and officials in the hall, whose fatigue would be dissipated as they heard the voices of the Nizam's attendants and palanquin bearers singing "Comes the Bridegroom at Dawn in Full Pomp." At the durbar hall, slipping in by a side door, he took his place and bowed in a low salute just as His Highness entered.

The ceremonies were not lengthy. All the nobles and officials presented nazar of a fixed amount. Five ashrafis was the largest amount; the nazar ranged as low as four or five rupeees for the smaller jagirdars. If anyone should give more than his proper amount, he would be thought presumptuous. The Raja felt surreptitiously for his own two nazars. Under Mahbub it had come to be expected that any coins dropped by mischance to the floor should be left there for the servants. This practice had not been enunciated as a regulation—by nature shy in a large gathering, Mahbub Ali Pasha rarely spoke more than was required of him on these occasions, but various small signs and gestures communicated his wishes and everyone recognized that it would be unlucky indeed to attempt to retrieve a wandering coin. It was, therefore, a wise precaution to carry two nazars.

His turn come, Raja Rameshwar Rao bowed deeply and held out both hands, on which his gold ashrafis lay on a folded square of white linen. Mahbub took them, placing them on a tray held by a man standing beside him. The offering of nazar was followed by the awarding of titles to those whom the Nizam desired to honor. Last of all came two young men, hardly out of their teens, dressed in gorgeous sherwanis of gold brocade. It was the custom that a bridegroom present himself in his wedding finery at the first durbar following his marriage. On each of them Mahbub bestowed a sarpech, an elaborate jeweled piece for the head. Throughout all this, the voices of men singing Persian poems in the halftones of Oriental music provided a pleasant background. Following these ceremonies the court repaired to another of the Chow Mahalla buildings for the birthday feast.

The morning star was fading by the time the Nizam departed

and the nobles were free to leave. Raja Rameshwar Rao returned to his house, Jambagh (Guava Orchard), across the Musi River. It was only recently that the family had acquired a house in Hyderabad, and even now it was used mostly as a residence for young relatives who came into the city to attend school. For them, as for the other chiefs of the principalities known as samasthans, Hyderabad and its rulers were part of recent history.

The samasthans were small and very ancient princedoms, some with origins fading back into mythology. The very name Jatprole, one of the three chief samasthans, is legendary and denotes "the place where Jatayu fell." Jatayu was the Eagle King who fought the demon Ravanna in a vain attempt to rescue Sita, the wife of the god Rama, from her abductor. The other two chief samasthans were Gadwal and Wanaparthy.

Wanaparthy Samasthan traced its origin back to the fourteenth century, when, as the Warangal kingdom crumbled, local chieftains established their ascendancy over surrounding territory and divided it among themselves. As the Hindu Vijayanagar kingdom was succeeded by the Muslim ones of Bijapur, Qutub Shah, and Moghul, successive rulers had found it expedient to maintain eight samasthans as buffer states along the Krishna River. Wanaparthy was bounded on three sides by other samasthans.

As peace spread over the Deccan, the original requirement of military assistance to the overlords came to be satisfied by the payment of an annual tribute, the peshkash. In the time of Aurangzeb, Wanaparthy became a feudatory of the Moghul empire and of the Nizam as viceroy of that empire in the south. The sanad issued by the Asaf Jahis, confirming the Raja of Wanaparthy in possession of his territory, concludes:

You should look after the old and new farmers (ryots) by providing for their welfare, construct tanks, and increase cultivation and revenues, and pay the government dues year by year and season by season regularly. Consider this as a deed of tenure on payment of peshkash, true and dependable in this respect.

By a sanad issued not long after this, the Raja was permitted to deduct from the peshkash the cost of maintaining 750 foot soldiers, 25 horsemen, and one elephant, this force being considered necessary for protection and for the maintenance of his personal dignity and prestige. He was also allowed to deduct the salary of the person who acted as his legal adviser and personal representative. That salary was later increased to include the costs of transportation, which meant the price of a palanquin together with the wages of the bhois to carry and the runners to accompany it. Within the bounds of his own samasthan, the Raja retained his sovereign rights, except that in the case of a death sentence an appeal lay to the Nizam.

Rameshwar Rao II, the incumbent of Wanaparthy under Mahbub Ali Pasha, was a good administrator, able, conscientious, progressive, a consolidator. But his chief claim to fame was his sons. For nearly a century and a half, the house failed to produce a direct male heir. Wanaparthy was not alone in this; three of the other samasthans were affected. Not surprisingly, a legend arose that these samasthans had come under the curse of a holy man who proclaimed that so long as the same houses ruled, they would not produce male heirs. Two of the houses, Jatprole and Gadwal, did in fact continue to have to adopt the heir for each succeeding generation until India became independent in 1947 and ended princely rule; in the next year both houses had sons.

True or not, the legend was believed by a great many citizens of Hyderabad, who tactfully refrained from discussing it in the samasthans. In Wanaparthy the customary blessing in the Raja's family was "May you have a thousand children." The adoption of heirs had become so thoroughly a way of life that a tradition had grown up that the heirs should come from a certain family, distantly related to the rulers, in Rangapur village. When it was necessary to adopt another boy, a few trusted family members were sent to Rangapur to find a likely candidate. Long before the beginning of the legend which supposedly made it necessary, the tradition was begun by a remote ancestor who had two sons, one by birth and the other by adoption. Before his death he divided the inheritance unequally between them, the larger, birth-right share, comprising 450 square miles, continuing to be the samasthan of Wanaparthy (or Suggur, as it was sometimes called), while the smaller was detached to form the samasthan of Gopalpet.

One result of these frequent adoptions to secure the succession was that there was in Wanaparthy more often than not a con-siderable hiatus between Rajas while the boys adopted after the death of their predecessors (or sometimes as infants just shortly before) reached the age when they could take over the responsi-bility of the state. In compensation Wanaparthy was blessed with a succession of remarkable women, dowager ranis who paid off the debts that their late warrior-husbands had accumulated, admin-istered the state, developed public works, and looked to the development of the family. In fact, it was largely because of the military as well as administrative prowess of one of the earlier ranis that Aurangzeb confirmed the family in their possession of the samasthan.

Rameshwar Rao II was the most recent of the adopted heirs. Whether through good luck or through merit accumulated by either the state or the incumbent, he had broken the curse. Two sons had been born to him, and the rejoicing in the state can be imagined: cannons boomed, fireworks illuminated the sky, and every household in the samasthan received a tray of fruits and sweets.

Aside from this notable accomplishment, his competence was often overshadowed in the public consciousness by the memory of his rollicking predecessor, Rameshwar Rao I, who reigned from 1845 to 1866. Had he lived in an age of mass media, that fearless, bold, and unruly chieftain would have been constantly in the headlines. For his adventures he needed an army, and this he supplied himself in part by buying slaves that Arab traders brought from Somaliland and sold in the market in Bombay. Along with them he bought women for their wives. These men were trained like soldiers and companions in arms; they were not treated like slaves, and apparently they did not consider them-selves as such. One of the Raja's hereditary titles was Bahiri Bul-wunt Bahadur, which means Brave Eagle, and many of the Africans gave themselves the name bin Bahiri, or Son of the Eagle. Many Sons of the Eagle still come to the present Raja for largess. The African Cavalry and the Wanaparthy Lancers, or-ganized and trained, formed the Raja's army.

As every ruler knows, an army is expensive to maintain. Living handsomely when not in the field, Rameshwar Rao I was fre-quently low on funds. When told that the treasury was empty, he used to say, "All right. Which direction shall we go?" Sometimes his target was another samasthan or a jagir. For the most part, however, with a sure instinct for where the money lay, he pre-ferred the government treasuries. One favorite was located at Nagarkurnool, in adjoining Mahbubnagar District. There revenue was collected for transport to Hyderabad in carts accompanied by heavily armed guards. At the climax of his freebooting career, the Raja and his troops ambushed these treasury wagons near Jedcherla on their way into Hyderabad.

When the report reached the Dewan, he resorted to the ruse of asking Rameshwar Rao I to come to Hyderabad. There he made him prisoner, confining him for safekeeping in a temple outside the city. Anticipating a long stay, some of the bin Bahiri hired a broken-down house about a furlong from the temple, where they cooked their Raja's food and brought it to him along with whatever comforts the guards allowed him. Unknown to the guards, the Wanaparthy men also dug a tunnel from the rented house to the prisoner's room in the temple. When it was all but completed, Rameshwar Rao sent word to his captors that as the death anniversary of his father was approaching, he should be allowed the assistance of a Brahmin from the samasthan in order to perform the obligatory memorial ceremonials. This was granted.

Early in the morning of the anniversary day the Brahmin

arrived with the supplies needed for the puja. For hours the guards smelled the incense and heard the chanting and the tinkling bell that accompanied the prayers. When these sounds continued into the afternoon, despite the fact that they customarily ended at noon, the guards began to investigate. Unlocking the door from their side, they demanded that the obstreperous Raja, who habitually defied his captors by barring the wooden door also on his side, should open up. Rameshwar Rao replied angrily that as he was not allowed to be in his samasthan, where the ceremonies could be properly observed, they must not interfere with his attempts to compensate for the deficiencies by additional prayers. By nightfall the guards had heard enough of the tinkling bells, and again demanded an end to the ceremonies. This time, receiving no reply, they broke down the door. Inside they found only burning incense sticks and a cat with a bell tied to its neck. The prisoner had long since gone underground and was well on his way to Wanaparthy.

Horses for the escape party had been kept in readiness at the rented house, with fresh mounts at the Raja's resthouses along the route. Safely back at the samasthan, Rameshwar Rao immediately deployed his troops among the rocky hills and awaited the appearance of the Nizam's army. It arrived promptly in the shape of Chaoushes under the command of the Kotwal, bringing with them two cannons bearing the latter's crest. Outfought by the Wanaparthy troops, the attackers fled, leaving behind them the cannons, which remain in the samasthan today. When the custom was established in the city of Hyderabad of firing three salvoes a day to announce the time, the same custom was adopted in Wanaparthy and the captured cannons were used.

Furious and helpless, Sir Salar Jung appealed to the Resident for advice. Wanaparthy, however, had little to fear from that side. The Raja was known to the British as an ally who had several times offered them his services and his troops: for the Crimean War, for fighting in Burma, and during the Mutiny of 1857. He had also maintained friendly personal relations with their representatives, particularly in the Madras Presidency. He had been educated in English as well as in his mother tongue, Telegu, and the court language, Persian, and had learned to speak five other languages fluently, so that he rivaled his ancestor with the title of Ashtabasha, or Master of Eight Languages. Before assuming charge of the government at the age of fourteeen, on the death of his mother, he had already become enamoured of European ways. A military uniform of European type was his favorite apparel; at his palace, British crockery and cutlery were used, and furniture of Western design had been installed during the 1830s.

At an early age he had seen and fallen in love with a young girl, Shankaramma, who lived in one of his villages. One day he found her in the village and, in good romantic style, carried her off, along with her two-and-a-half-year-old sister, Janamma, who happened to be with her at the time. Since this action left no choice for Shankaramma's parents the marriage was performed. A charming contemporary painting shows the Raja "and his sweet heart Ranee . . . taking the report of the Day Officer."

After her sister's marriage, Janamma continued to live at the palace. When she was a few years older, Rameshwar Rao renamed her Caroline and sent her to a Presbyterian mission school in Madras. From there, on a holiday, she brought home a copy of *Pilgrim's Progress* which she had received at Prize Day for her academic achievement. As the marriage to Shankaramma was childless, the Raja eventually took Caroline for his second wife, with no better luck. So long as her husband lived, Caroline led a Europeanized life, even having to learn to waltz. He dressed her always in crinolines, and her small nieces and nephews used the hoops to roll or jump through.

Even to his staff, Rameshwar Rao gave Christian names, which many of the families still retain, sometimes followed by the original caste name of Reddy: Henry Wahab, Charles Wahab (his wives' brother), William Wahab, James Wahab, Edward Wahab. The fact that most of these people were Hindus and that Wahab was a Muslim name gave the whole proceeding a fine non-communal flavor.

More importantly than in his personal life, Rameshwar Rao I found much in the British system of government to emulate, reforming his own administrative system along the lines current in British India. He was the first in the Nizam's Dominions to introduce revenue survey and settlement. This means that Wanaparthy was mapped for the first time, no mean feat in 1862, over undulating, forested countryside. When it was resurveyed in 1936 the original calculations for individual fields were found to be accurate to a maximum error of three percent.

Until that time, land taxes varied yearly. While the crops were still standing, a representative of the Raja, together with some village elders, inspected each field, estimated the harvest, deducted the cost of cultivation, and fixed a portion of the remainder as the samasthan's dues. The tax varied with the crop and was levied only on land actually cultivated, so that it was economically feasible to leave some land fallow. All standing trees belonged to the samasthan.

With the survey completed, Rameshwar Rao classified the lands according to the type of soil and also according to whether water was provided by the state and, if so, whether it was provided by well, which was a reasonably certain supply, or by tank, which failed in repeated seasons of poor rainfall. Under this system of classification, fixed revenues could be established. In bad years, revenues were remitted and food grains were brought in from other areas and distributed at subsidized rates, the excess charge being borne by the samasthan; fodder for the cattle was supplied in the same way. Those who could not buy food for themselves or their cattle were supplied free when the village official (patwari) certified that they were destitute. Because of this system there were in Wanaparthy, as in the rest of Hyderabad State, no known deaths from hunger, even during the disastrous famine of 1899–1900.

Rameshwar Rao I also organized a regular judiciary with inde-

pendent civil and criminal courts, issued judicial stamps, and
organized a police system along British lines.

With this background it is not surprising that when the Dewan
asked the Resident's help in dealing with this thorn in his side,
the latter advised against a frontal assault. In dealing with such
an intrepid warrior, tact was a better weapon than opposition,
he suggested. Consequently the Nizam appointed Rameshwar
Rao as a regional officer (Zilledar) to help maintain order in the
Dominions. As such he was occasionally sent by the Nizam to
subdue rebel chieftains and to level their forts, or even to collect
the tribute (peshkash) due the Nizam from the other samasthans
when they fell into arrears. On one occasion he exacted a famous
gem from Jatprole Raja in lieu of cash. After the uprising of
1857 he helped Sir Salar Jung restore order in the Nizam's
Dominions. Seeing the quality of Rameshwar Rao's trained
troops, the Nizam made him first inspector of his own cavalry
and, a year later, inspector-general of his army. In this capacity
Rameshwar Rao produced a model manual of arms and reorganized the army into an efficient fighting force. Its core was the
Wanaparthy Lancers, presented to His Highness and rechristened
the Golconda Lancers, together with an infantry arm.

When Rameshwar Rao I died, in 1866, the year of Mahbub Ali
Pasha's birth, the Dowager Rani sisters divided the responsibilities between them. The senior, Shankaramma, ruled the state,
and the junior, Janamma, the erstwhile Caroline, ruled the family.
Trouble was not long in finding their address. Some opportunist
among the African Cavalry promoted the notion that since the
Brave Eagle had died childless, they as Sons of the Eagle should
be his heirs. Before they could dismantle the samasthan, Shankaramma moved quickly: her brother and adviser, Charles Wahab,
was dispatched to persuade Sir Salar Jung to take over the African
Cavalry. Under the new name of the African Guard, it became
the bodyguard of the Nizam.

With her brother steadfastly standing by to advise, Shankaramma spent the remaining thirty-five years of her life adminis-

tering the samasthan, training the heir, paying off the debts and investing the surplus in public works which are a monument to her prudence. One of these was an extension of the system of tanks with the addition of a network of feeder channels which brought several thousand more acres under irrigation. For the time it was a sophisticated system.

During the construction of Shankarsamudram, the large tank which bears her name, Shankaramma spent her days in the fields personally supervising the activities. Its banks were built of rubble masonry, by laborers who brought headloads of earth and stone. So solid was the construction that for nearly a hundred years it withstood every storm and flood without a breach, while holding enough water so that land irrigated from it can produce three crops a year. Many of the laborers bearing these heavy loads were women, and Shankaramma decreed that so long as a pregnant woman worked she should receive double wages.

High in priority among Shankaramma's concerns was the succession. Rameshwar Rao I had fathered only one child, which died at birth. To help his wife through this tragedy, he sent to Rangapur for another infant. Only one, a twenty-one-day-old child, was available in the traditional family, and so he was adopted without waiting for the astrologer's predictions. Unhappily this child, Ramakrishna Rao, was thrown from a horse and killed at the age of fourteen years, precisely as had been foretold when his horoscope was eventually cast. After this, horseback riding was forbidden to members of the ruling family. The prohibition continued until the mid-1930s, when Rameshwar Rao III, an active youngster, used to take rides on the sly. After he fell off and hurt himself beyond disguising, his mother decided it would be better for him to learn to ride properly, so he was sent to the African Cavalry for instruction.

After the death of Ramakrishna Rao, a commission of Wahabs again went from the palace to Rangapuram. They returned with a five-year-old boy whom they had noticed on approaching the village. This child was riding on a buffalo and had thrown a cloth on the back of the animal for a seat. "This is my elephant," he explained proudly. Examining his hand, they found in his palm the seven prized astrological signs. When it turned out also that he came from the family that traditionally supplied adoptive heirs, it seemed clear that he was meant to be a ruler. Thus the future Rameshwar Rao II was chosen.

When the boy was old enough to go to boarding school, Shankaramma sent him to Madras Christian College. As a youngster, Rameshwar Rao II was so frightened of the imposing Shankaramma that he would hardly speak in her presence, but he learned well the lessons she wished to teach him. When the young Raja began taking over active charge of the administration, in 1892, he reorganized the government to keep pace with the times, the essence of which was a transition from personal to institutional administration. He introduced a departmentalized form of administration, separated the executive from the judicial functions, personally supervised the alignment and building of roads which were so good that many are still in use and motorists today drive in the shade of the trees with which he lined them. Before the coming of the rains each year, the Raja personally inspected the paddy fields to see that the peasants had prepared the drains adequately. Electricity was introduced into Wanaparthy before it came to many of the major cities. It made possible the early installation of X-ray equipment in the Wanaparthy hospital.

The village remained the basis of administration, no matter what the superstructure became. Under a headman, twelve classes of artisans held land at reduced rates in return for work of varying amounts which they performed for the benefit of the village community; special skill received special remuneration. In addition, they received a fixed fraction of the total produce of the village in return for discharging all public functions. In this way an equitable distribution of the fruits of production was achieved in proportion to the needs and contributions of the various kinds of workers. The twelve classes of artisans were skilled farmers; carpenters; blacksmiths; watchmen; potters, barbers, and washermen; goldsmiths; masons; toddy tappers; shepherds; priests and others attached to the temples; and some specialized functionaries.

Rameshwar Rao II anticipated the cooperative movement in providing cheap credit (at a nominal rate of interest or none at all) to ensure that no agricultural development should fail for want of funds. Security for these loans was not immovable property but the capacity of the borrower to work. The advantage that the samasthan had over present-day rural credit societies lay in personal acquaintance with the borrowers and their community.

These activities and related ones kept Rameshwar Rao II close to Wanaparthy and his people. Every morning a runner arrived at the capital from each of the 150 villages, bringing news and reports and receiving instructions to carry back. The runners were chosen in turn from the Harijans of the village, and in payment they received a measure of grain for each day's work. But long before these messengers began showing up at the capital, the Raja had begun his daily contacts with his people. Those who wanted a personal conference with him had direct access. He used to sleep in the open, on a verandah at the front of his palace. Early in the morning he would be awakened by voices calling to him from the bottom of the stairs. A yawn, a stretch, a descent of ten steps, and he was in conference with his people. Occasionally someone who could hardly contain his emotions called out his story while Rameshwar Rao was being shaved; before he had patted his face dry he appeared at the window with a response.

When not in the capital, the Raja was often to be seen in the villages, where his coming could hardly be missed by anyone even moderately interested in knowing of it, for he came by that novelty, a motor car. Debt was one of the major legacies of the flamboyant Rameshwar Rao I to his heirs. The Dowager Rani had worked hard to remove it, and had succeeded and even managed to achieve surpluses which were plowed back into the samasthan. Rameshwar Rao II, whom she had trained up carefully, was quite aware of his duties in this regard. Impulsiveness was not a part of his nature and he carefully weighed every expenditure before committing it. One of the few luxuries he allowed himself was the purchase of one of the first cars in the Nizam's Dominions. It was of French make, a De Dion-Bouton, and for years "De Dion" was a synonym for automobile in the family. When he went on inspection tours of the villages, he used to go in the De Dion. Alas for the chief revenue officer, who had to accompany him! That gentleman had the most intense suspicion of the mechanical monster. Refusing to commit himself to its care, he used to ride through the samasthan on the running board, holding onto the doorposts as to life itself. Relief gave enthusiasm to his stride at those times when they got down and proceeded on foot to examine the irrigation systems.

Wanaparthy was made up of fertile lands, but an annual rainfall of only 28 inches focused attention early on the possibilities of irrigation. The samasthan's 450 square miles contained more than 600 tanks, with networks of channels for collection and distribution of the water. It was the ambition of the ruling family not to allow a single drop of water to leave the samasthan unutilized, except for the Krishna River on its border, where the banks were too steep to make the river a practicable source. So thoroughly was this aim pursued that in 1936 a renowned irrigation engineer, called in by Rameshwar Rao III, could find in the entire samasthan possible spots for only two additional tanks; both were in process of construction when princely rule was abolished in India.

Though careful with his funds, Rameshwar Rao II was by no means ungenerous. Anyone in the samasthan who approached him with a wedding invitation received on the spot a gift of ten rupees, an amount of cash money not normally seen by a villager in several months. Shortly after the death of Rameshwar Rao II, his son Krishna Dev was called on by a peasant whose daughter was to be married. The young Raja presented the peasant with 100 rupees. Startled, the man remarked that Raja Rameshwar used to give ten. "My father," the new ruler explained, "was born in a village. How could he give more than ten rupees? But I was born in a palace. How could I not give a hundred?" In America at this time, John D. Rockefeller was explaining that his son could give more than a dime because he had a rich father.

Five annual festive occasions brought the people of the samasthan together with the ruling family. The first and most important was Dassera, the ten-day festival celebrated all over India under various names and with a variety of traditional observances, which basically rejoiced in the triumph of good over evil. Dassera usually falls sometime around October; the monsoon is over, the crops have been harvested, and six months of clear, cool sunshine lie ahead. From all over the samasthan people flocked to the capital to present nazar to their Raja at his durbar, to listen to the music and watch the dancing and partake of the general gaiety. One of the days had an additional significance. On that day the Raja on his caparisoned elephant, the army, and the guards would go in procession to a sacred tree, where they did obeisance to their weapons and then, symbolically acting out the tradition that Indian kings used to go to war on that day, crossed the frontier of Wanaparthy before returning home.

Not only the military performed this act of reverence. Every man and woman who worked worshiped the tools of his trade. Cooks lit incense and dotted the red kumkum powder on their pots and fireplaces; carpenters their saws and chisels; farmers their ploughs; potters their wheels; and so on through the occupational spectrum. In this Way Hindus still annually acknowledge their indebtedness to the contributions of preceding generations.

This festival was followed three weeks later by Diwali, the Festival of Lights, when the prosperous families outlined their homes with rows of tiny oil lamps and even the humblest put out a light to welcome the Lord Krishna. On Diwali the women came from all the villages to do arati to their Raja, which meant ceremonially waving a lamp before his face in the same way they did before the image of the god in puja.

The third festival was New Year's, which fell six months later, when the winter harvest had been gathered and the people were preparing for the long, dry hot season. On New Year's, prominent people from the villages of the samasthan gathered in the capital for community worship services and to hear Brahmins read the astrological forecast for the coming year.

The other festivals were based at two temples in different parts of the samasthan. To these, pandits from all over India, particularly from the South, came for a kind of convention of philosophy, at which they were rewarded with cash gifts and a shawl of honor. Poetry also received its due; Rameshwar Rao II was so active a patron of Telegu and Sanskrit poetry that he established a press in Wanaparthy to print his protégés' books. Relieving the serious intellectual burden of these festivals was an accompanying mela for the common people. Cattle from all over South India were brought, for these were famous cattle markets. Music, dancing, wrestling, shadow plays, recitals by religious storytellers and minstrels, and cockfights provided amusement and interest for nearly every taste.

Occasions such as these both strengthened and symbolized the ties that kept Raja Rameshwar Rao close to his people in the samasthan; at the same time he recognized that modern developments were increasing the importance of his contacts with Hyderabad, and that he needed more convenient access to the city. His position is illustrated by his attempts to build a house in Hyderabad. Selecting a handsome spot of land overlooking Husain Sagar, he requested Mahbub Ali Pasha's government to allot it to him for a city residence, but the long shadow of Rameshwar Rao I reminded them that guns placed on the hill could command the city. He was granted instead some low-lying land at the bottom of the hill.

Still, his presence in the city was significant, for Wanaparthy, like the other samasthans, represented an important strain in the state. Tied to Mahbub by duty and affection, these indigenous Telegu-speaking Hindu people were the warp, to which the largely Muslim and Moghul Asaf Jahis were the weft. Together they made a durable fabric which was also, with the brilliant colors of the latter against the deeper tones of the former, handsomely iridescent.

Chapter IX

The Unworldly Ones: The Hijras

THE guns boomed across the city for the second time in a day. At first there was an incredulous silence as people counted, "Nineteen. Twenty. Twenty-one." Suddenly the streets came alive with laughing, shouting throngs. Even the blind and lame beggars hastened their steps in the direction of Purani Haveli, mouths watering at the thought of the feast to come. Two royal births in a single day were a rare and auspicious event and would be celebrated with largess.

Inside the palace, Mahbub Ali Pasha continued his instructions to his courtiers, his face bright with joy. "When the Hijras come, instruct them to go at once and bring their entire community. I will give for both my son and my grandson. As it is their work to dance and sing in rejoicing that a child is born, let them come through the streets dancing and singing, that the city people may be happy with us." Then he added as an afterthought: "Send troops with them that they may not be molested in the streets."

For eight days Mahbub Ali Pasha kept the Hijras at his palace, singing, leaping, dancing. Then with "the army on this side and the army on that side," and having put 5,000 rupees on the rath cart that carried the elders, he sent them dancing to their homes again.

One person's rejoicing was soured by the extended celebration. The heir apparent, Mir Osman Ali Khan, had also called for the Hijras, that they might come to King Kothi palace to enliven the sixth-day celebration for his first son, Mahbub's grandson. But, detained at Purani Haveli, they were not able to respond to the summons. For this he bore them a grudge. "These people have become too arrogant," he is believed to have said. That was the beginning of the end of the Hijra community in Hyderabad, for Osman never called them to celebrate the birth of any of his subsequent children, and after becoming Nizam he issued a law, the Qanoon Muqanissan, which forbade the Hijras to take into their group any newcomer under the age of thirty. It has been claimed that the Qanoon Muqanissan sprang from Osman's zeal as a reformer, which he certainly was in many ways, but the story of his grudge is what the Hijras themselves believe.

Who were these Hijras? The determining fact of their lives was that they were deviates, that is, they did not follow the generally accepted pattern of behavior. What a society does with its deviates tells much about it. If an individual defies the social expectations, whether in regard to sexual behavior, length of hair, or religious observance, the most common response in many societies has been increasing pressure for conformity, culminating in rejection of those who refuse to capitulate. So it was in India, in a way. The paradox was that a fearful price was exacted from the Hijras for their deviance, but once that price had been paid they were permitted an honorable place in the society.

Born as males, the Hijras rejected sexual activity of all kinds but indulged their preference for the clothing, the cosmetics, and the domestic activities of women. Without the Hijra community to shelter them, they would have had no choice but to become zenanay, practicing homosexuals, who were cast off by their families, despised by society, and used by any male with a taste for pretty boys. But there was a difference, for the zenanay made up their eyes and wiggled their hips when they walked in order to advertise their availability, but the true Hijra was incapable even of desire. With one door after another closed against him, the Hijra turned the violence born of his agony against himself and cut off his external genitalia. Some performed the deed where they could be nursed by Hijras; others faced their dispair alone in the jungle. In either event there is no way of knowing what the mortality rate may have been. Those who survived recovered their health and strength with only sexual characteristics affected. Perhaps some lingering trace of ambivalence can be deduced from the care with which they buried the rejected organs.

The self-mutilation of these impotent wretches and their acceptance into the Hijra community is a kind of allegory of suicide and rebirth, while their manner of speech suggests a yearning for identity and identification with a social group. So together they have built a world for themselves. In Hyderabad, as in most of India, people are addressed less often by name than by the title which shows their precise status and relationship within the extended family. So also with the Hijras, with the added detail that the confusion of their terminology is a constant reminder of the sexual confusion which brought them into the group. Most of the senior members of the community become gurus, and a common usage involves such titles as Grandmother Guru, Guru Aunt, Guru Brother, Son. They use "he" and "she," "him" and "her," indiscriminately. Cementing them to the community is a common name, "Baksh," which they add to the masculine name given them in infancy. In addition, those who are heads of Hijra houses add "Naik." This results in names such as Abul Baksh Naik, Vijay Baksh, Rahman Baksh, Nirmal Baksh Naik, the first and last being heads of houses.

As most of the Hijras came from the lowest rungs of the social and economic ladder, they could neither read nor write; and as fear of abuse or reprisals put a value on anonymity, a little of the past died for them with the passing of each elder. Only their way of life was passed along intact. In many ways they were comparable to a monastic order under the threefold discipline of poverty, chastity, and obedience. Poverty was no problem: their birth had assured them of that. Their capacity for chastity and obedience was tested before they were accepted into the order; their courage also. After that, they learned the simple life of the order: to scrub and cook for themselves, and to maintain with a minimum of friction a careful balance between individual and co-operative living; to sing songs to the newborn in a variety of languages, to accompany themselves on the dholak (a two-ended drum), to dance, and to go out daily on the rounds by which news of births was collected. Thus they plied their ancient trade, following a practice which they believe goes back to mythological times.

It is worth letting them speak for themselves. Among them seniority is very important and the juniors do not speak in the community meetings. The story that follows is compiled from conversations with the heads of four houses of Hijras in Hyderabad. The conversations were in Hindustani, which the Hijras speak with many archaic expressions and constructions. Often ungrammatical, their speech is full of imagery and sometimes has a rather poetic quality.

*　　*　　*

Listen to my words. This has come down from the ages. We have heard from the mouths of our elders that there have always been Hijras. They are all over India. It is written in our people's fate that we must eat of the charity of the worldly ones.

For us down through the ages this has become our livelihood. So we go to give blessings. This is the only work of the Hijras, that in whatsoever house there is a child born, be it a son or a daughter, we take our dholak, we sing the song of the newborn, we take our due and bring it back. So we fill our stomachs. Throughout Hindustan, only this is the occupation of the Hijras. In peace we go and bring our rations and cook and eat and live in peace at home.

They say that our first guru came from Delhi in some early time. It may have been the first Nizam; what time that was is known only to God. As though any of us could read or write, to say, "It is like this; he came on such a day and date!"

After my father died—when I had reached the age of understanding he died in front of me—I lived with my uncle. I used to play among the girls, borrow my sister's sari and play with dolls, stay at home doing woman's work. My uncle used to say, "What do you mean by walking like that? If you walk in the street and swing your waist like that, somebody will accost you. I will not like it. If somebody makes a rude remark to you, I will not like it. It will spoil my name." For this he used to beat me, beating and hammering. I received good blows. They used to put ground chilie in my eyes. For two days at a time, they didn't give me food to eat.

Enough. I realized, "My life is not with you people," so I left home. I wandered about, stumbling, begging in the bazaars, sleeping on the streets: "Let's see if anyone is coming in that lane. Some one of my relatives will see me and they will beat me. They will catch me and take me away." So, smitten with fear, I slept here and there.

I lived with the zenanay for some time. Having begged, I would return and it would be nighttime and some rough fellow who had been drinking would catch me and pull me about, slap me, show me a dagger or a knife. Then he would take me off and when once or twice I had been spoiled, I said to myself, "Creature, this is no good."

Whenever I met a Hijra, I used to talk with her: "Where do you live?" One gets to know; so one goes. Those zenanay people also used to say: "Hijras live there. They do like this; it is like that with them. One has to live respectably with them. If one goes there they close the door like a prison. At nine o'clock the lock falls on the door; nobody can go and come there." The zenanay used to talk like this, and I used to listen. I thought, "It must be good there," so I went.

Now, when a fellow came among us, we used to say, "Well, son, you have come here wanting to join the Hijras, but first you must sit on the Lal Gundaiji (kootah, an instrument of torture)." If he said, "Oh, my! Who would sit on that?" and ran away, we knew he had only come to harass us. Who knew whether fellows like that might not be thieves or deceivers? But if he said, "Keep me, I don't like wandering about. You can do whatever you like, I will stay with you only," then we knew he was a true Hijra and would be obedient. We only said it to frighten them. We did not have a Lal Gundaiji; we only called out, "Ho, inside, bring the Lal Gundaiji!" and if he was not a good, courageous fellow he would run away. Those who stayed, stayed.

It is thirty years now that I have stayed among the Hijras. My family do not let me come near them. They say, "This is a bad fellow. It is a disgrace to us. If he keeps coming here it will be a reflection upon us." When I walk about the town we come face to face with each other but do not talk. Now if there is sorrow or gladness in their hearts, will I know it? Did I tell them what was in my heart?

When I joined the Hijras I had, just as a man has, everything. So I thought I would live like that with the Hijras, wearing a sari and going to dance, still keeping all that. But there are some women, if they call us to dance, when we dance they also dance. While they are dancing they twirl money over their heads to avert the evil eye and give it to us. So if an elderly woman is there, while we are dancing, suddenly—gup! she puts her hand there to see if one is a true Hijra. So each of us voluntarily becomes castrated.

With me it happened like this. There was a man in our house. When I first came to the Hijras, he had fallen down and broken his hip. I was the one who massaged him and took care of him until it got a little better and he could walk and move about a bit. So he said, "Come, son, it is several years that I have not asked in the villages. Come with me and we will go for a month or two and ask and come back again." "All right," I said, and we went.

That old man could not walk very much, so I left him in the village where we slept and I used to go to the villages nearby and ask. Now in every village there are one or two smart alecks who say, "If you are a Hijra, show us." In that village also there was one. So no one in the village would give me a single paisa because they said, "What kind of a Hijra are you? Get out! We won't give you anything. Get out!"

So I got into a fury. "What is life?" I thought. "It is a useless thing!" So I went into the jungle between the two villages and I had a knife with me and I cut my organ off at the root. When it is not of any use, when there is no strength in it, what are we to do by keeping this? If we do not have the courage, how will our stomachs be filled?

If one dies in the jungle, who is there to see? If we know soon enough, we look after him. In short, it is like this: if one has to remain in this world, if one still has air and water left in one's portion, one lives.

The next day I took a bath and put on an oil bandage. I invoked the name of the goddess, Besraji Mata, soaked the bandage in the oil in her lamp, and applied it. After that, slowly limping, getting up and sitting down, I went to the village to the house of that smart aleck fellow. "Say, fellow, now will you give?"

"Arrai! What have you done!" So, frightened out of his wits, instead of giving me four annas he gave me two rupees. When he had given it to me I slowly went around the whole village asking, and they gave. Then slowly I limped home. For two weeks I stayed at that place and the old man took care of me. After that I was all right so we left and went to another village. It was like that.

When we do this thing we invoke the name of our goddess, Besraji Mata. If we are Mussulmans we take both names, the name of the goddess and the name of Allah. It is a matter of one's liking. Whatever one's faith is, his faith is with him and he does accordingly.

When I was first with the Hijras I had to sweep and dust the house, wash the vessels and plates, and do all the work, grind the chilies and spices, and they watched me for six months or more and thought, "Yes, he is all right. He will stay." After that they put a sari on me. As for that, one comes there wearing a sari, but they put their own clothes on you.

Now I get up in the morning and wash my mouth and hands and drink my tea. Then, whatever lanes are mine to cover, I cover them. I take my dholak on my shoulder and wander from morning till evening. "May my raja live long! May my master live long! May my father live long!" I ask children and older people, "In your lane, who has delivered a child?" Then if anybody shows us, "It has happened in that house," we go there and call down blessings. We stand by the gate and clap our hands and say, "May the new-born baby live long; may his father live long; may his maternal grandmother live long; may her paternal grandmother live long!" we say.

When we call down blessings, the worldly people come out. "Oh, so you people have come? All right. Go now. Come on the sixth day." So I put my mark on the house and go. On the day they call us for, that day we sing and play and earn. We play the dholak. We sing to the new-born baby. Some of us tie bells on our ankles and dance with the baby in our arms. While we dance and jump, we imitate a pregnant woman, and when the baby is born we dance how the trays are filled. Come then! We take them and come away.

The Telegu people give soon, as soon as the child is born. Often among the Marwaris they don't give soon. Until the newborn is named, they don't give. Often they call us on Sundays, for then the shops are closed and the men are at home. When the men are not there and they want dancing, they have it on Tuesdays or Thursdays. Now if a girl is born, they say, "After all, it is only a girl; it can be any time." Saying this, they call us any time and give to us.

We also go and sit in the hospitals. If a newborn goes from there, we go behind and put our mark on the house. And if we

go to a house where Shri Kishen has not given a child to rock
and bring up, we pray, "Oh, God, give this house a son or daughter so we may get something that we may eat." So we beg for
paise and fill our stomachs and even so are all right. Even that
occupation is honorable.

We divide up the city so each of us has an area. But after they
tell us when to come back, then for fear someone else will come
and earn we put our mark. Every Hijra has her mark that we
make on the door. If someone else comes to that house, she recognizes my mark. Now nobody will go and do that house except
the person whose mark is on it.

They pay us like this: they take a tray and they put five seers of
rice, one and a quarter seers of fine lentils, copra, spice, and condiments and the red kumkum powder for worship on each tray.
Now don't some of the wealthy people wear saris with brocade
borders made with gold or silver thread? They used to give those
to the Hijras. A plain sari with brocade borders. They also give
money. According to the house, so they give. According to custom ordinary people give five rupees for a son and half that for a
daughter. If they are of the poorest, they give two and a half
rupees for a son and half that for a daughter. If among Marwaris
there is a safe delivery and a first son is born, they say, "You must
bring your whole brotherhood," and then we all go, from the six
Hijra houses.

If we go to a house where a son or a daughter was born and
they do not give, we say, "Wah, wah! But you had a son, did you
not? Come on, give!" We can do that. But if they don't let us
dance, can we force them? Are they in debt to our fathers and
grandfathers? If they give, they are the givers; if they do not give,
they are still the givers. If they say no, then we say, "What are we
to eat and how are we to live? May your children live long; may
your stomachs remain cool. God has given you children—why are
you sending us away empty?" Sometimes the neighbors say,
"What? Have you not even the money to give to the Hijras? Shall
we lend you a rupee? We gave; why don't you give?" For our

work is only this: that from the harvest of someone's stomach our stomachs are filled.

When the heart gets weary staying at home, we say, "Come, let us go and ask in the villages." We take four annas from each house in the village. The person who has no money gives paddy, or he gives jowari (food grains). You can say beggars, or you can say Hijras. It is called Hijra's alms. We must go at harvest time. They cut the paddy, don't they? After Dassera festival. "It is two or four days to Dassera," we say, and we go. We used to go to the jagirdar and say, "Sahib, we are going to the jagir. Give us a little note." So he wrote a letter to the patel or the patwari saying, "Brother, the Hijras are coming. You must look after them."

Two or four go together. We stay with someone in the village: a patel or a toddy tapper empties a room for us. When we go to the villages we take our eating and cooking vessels with us. When we alight there, we ask in the neighboring villages and hamlets, come back, wash our hands and faces, light our fires and cook. We cook some vegetables, eat and fill our stomachs. That would be at about two o'clock. Afterward we just walk about in the village where we are staying. "Come, give! Come, give!" we say.

It used to be that when the villages were completed, we would say, "Patel, we are going." So he said, "All right." There are washermen in the villages, and he would say to them, "Take these people and conduct them to such and such a village." So the washermen took us from this village to that one, loading what luggage we had on their donkeys. Because of that we gave them a rupee or eight annas.

When I began to learn the work of the Hijras, I saw who was good, among four or five, and I said, "I want to be a disciple in his name." So she makes me one. Or she says, "No, brother, why in my name? There is no disciple in that person's name. Become his disciple." But if I say, "No, I want to be your disciple only," then he makes me one. The brotherhood is called and seated, and he says to them, "Look, this is my disciple," and covers me with a cloth. That is all.

Now I am a guru; according to my liking I take disciples. I go and make the rounds of the lanes. Sometimes I am called by appointment. So I say to my disciples, "Let us go, brothers; they have called us." Now that I am old I am no longer able to dance, am I? So I take the disciples and make them dance and sing, and what is given I bring back and share with them. If three people go, it is divided into three shares; if four people go, into four.

This Hijra's guru is Grandmother Guru to me, the guru of my guru. She is my Aunt Guru; even if he is younger than I, I call her Aunt. My brother guru had the same guru as I. Suppose I join the Hijras today. If tomorrow another joins, he has to defer to me. Among us it's like this, that if one becomes a disciple at this hour and another comes an hour later, the second one has to defer to the first even though he may be younger in years and the one that came after is older. Suppose tomorrow my Guru Aunt takes a mere child for a disciple. I must call him only Brother; I cannot call him Son. But if my Guru Aunt's disciple, whom I call Brother, takes a disciple, then I call that one Son.

If my guru gives me abuse and even strikes me four times, it is nothing; he is greater. So if he beats me there is no fine. But if I so much as touch him lightly with one finger, there is a fine against me. We have to show respect.

Out of respect also we do not tell names except when Hijras come face to face. If the Hijras stay, they stay. If they get into trouble and go someplace else, they may use our names as terms of abuse. Now as long as I am alive, they have heard my name. After I die, new disciples come. The Hijras will not tell my name. They say Grandmother Guru, Great-grandmother Guru, like that.

In this house there are thirty Hijras and so there are not enough rooms for everyone to have one room. Three or four have rooms; for the rest, those who get on together in words and ways live together in one room. But eating and cooking are separate. One makes tamarind water; another prefers chutney; the day a third gets money, she brings a ration of meat and cooks it. When one has nothing, "Today I have not a paisa, Guru Brother," I will say, and if he has a rupee or two he will give it to me. When he has nothing, I will give to him. It happens like that.

Our dying and living is in three houses here near the High Court, so we are called city people; the other Hijras live in three houses in Lud Bazaar. Each house has a Naik. Suppose the Naik dies. After they bury her, the brotherhood sits. They say: "This one's ways are good; that one's ways are good. This house needs repair. Some guest will come from outside; he has to be looked after, given food and drink. Does this one look as though she can manage this household?" They look for someone in this way.

There may be four or five of the dead Naik's disciples living in the house. They ask these four or five, "Well, which one of you will take the place? Which of you is capable of looking after this household? Will you manage? Will you manage?" Some will say, "No, we will not be able to manage; install so and so." So they ask them all, "Are you willing that he should be installed?" If they say yes, they install him, saying, "We will seat this one."

They say this and they take her hand and raise her up and make her the head of the house. So that one looks after the house. I have a dholak and bells, don't I? They put the dholak and bells in her lap and say, "Look, this is the house and the household; these are the bells. Take them and look after them." Then she is the Naik and she changes the name of the head of the house on the municipal records, so she is responsible. But the house cannot be sold. Among us it is a disgrace to sell it.

Now I am Naik. It is like this. Sometimes I stay at home. Now there are others: my disciples, my guru brothers. These people go to earn. So the disciples bring me a share. If they earn eight annas, they give me four. Out of that, I must eat something and keep something with a thought for the future: that someone may come and go as a guest, that the house may need repair, that there is the tax to be paid. All this has to be seen to, so I must keep four paise for a time like that. If I do not have the money when it is needed, then I must borrow it, complete the work and then afterward repay it.

Suppose someone of our house becomes very ill. If he cannot bear the expenses of the doctor and the medicines, then he is admitted into the government hospital. After he is admitted, if he gets well, then he gets well. If they say it is not possible, then we bring him home and go on giving him medicines. If he dies, we bury him. Only one person, I alone, am responsible for these expenses.

As far as burial is concerned, it is like this. Now this is my Aunt Guru; she is older than I. So perhaps she thinks, "He is younger than I. Why should I saddle his hands with this burden? Tomorrow, if not today, he will curse me after I die." So she saves a hundred rupees or two, and from that hundred or two all the expenses are met. Her third- and tenth-day ceremonies are all done, taking a little at a time from that amount. If she doesn't save, then I have to do it, in a poor way. Like, if she leaves one or two hundred I will do it in good style. If there is nothing, then within a hundred somehow I will do it.

For the ground they want a lot; if you mix earth with earth, that is one thing, but if you want the grave lined with brick or stone, and stones placed on top, it is another thing. For the third-day ceremony, as much as you spend it costs. We send for gram (lentils), fruits, and incense sticks and coconuts and put them all there where his breath left him. Then we break the coconut. When we get up in the morning, the first thing, if he was a Mussulman, we send the food and incense to the mosque and a prayer for the dead is read over them and then they are distributed to children. Those who live in the house pop two or three grains of gram from it into their mouths and eat a little bit and it is over.

Now comes the tenth day. We cook wheat bread and fry a little halwa, get it prayed over, and the ceremony is over. Will we not distribute two or four breads to the poor in his name? We give that and the people of the house eat the rest. Of course, as the person was, so it will be done. If an old person who has been living in the house for so many years dies, we must act according to her age. If a young person dies, "Hmm," we say, "What did he earn?

What did he leave that we should do all that?" Saying this, we do it in a poor way.

When the guru dies, the disciples are the heirs. While I live, my disciples wear glass bangles; they wear all kinds of ornaments and cosmetics, and even use attar, and wear everything women do. If I die, they will not wear these things; they leave off wearing bangles and wear white, as widows do. Now, don't people believe that where there is rejoicing, the presence of a widow brings bad luck? But the stomach is a tyrannical thing. If they go to donors' houses, the people may say, "Eh! Why have you come here wearing white clothes? You are widows!" So just for going to births, they will wear red and yellow, and when they come back home, they will take it off.

When a Hijra dies, he is buried [not cremated, which would be the more common Hindu practice]. We build the sign of the man on his grave, but put no name. If anybody among us dies, we keep the dholak silent for only ten days. If we kept it silent for forty days, how would our stomachs carry on? But for ten days, none of the Hijras from any of the houses go out; the whole brotherhood is silent.

Now suppose somebody turns up carrying a bundle and seeking hospitality. We will ask, "How did you come here?" He will answer, "Like this." We ask, "From which place are you?" and he will say, "Such and such a place." We will say no, and drive him away. But suppose he comes with a tin suitcase and bedroll. We think, "Yes, this is a Hijra from a respectable house," and accommodate him. When we take him in, we ask him, "Which place are you from?" I know that in such and such a place there is a house of the Hijras. So when he says, "I have come from that place," I say, "Yes," and we give him water to wash and tea to drink. Then we quickly cook food and give it to him to eat.

Then we keep him for as many days as he wishes to stay. If he wants to stay four days, we keep him for four days and hold him back for another four days. "How, now, why do you leave so soon?" we say. Then we give him a sari—not a new sari from

the bazaar, but one that has been given to us new in charity—
and a blouse and one-way fare. It is the same when we go for a
visit. For instance, I am the head of the house, am I not? So
they will give me that. If my disciple goes, they will give her
eleven rupees, a sari, and a blouse. If a disciple's disciple goes,
they will give five rupees, a sari, and a blouse.

For questions that affect the brotherhood, the Naiks of all six
houses sit together and talk. The rest of the Hijras sit at a little
distance; their opinion is not taken. "You are children; you sit
silent." If one of them says something, then another's disciple
will also speak and then a third person's disciple will also speak
and then there will be quarrels among us. So we do not allow
them to speak. The method is this: when the brotherhood comes
together, the Naiks sit in one place. "Look, brother, it is like
this," one will say. If I do not agree, then another will say, 'It is
not like that; it is like this. Do it this way." Then I say, "Yes,
that is correct. He speaks correctly."

For fines also the brotherhood sits. Like, if my sign is on a
house and another Hijra does the house and earns. "Why did you
do my house?" I say to her, and so we quarrel. When we quarrel,
we clap our hands in each other's faces. That is our way of quarreling. We do not beat and break; beating and grinding is simply
not the way of the Hijras. Our fight is of the claps. But when we
have quarreled, if she does not agree, then for that, too, we must
call the brotherhood. "Why did you do it? You mustn't do it
again," the Naiks say, and they relieve her of a good amount of
money. Or suppose I may have said some wrong words; I may
have said something bad to my Guru Aunt in anger, so she reports it and gets the brotherhood to sit. So I am fined ten rupees,
five rupees, eleven or twenty rupees. "Then don't say it again,"
the Naiks say, and we are reconciled.

For stealing, heavy fines are given. Among us, we do not keep
the one who steals or does bad things. Suppose this match is lying
on the floor and a new fellow picks it up and says, "Whose match
is this?" Then we say, 'Yes, brother, this is not a thief; this is a

good person." And saying this, we keep him. Among us, we go and come all over Hindustan. So there is a guest's suitcase or bed-roll, or someone forgets something inside the house. If one picks that up and hides it, he is called a thief among us. For that, there is a fine. So if he commits theft, we will fine him once or twice. We will admonish him, "Look, son, you must not do this kind of thing." Otherwise the head of the house must pay the com-pensation. Suppose there is a guest in the house. If a match of his is stolen, the Naik must replace the thing. If it is a silver ring, and that is taken, he must be given as much back. Even if twelve and twelve, twenty-four, years pass, this thing will still be talked of among us. "When I went to your house, my property was stolen." That is why compensation is paid immediately.

The Mussulmans recite their prayers in their houses on their festival days. The Hindus celebrate Divali. After Divali comes Doopki Poonam, and on that day we all do the puja of Besraji Mata among us. Those who pray, pray, but mostly on big days. How every day? Are they going to earn their bread or are they going to sit and pray? On the day they bathe, that day they pray; otherwise once or twice a year. We do not have communal quar-rels. If anybody prays, I stand behind them and I bow down. He who created me, what should I hide from Him? But I cannot read or write and I have not been taught how to do the prayers. I have kept the fasts, but I do not fast any more because now I am old and can no longer cleanse myself ritually in the proper manner.

It sometimes happens when we go about that men accost us and we get angry. "Why, brother, can you not get a woman, that you are accosting a Hijra?" We get very angry and we come away. Or it happens that when they accost us and we curse them, they raise their hands to beat us. Then there are fights and fisti-cuffs. The bystanders often interfere and say, "What, brother! Why do you quarrel with the Hijras?" and they go on with a scolding. But if we go to a house and see a zenanay trying to sing and earn our money, we beat him up. "Why are you stealing our living?" we say and, saying, beat him and snatch away his dholak. Why should I lie?

Sometimes it will happen that someone swears and curses us. They say, "Arrai! You ———! Ruined your parents' name!" What harm is done to us? Their mouths are spoiled. We remain quiet and go on our way to earn bread for our stomachs.

If we go in the train, we sit in the women's compartment. Nobody questions us. If a man sits there they say, "Here, you! Why are you sitting in the women's compartment? Come on! Get out from there!" and they get him out. But if we people go, who asks us? We have luggage and bedrolls with us and we are respectable travelers.

There is no shame in asking and eating. If I hold out my hand before you, if it comes to your heart you will give me a paisa or two. With that I will fill my stomach. We cannot steal or deceive. In our house, at nine o'clock the lock falls on the door. No man over twelve may enter. We can live there with respect. There is honor there. By asking and living, does one lose one's honor?

* * *

Near the top of the wall surrounding the Hijra's house is a stone marker which shows the height reached by the waters during the flood of 1908. Only once more after that, on the occasion of the double celebration, did the Hijras dance at Purani Haveli. Once more they shared in the happiness of their sovereign. Once more, a new life at the palace was blessed by those who were themselves unable to give life.

Chapter X

Middle-Class Wife: Rukmani

RUKMANI had heard of the Delhi Durbar, though she could scarcely imagine why anyone should choose to travel so far. For her the occasional journey by rath between Hyderabad City and her village was ample. She knew that everything would be done to make His Highness comfortable on the trip; her husband had said so. As a government servant, he had worked on the papers which detailed elaborate plans to ensure that this would be so. Keshow Rao, her husband, was one of the new wave of young men; since the revival of the Hyderabad Civil Service, increasing numbers of families were educating their sons for government positions. Many of these young men represented the first generation of education in their families. In the case of many, also, government service involved going to live in the district or village to which they were assigned and was the first step in loosening family ties.

These families thus propelled their sons in the direction of coming developments, but the opposite tendency existed side-by-side in them. Indian women have generally been the guardians of tradition and the most conservative force in Indian life, and so it was with the women of these families. The wives of their sons were similarly conservative, but paradoxically they became almost prototypes of the "average" housewife of today. Who now leads the kind of life that Begum Fakhr ul Mulk cherished? But the mode of life of the Rukmanis of today is virtually indistinguishable from that of their grandmothers in Mahbub Ali Pasha's time.

*   *   *

"Amma! Amma!" The call at the door, addressing her as "Mother," woke Rukmani almost with the first syllable. She had been about to wake herself, for her body had become attuned to being alert at this time of the morning for almost ten years now. No drowsy stretching and lounging in bed for her. There was so much to be done in the next three hours.

With a twist of her young body, she was on her feet. Stooping, she rolled her bedding into a neat sausage encased in the bamboo mat which had protected it from the floor, and placed it against the wall at the far corner.

"Amma!" came the call again. Rukmani went through the narrow passage to the tiny verandah and opened the door to let in Sathi, the little servant girl. The sky was milky outside, promising a fine day when the sun came up.

"Namaste, Amma," said Sathi as she squeezed past Rukmani in the passage between the single room of the house and the common wall it shared with the dwelling next door, where Purushottam, the Revenue Office clerk, lived with his young wife, Indira, and their new baby.

"Namaste, Sathi," returned Rukmani, reentering the room. Her husband, Keshow Rao, still slept on the string cot beside the place where her mat had been, his head pillowed on a folded arm. In a little while he, too, would waken. The room was dim; the only light filtered through the door into the passage and the single small window, whose wooden shutters had shrunk during the summer heat. The two children, Madhusudhan, nine years old, and Urmila, four, slept across the room from their parents. She glanced briefly at them, feeling the stab of pain she had felt every morning for nearly a year. But the wound was healing now. Less than a year ago, there had been three children on that side of the room, until Krishna Kumar was taken away from them.

It was only a cold, caught because he had played about in drenched clothes instead of coming straight home from school. A cold was nothing to worry about; most children got one soon after the start of the rains and Krishna Kumar was simply being his bright, mischievous self, the child that always needed correction. Once Keshow Rao had to slap him for nearly setting the kitchen on fire through his prankishness.

Rukmani at the time had been preoccupied with the arrangements for her sister's impending marriage, which was to take place after the rains. The groom's people were in a hurry; it must be celebrated at the very start of the marriage season, on the first auspicious day after their crops were harvested and stored. Rukmani's mother had come to the city to wrangle about the jewelry and brass vessels that must go with the bride and to look at the clothes that must be bought later. The house had been full, with her mother, her sister, and Lakshmi, her brother's wife, all milling around, excited at being in the city after years of quiet village life.

The childless Lakshmi had made a pet of Krishna Kumar and begged Rukmani to give him to her in adoption, but Rukmani could not bear to have the lively, impudent boy out of her sight. For all his mischief, he was like a light in the house. "We will see later on," she replied to Lakshmi's repeated requests. "He is still so small now, and he must go to school and be a big man like his father."

Lakshmi was crestfallen. Who would look after the land when her husband grew old? There was a good life to be had on the land; even better now that the new well was dug and a second pair of bullocks had been bought to draw up the water in great leather buckets which emptied themselves at the top of the well into stone irrigation channels. Why should the boy need to take government service? Did not her husband, Seethapathi, have a respected place in the community? Since last year, he had been called to sit with the elders under the great banyan tree at the crossroads to decide village disputes!

She looked across the tiny enclosed back-yard from her place in the detached kitchen where she was helping Rukmani make moorkuls—the coils of savory, spiced gram flour paste that would be fried in ghee. Krishna Kumar was sitting in the corner of the platform that held the pot of sacred tulsi (basil), making deep lines with a stick in the smooth yard. "Krishna Kumar," she called, "don't spoil the yard with your drawings. We have no time to sweep it again before our guests come."

The boy had been apathetic for a couple of days, walking instead of running, sitting about instead of wrestling and teasing neighboring children in the lane, but everybody had been too preoccupied to notice it. Now he got up listlessly and dragged his feet toward the verandah, coughing and holding his side. Lakshmi, holding the brass moorkul mold poised in mid-air, watched him go. "Hurry up, Akka (elder sister)," Rukmani urged in the staccato syllables of the Telegu language which was their mother tongue. "The ghee is already smoking."

"Wait, Rukmani," Lakshmi said. There was a note of anxiety in her voice. "I think Krishna Kumar might be having fever."

Rukmani took the vessel off the fire quickly and went to the kitchen door. Krishna Kumar sat on the step of the verandah holding his side and breathing with difficulty. She felt his forehead; it was burning hot. "Come," she said, taking his hand and leading him into the room, where she spread his bedroll in a corner. "Lie down," she told him; "this evening all this fuss will be over and everybody will go home tomorrow. Then we will call Raman Vaid and he will make you well." A vaid was a practitioner of ayurveda, the Hindu system of medicine.

But late that night the child was delirious, his body flaming hot, a bluish tinge about his lips, his breathing shallow and noisy. Early in the morning Raman Vaid came hurrying at Keshow's desperate pleading. "He only had a cold," Rukmani told the vaid almost apologetically. "We were all so busy; the house was full." Her large, soft eyes were dilated with fear.

Raman Vaid took the boy's wrist between his thumb and fingers. "He has much fever," he said. "The cold went to his lungs. We must apply heat."

Rukmani got up quickly and went to the kitchen, calling Lakshmi to accompany her. From the shelf above the fireplace she took down four bricks. "Light the fire and heat these," she told Lakshmi. "I will get the cloths." Lakshmi soaked a rag in oil and put it in the fireplace, building a neat stack of shavings and kindling over it. The fire caught at once and she fanned the little flame with a palmyra leaf fan. Soon the dry wood blazed up. Across the top of the fireplace she placed a piece of iron grating which they used for grilling kabobs and set two bricks on it. Rukmani returned with strips of cloth torn from an old sari. "Hurry, Akka," she urged, holding out first one cloth and then the other. Lakshmi took the bricks off the fire with a flat strip of metal bent to form tongs and placed them on the cloths. Wrapping each piece quickly round a brick, Rukmani ran from the kitchen to the room where the family had gathered, the elders around the boy's pallet, anxiously touching one or another part of his body, the other two children sitting hushed at a distance. The vaid turned the child on his side and placed one brick to his chest, the other to his back, and pulled the shawl over him. "Put something under his head to raise it a bit and keep the door and window closed. Don't let the air get to him," Raman Vaid said. "I will go back and prepare the medicine for him. Let Keshow Rao Sahib come and fetch it in three hours' time. I have to buy the ingredients from the herb shop when it opens."

Lakshmi came in carrying three or four long, dry chilies and a rag which she passed above Krishna Kumar several times, from head to foot and from side to side, meanwhile muttering under her breath, removing the effect of the evil eye which had lighted on the boy and made him ill. Then she went back to the kitchen and threw them into the fire. The chilies crackled and flared up suddenly; the rag shriveled into nothingness while she watched. Her mother-in-law, in the doorway, exclaimed, "Arrai, Ram! Not even smoke!" Truly the evil eye had been put on the boy! Lakshmi put the second pair of bricks on the grating, to be warm when the others needed changing.

But the bricks and charm did no good. By the time Keshow Rao brought the medicine, the child could not be roused to swallow it. His breathing became more rapid and shallow by the hour, and by next morning the little body lay still. Rukmani had sat by the child, not moving, dumb with fright, too agonized to weep as she watched his life flicker away. Keshow Rao sat on the edge of his cot in the dim room, speechless and still, roused only twice a day when one of the women gently whispered that he must eat something, a request they did not dare put to Rukmani after her first refusal, shaking her head slowly, her eyes never leaving the child. Eventually the rasping had stopped and the little body had grown cold, and Rukmani was led gently away while the others did what was necessary. Then, placing the body on a bamboo cot which had been brought from the bazaar, Keshow Rao joined the men of his family and neighbors in carrying his son to the burning ground. For an adult the funeral procession would have been preceded by music, reminding the mourners that the one who had gone had shed the cares of this life. But for Krishna Kumar they kept silence; being a child he had not yet tasted life and its cares.

Well, God had taken what was His and the mother must put

a stone on her heart and face life with all its demands. But Rukmani could never look at the sleeping children without remem-
bering that they had been moved together because the place between them had been vacated. Perhaps in time God would give
her another baby to fill the empty hole in her heart. Meanwhile
there was today to be lived.

She moved aside the dark green curtain that covered the open
shelves in the wall and took out a clean sari and choli. Then she
made her way to the bathing room, a small area partitioned off
from the kitchen, the smooth floor sloping down to a hole in the
outside wall which let the water through to the gutter in the
street behind the house. Sathi had already filled the big brass
water vessels which Rukmani had brought with her as part of
her dowry.

Undressing, she threw her soiled clothes over the partition wall
and poured the first "chumboo" of water over her body, the sudden chill sending a shiver through her. Keshow Rao and the
children must have warm water from today, she thought as she
scrubbed. Drying herself with an end of the sari she had removed, she quickly wound the fresh one around her and tied her
fresh choli. Entering the kitchen, she picked out a piece of char-
coal saved from the fireplace and a couple of grains of coarse salt.
These she chewed to a smooth paste which she rubbed briskly
over her teeth with a forefinger. She rinsed her mouth several
times, spitting into the yard, and washed her finger. Having
combed her long black hair and wound it into a loose knot, she
took her little silver kumkum container from the shelf and
crossed the room to open the window. She lifted her little round
mirror off its nail and propped it against the wooden shutter,
where it glinted in the early sunlight. After carefully dipping
the tip of her third finger into the kumkum, she wiped the edges
of the red powder to form a circle and applied it to her forehead
between and just above her eyebrows, making the red dot, or
bindi.

Behind her in the room, Keshow Rao was awake. He swung

his legs to the side of the bed and sat up. "Madhu," he called, "come on, get up and let me see your books." The child did not stir. He crossed the room and shook his son. "Come on, Madhu," he said, "I must leave early today. We are arranging for His Highness's trip to Delhi to meet the king from across the black waters, and I must get the papers ready to go to the Secretariat today." Madhu got up and rolled his bedding, placing it beside his mother's against the wall.

"Go and wash your mouths," Rukmani said to her husband and son, "and I will bring you your tea."

"I have to go early today," Keshow Rao began. "The papers———."

"Yes, I heard you," Rukmani interrupted. "Besides, you told me last night. The food will be ready early. It is Saturday, so no meat."

Keshow Rao made a little grimace. He liked to have meat, and their vegetarian diet on Saturdays was a sacrifice, but Rukmani felt she must make him observe at least this one religious custom.

Out of the room and into the yard, Rukmani faced the rising sun and greeted it with palms touching in a namaste. Sathi had washed the platform of the tulsi plant and placed a small vessel of water beside it. Rukmani poured the water over the plant, anointed the pot and platform with small dots of kumkum and turmeric, and made namaste to it. Now she was ready to handle the food for her family.

Filling a shining brass vessel with water, she put in tea leaves and sugar and set it to boil. Another vessel, covered with a square of net weighted down with beads to keep out flies, stood in a pan of water to discourage ants. From it she poured milk into three silver tumblers. Then she strained the boiling, sweet tea into them, set two on a tray, and carried them to her husband and son.

Returning to the kitchen, she resumed her working posture: squatting, her utensils and supplies around her on the immaculate floor, the work between her widespread knees. Into a large thali, a flat plate with a small upright rim, she put two handfuls of wheat flour and mixed in a sprinkling of salt, a spoonful of ghee, and a half cup of water. Then she began to knead, pressing down with her knuckles while rocking forward so that the weight of her body helped to flatten the firm dough, then folding and rolling it with the heel of her hand, sprinkling additional water when it became too dry, until it was a smooth, golden ball. Covering it with a bowl, she set it aside to soften and took a sip of hot tea. Then she took the vessel of rice which had been picked over and washed and set it on the fire.

"Bring your glass for tea, Sathi, but first take his hot water into the bathroom," she called, "and tell him his bath is ready." Rukmani never spoke her husband's name; no Hindu woman did. It was unthinkable bad luck, apart from being forbidden. She had referred to him as "Munshi Sahib" (Mr. Clerk) until last month, when he was promoted and she had to accustom herself to calling him "Muntezim (Supervisor) Sahib." In talking to him directly, she used no appellation at all. To the children, she referred to him as "your father."

Rukmani poured tea and milk into the tumbler for the girl and set the vessel aside for washing. Then she reached up to an open-work basket which hung in a rope cradle from the low ceiling and took out vegetables—potatoes, carrots, flat, pale green beans, stalks of curry leaves, a bunch of coriander greens—and put them on a bamboo tray. From a basket in the corner, she added two large brown onions and set herself to peel and cut and wash the vegetables for the curry that would be served with the rice and dal, the gravy of spiced lentils, for the meal in a couple of hours' time. Occasionally she paused in her work to take a sip of tea.

By this time the neighborhood was awake and bustling. Vegetable vendors, pushing their barrows along, called their wares; children shouted in play in the street; carts of firewood rumbled by; the sound of fluttering, squawking hens, tied upside down by the feet to a long pole, announced the egg seller. The burly milkman with his great spreading turban, gold rings in his ears, a stuffed calf under his arm advertising his trade and a shallow iron basket of fodder balanced on his head, drove his buffalo along, knocking on back-yard doors to deliver milk for the day. Doors opened as housewives stood to watch him milk the animal, alert to detect the sleight of hand that would leave a little water in the milking pot after the udders were washed.

Sathi went about her work methodically. She sat down by the grinding stone and ground the spices to be used in the day's cooking, leaving them in little heaps on the lid of a cooking vessel. Then she took the bedrolls out of the room to the back verandah, swept the room and dusted the bed, replaced the bedrolls, swept the front verandah, the passage, and the back verandah, swept the back yard and took the sweepings in a square of iron out the back door and threw them into the lane outside. As she did so, the cannon boomed the hour of eight. It was some miles away but could be heard all over the city, and the vibration in the air sent the pigeons fluttering from the minarets of all the mosques around.

Placing her broom against the wall in the corner of the yard, she went out to call Madhu in from play. As he came in through the back door, Sathi took the water from the kitchen and put it in the bathroom for him. Then she took up the cleaning of the rice and dal for the evening meal. When the bathroom was free, she would bathe the little girl and wash the clothes the family had worn yesterday. By that time, the meal would be cooked and after the family had eaten, she would be given her meal. Her last jobs would be to wash the thalis from which the family had eaten and then scour the cooking vessels, rubbing them with tamarind until their brasses shone like gold. In her own home they were rubbed with wood ash, which was slower but more economical. Then she would sprinkle the yard with water and smooth cow-dung paste over it. Years of this treatment, in the hot, baking sun, had given the yard a smooth, hard, clean surface.

Sathi worked hard all day. From Rukmani's house, she would

go to the two shops which she swept every morning. From there, she went to yet another house to wash clothes. They gave her a cup of tea and a snack. At five, she went back to Rukmani to help with the evening meal at six, which she also shared, and to clean up after it. Then she was free to go home to her family. Her father drove a bullock cart for a grain merchant, delivering sacks of wheat and rice, dal, and tamarind and tins of ghee and oil to the great houses of the nobles whose retainers ran into hundreds and consumed vast quantities of provisions.

Sathi had been married when she was seven years old to a young man of sixteen from her father's village. Now she was twelve and it would not be long before she reached puberty. Six months after that event, her husband's family would come to claim her. Meanwhile her work kept her adequately fed. Food was cheap and Rukmani was generous with her helpings and gave her two whole rupees a month as salary. Besides, she sometimes gave her an old sari which could be worn by her mother or cut and made into two of the long skirts she herself wore. Between the two shops, she earned another rupee every month and yet another from the house where she washed clothes. In all, she earned as much as an adult woman; counting all the food she was given, she earned as much as a young man of her class.

The money was useful at home, for Sathi's family had been forced to borrow for her dowry. In the three years since she started working, at the age of nine, she had assisted in paying off the debt. Her two older brothers had disappeared three years before, the night of the flood, along with her father's brother. They had worked along with him in the Afzul Gunj market, unloading grain during the day and sleeping in the godowns as night watchmen, getting their food from the merchant's family.

Rukmani cleared the space by the kitchen door, spread a bamboo mat, and called to her husband and son. When they sat down, she placed a thali in front of each and served them generously with rice, pouring a little ghee over each portion. Then she filled little brass bowls with vegetable curry, dal, and curds

217

that she had set in a black earthenware pot the night before. From a large, glazed earthenware jar she took two spoonfuls of the mango pickle she had put down in the summer and added them at the side of each thali.

Keshow Rao ate quickly; the boy Madhu dreamed between mouthfuls. "Come on, Madhu," she reproved him; "boy children must eat their food quickly. You will not be ready by the time your father leaves and you will have to walk all the way to Panthulu's house." Turning to her husband, she said, "Madhu will be late today. Don't wait for him in the afternoon; he goes to the wrestling class."

Keshow Rao nodded, his mouth full. "Have you started learning to twirl the stick yet?" he asked.

"No," the boy replied, "only when I am fourteen. The stick is too long."

Rukmani smiled at him, helping her husband to more rice. "You will be big and strong enough before then, son," she said. "Already you have grown and your shoulders have become broad since you went to the wrestling class." She refilled their tumblers with water and turned to roll the dough into rounds which she placed, one after the other, on the hot tawa—a round, slightly concave iron griddle—and pressed down with a cloth, twirling them round and turning them over until they puffed up. She made nine of these rotis every morning. The brass toshdans in which her husband and son carried their food were beside her. Four rotis went into her husband's, two into Madhusudhan's, and three she kept back for her own mid-afternoon snack. In the toshdans with the rotis she put a helping of the vegetable curry left over from the morning meal. She watched her husband and son finish their meal, and handed each a banana from the hanging basket.

Keshow Rao and Madhusudhan washed their hands, rinsed their mouths, and went back to the room, the one to collect his papers and quills, the other his books and slate. Sathi had gone to call a tonga, a two-wheeled, horse-drawn carriage in which driver and passenger sat back to back. Presently the cry of the tonga-wallah, punctuated by the bells on the horse's collar, could be heard coming up the lane at the back of the house. Keshow Rao and Madhu hurried out, the former calling, "We are going," as he went.

Following them to the back door, Rukmani called Urmila in from the lane and washed her hands. Setting her on the mat, Rukmani refilled the thali in which her husband had eaten, as a Hindu wife should do. Deftly she moved the tips of her fingers to mix the rice and its accompaniments into firm mouthfuls and fed them to the little girl, taking a mouthful for herself while the child chewed. The last mixture, traditionally, was of rice and curds, which cooled the stomach and aided digestion. To this mixture for the child she added a banana, which she mashed with her fingers, and a sprinkling of sugar.

It was Saturday, the day she would go to the temple of Hanu-manji, the Monkey God, a few hundred yards away, taking Urmila with her in a tonga fitted with a curtain to hide them from the prying eyes of strange males. Hindu women of her class did not go about the streets at all; even the marketing was done for them by their husbands. They spent their lives within their homes unless it was necessary to go out, when they went with their husbands, the curtain of the tonga lowered for them. Only to the temple did Rukmani and the others like her venture out, the ends of their saris pulled across their heads and covering their faces. Muslim women, too, led lives sheltered in their homes, but they were able to go short distances because the all-enveloping burqa with the peephole or square of net across the eyes was sufficient to hide their charms.

Rukmani did not have time every day to do her puja, the ritual morning prayer before the little images of Ganesha, the Elephant God, and the Lord Krishna, whose devotee she was. Only on Friday, the official holiday, when the cooking was not so urgent, was she able to spend a satisfying twenty minutes after a headbath, her long hair only partly dry and hanging down her back, sitting before the puja pandal, the little painted wooden canopy under which a pot-bellied and smiling Ganesh and a silver Krishna playing a silver flute had their abode. The pandal was placed on a low wooden stool on a small square of carpet at the far end of the back verandah, the area partitioned off with a painted wooden railing.

The first prayer must be to Ganesh; the obstacles of life could be overcome only by praying to him, for the Elephant God was the darling of the Lord Siva and his consort, Parvati. This is how it came about that Ganesh had that importance. Once Parvati received word that her husband, Lord Siva, was on his way home after a particularly long and anxious absence. Parvati wanted to bathe and deck herself out for her husband's return, but there was no one to guard the door for her, so she made the figure of a little boy out of mud and breathed life into him. While she was still engaged in the long process of her bath, Siva returned, but the boy guarding the door did not know him and forcibly prevented him from entering. In the fight that ensued, Siva cut off the boy's head, which went rolling far away into the undergrowth.

When Parvati saw what had happened, she was distraught. To pacify her, Siva promised to bring the boy back to life. Having searched in vain for the head, he sent an emissary to earth with instructions to return with the head of the first creature he saw moving. Predictably, he returned with the head of a baby elephant, for it had been night when the emissary reached earth and everything was sleeping. But there is an old saying that elephants and babies are never still. Attaching the elephant head to the boy's body, Siva breathed life into him again and named him Ganesh.

The boy was the darling of his heavenly parents, who spoiled him and gave him so many sweetmeats to eat that he grew a great, protuberant belly. On his first birthday, Ganesh bent to touch his parents' feet in the traditional gesture of reverence, but his belly was so big that he could not bend over far enough to reach them. The new moon, observing this, burst into laughter and Ganesh, hearing the scorn, forced himself down so that his belly burst, forcing Siva to save his life yet once again. Parvati, furious at the moon, cursed it and said that he who did not pray to Ganesh on the night of the new moon would never overcome the obstacles of life. And so, moon or no moon, the precaution of praying to Ganesh first must not be omitted. But this was not onerous, for Ganesh was a jolly little god who had done his best, and so it was easy to feel a sense of kinship with him.

Rukmani sat cross-legged on a low prayer stool, made a namaste to the Elephant God, and put red kumkum powder on his forehead. Then she lit the oil lamp and two sticks of incense and, placing flowers around him, prayed from the Sanskrit text:

I pray to the white-clothed, white-skinned Lord who has four hands and a smiling face, to ward off all obstacles. I pray day and night to the trunk-nosed God endowed with only one tooth. I pray to the God who is endowed with the Goddess Parvati's hearty blessings, who corrects mistakes and destroys obstacles, to the God endowed with sweet speech, who is pleasing to all and who eats cooked rice balls and rides on a rat.

The prayer ended, she offered the god turmeric powder and broke a coconut before him. Then, moving the lamp in a circle before him for arati, she rang a little bell. Her worship of Ganesh over, she prayed to the Lord Krishna, performing the same ritual:

I pray to the Lord Krishna who has the kasturi on his forehead, who has a diamond in his heart, a fresh pearl at the end of his nose, and a bangle on his wrist, who handles a flute and who is painted all over with sandalwood paste, who has a garland round his neck and is surrounded by milkmaids; to that Lord I pray. Having been born to the Princess Devaki in the beginning and brought up in the house of a milkmaid, he killed the pretentious Pootana, lifted the mount of Goranthan, killed Namsa, slaughtered all the Kauravas and brought safety to Kunthi's sons, the Pandavas; to that Lord I pray.

In this way, on Fridays and Saturdays, the first and last days of the week, she nourished her soul. Keshow Rao did not join her in these prayers, although occasionally he went to the temple to offer thanks for a joyful event in the family. Madhu did not concern himself with his soul, though he liked to go to the temple with his mother and did go during the summer and the Dassera, Ramadan, and Moharrum holidays.

"Today we go to take the darshan (blessing) of Shri Hanumanji," said Rukmani, stroking the top of her daughter's head. The child gave a little jump of joy and started to run across the yard. "Not yet," called the mother; "your father and brother left early today. It is not yet ten o'clock, so we have time. When we get ready we will go next door to see what Indira Akka is doing and you can play with the baby. Just listen to him crying!"

The heat of the fire had brought a glow to her face and the rush of work had disarrayed her hair. Besides, she had not yet oiled it after her head bath of the day before. Hair was left in its natural state for twenty-four hours after being washed, and the free softness of it framed Rukmani's face, taking another year or two from her twenty-three years. She washed the child's face and then her own and went to the room, taking the little girl by the hand. First, she changed Urmila's clothes, dressing her in a long, fully gathered skirt tied at the waist and a fresh "jacket," a round-necked, short-sleeved blouse which buttoned down the front and reached below her waist. Then she oiled the child's hair, parted it in the center, and pulled it back into two braids, each so tight that the child's head jerked backwards with every twist. This not only kept the hair well in place all day but gave it more root strength and caused it to grow faster.

On temple day, clothes must be special: Urmila's flowered skirt and the sleeves of her jacket were edged with tinsel and her braids were tied with tinsel to match. Rukmani lifted the child onto the string cot and turned her attention to herself. When she had oiled her hair and done it up, she put on a fresh sari, of fine handwoven natural cotton with a wide gold border, and a brocaded choli, of red silk, neatly folding the clothes she had worn since morning, for they must be used again on her return from the outing. Pulling a tin trunk out from under her husband's cot, she unlocked it and took out the little wooden box which held her jewelry. It would never do to go to the temple without jewelry. She would meet so many women of her acquaintance there and they would inspect her surreptitiously. They must not be allowed to imagine that Keshow Rao Sahib could not afford ornaments for his wife and daughter, or that the ornaments had perhaps been pawned to meet a family need. Kehsow Rao Sahib was a man on his way up, and his status must be proclaimed in this silent manner. So she took out a little gold chain for Urmila and a long heavy one of quarter ashrafis for herself. A fresh bindi between her brows, her bare feet in pretty sandals, and she was ready. She tested the bolts on the front door, locked the room and the kitchen. With one last look around the yard, she led the little girl out the back door and locked it securely behind them.

A few steps down the lane took them to the back door of the adjoining house, where Purushottham, a Revenue Office clerk, lived with his young wife, Indira, and their new baby. Finding the door slightly ajar, she entered the yard with Urmila. The house was a duplicate of her own. Mangaldas Sait, the cloth merchant, had built the two semi-detached houses two years ago. The rent of five rupees a month each was rather high, but they were new and solidly built and had roofs of the new tiles that were being made in far-away Mangalore. Besides, Sathi could conveniently fill the vessels from the tap, at the end of the lane, which served the neighborhood. It had been set there when the new water-supply line was laid after the flood. Memory of that catastrophe still caused people to catch their breaths, but His Highness had done everything to wring a blessing from it. One must surely be thankful for the tap: no need any more to buy water from the water cart and use it as though it were precious.

Indira's tulsi plant was flanked by two jasmine bushes and she had several pots of yellow marigolds along the wall. The two neighbors had become good friends, and on Fridays Indira sent a handful of flowers for Rukmani's puja. Indira was sitting cross-legged on the floor of the back verandah, the baby across her lap screaming in a temper tantrum. "What is the matter with him?" asked Rukmani. "We have been hearing him cry for so long now. He is not ill, I hope."

"God forbid!" Indira replied. "He is only angry. He has a temper up to his nose, just like his father. I am trying to get him to sleep so that I can change and come with you to the temple." She bobbed her right knee so that the baby's head bounced up and down, and he cried all the louder.

"Give him to me. I will hold him while you change," Rukmani said, holding out her arms. Indira handed the baby over and got up off the floor. The baby hiccoughed a bit, stopped crying, and stuffed his fist in his mouth, a drool of saliva running down his chin. "Oh, Raja," Rukmani said, cooing and bouncing the child in her arms. "Have you heard the story of the other baby who cried?"

"Let me tell it to him! I'll tell it to him!" Urmila exclaimed, tugging at her mother's sari and jumping excitedly.

"All right, you tell it," Rukmani said, and squatted on the verandah, with the child seated on her thigh while she held his little hands ready to make them clap when the narrative fell into rhythm. Urmila squatted opposite, leaning forward, her hands ready to clap in time, too.

"A fisherman caught three prawns and set them out to dry," she began. "Two dried, but the third did not." Then she chanted:

> Why, prawn, why didn't you dry?
> *The straw was across me.*
>
> Why, straw, why were you across him?
> *The horse didn't eat me.*
>
> Why, horse, why didn't you eat it?
> *The groom didn't feed it to me.*
>
> Why, groom, why didn't you feed him?
> *The slave didn't give it to me.*

Why, slave, why didn't you give it to him?
My mistress didn't tell me to.

Why, mistress, why didn't you tell her to?
My child was crying.

Why, child, why were you crying?
The ant bit me.

Why, ant, why did you bite him?
If he puts his hand in my nest, then won't I bite him?

The baby struggled at first, but as his hands were made to clap to the rhythm of the jingle, he began to coo and gurgle, dribbling streams down his shirt. With the last, long-drawn-out syllables, Rukmani swung him high above her head and brought him down again to pat his bare bottom.

Indira came from her room, her seventeen years and her new motherhood glowing, a roll of cloth under her arm containing a change for the baby. She went to the back door and looked up and down the lane. Then she called to a boy playing in the gutter, "Son, just go down to the end of the lane and call a tonga for me." In a few minutes, the bells tinkled up the lane and stopped outside the door. The tongawallah let down the curtain between himself and his passengers and the curtain to shield them from the public gaze. Then he got down and stood holding the horse's head, his back discreetly turned so that he would not see the ladies when they left the house and climbed into the vehicle.

As the tonga drove up to the temple, Rukmani, peeping from behind the curtain, could see the long lines of beggars on either side, some lame, some afflicted with leprosy, some blind, some bent with extreme old age, holding out their bowls and calling down blessings upon the almsgivers. There was quite a crowd of ladies and children at the temple steps, some of whom she knew: the wives of clerks and accountants, the doctor's wife and daughter, ladies who had been neighbors before she moved to the new house.

Rukmani and Indira alighted and each bought a coconut from the peddler sitting beside the steps, shaking the nuts in order to hear from the sound of the water inside whether or not they were good. Then each bought a handful of flowers, some kumkum powder, and a couple of tiny squares of compressed camphor. Leaving their sandals outside, they climbed the short flight of steps and entered the verandah surrounding the room in which the god was installed. The interior was windowless and dim, but the god was plainly visible, surrounded by deepams—small earthenware saucers full of oil which fed lighted wicks made of twists of raw cotton—and tall brass lamps which threw their glow all around. Hanuman's smiling, benign monkey face rose above garlands of flowers, and his forehead was streaked with red kumkum. As women were not allowed to enter the sanctum, they joined their palms and bowed their heads where they stood in the doorway. Then they started on their rounds of the encircling verandah, ringing the bell which hung outside the sanctum each time a round was completed, to attract the attention of the god and to notify the priest that they had come for worship.

As they completed the third round, the pujari met them at the door of the sanctum. Rukmani placed in his hands her coconut and the other articles of worship she had bought and remained standing at the door while the pujari returned to the god and performed the ritual on her behalf. She watched while he intoned the prayer in Sanskrit, anointing the god's forehead with kumkum and offering the flowers. Hanuman gave the blessing of courage in one's undertakings. He it was who had served the Lord Rama and fought Ravanna to free Sita. He was the victor of many battles, the embodiment of fortitude and bravery in adversity.

The pujari broke the coconut exactly in half on the stone at Hanuman's feet. Then he picked up a brass tray holding the camphor squares, which he had set alight. With one hand he gave arati to the god, moving the tray in a circle before the image; with the other he rang a little bell. While he did this inside,

Rukmani tolled the big brass bell outside the sanctum. The puja completed, the pujari emerged with a vessel of holy water which he spooned into Rukmani's curved palm. She drank out of her palm, fingers up and wrist touching her chin, and wiped the drops across her hair, then took from the pujari half the coconut, the prasadam which had been blessed by the worship. The other half would remain in the temple. Her worship over, Rukmani stepped aside to allow Indira to go through the same ritual.

Descending the steps, the women greeted and chatted with acquaintances, but today they could not dally. Indira had to return promptly, to make her store of badian before the rains set in, while there was a strong sun to dry them. Tonga drivers, alert for customers, called to them as they walked past, throwing small coins to the beggars, but they chose the vehicle which had brought them and was waiting to take them back. "I will come in a moment and help you with the badian," Rukmani said as she headed for her own door.

Indira quickly changed her clothes and, spreading a mat in the kitchen on which to place the baby, took down the vessel of broken rice which had been cleaned and kept ready for boiling. Between turns at stirring the pot, in which the broken rice was rapidly becoming a thick gruel, Indira set out snacks for Rukmani, Urmila, and herself; squares of a confection made of milk solids and sugar, and savory puffed rice fried with dal and peanuts. "If it stays fine today and tomorrow," Rukmani commented, "the badian will dry. You really left it very late, Indira. The first rains have fallen and who knows when the monsoon will set in?"

"I know," Indira agreed ruefully, "but my mother-in-law stayed so long after the child's head-shaving ceremony and they have so many relations in the city that there was always something to keep me busy. I was late with making the pickles and that upset everything. The Accountant Sahib has been so busy lately that he kept putting off buying the oil and the green mangoes until the season was nearly over. I was afraid to remind him too many times as he becomes annoyed very quickly. These clever men are difficult to approach, my mother-in-law says. But he is good to me."

"That is a very beautiful pair of bangles he bought you. How many tolas do they weigh? There must be at least four or five tolas of gold in them."

"No, only three," Indira said. "They look heavier, but there is resin inside them. Come on, the rice is ready now." She took the pot off the fire. The women each held two corners of a long, clean cloth and spread it in the sun in the yard. Then, each of them took a bowl of the boiled rice mush and with a spoon put little heaps of it in neat rows on the cloth. In two days, the badian would be dry and ready to put away, to be fried in ghee when needed. They would puff up into crisp, savory mouthfuls to be served with a meal or as a snack.

"What needlework are you doing these days?" Rukmani inquired as they worked.

"I have nothing on hand," the younger woman replied. "The baby takes up so much of my time. I wanted to keep a servant girl to do his washing and carry him so that I can be free, but the Accountant Sahib does not seem to be willing. He did not say no; he just didn't answer when I suggested it. Men are very strange. It is difficult to know what they are thinking, especially the clever ones. My mother-in-law says so."

Rukmani raised her eyebrows. Of course, mothers-in-law always twisted their sons' faults around to make them look like virtues. That was their way. But better not say anything to Indira. She had to make her life with her mother-in-law and probably, when the old man died, would have her permanently in the house, since Purushottam was the only son. So the less said to make her suspicious of the old woman, the better. Indira would find out for herself how to deal with silent negatives. She was still timid. After all, she had only been with her husband two years and was a second wife. Purushottam's first wife died during the plague: perhaps that had made him silent and reserved. Besides, he was so much older than Indira, whose parents had considered him such a good match since they could not afford a big dowry, having three other girls to marry off and no sons to help.

"I must go now," Rukmani said, setting her reflections aside. "Look, the child has fallen asleep on the kitchen mat." Picking up her daughter, Rukmani carried her to the door, but turned back at the sound of Indira's voice.

"Akka," the younger woman was saying, "next week shall we just go to the temple of Lord Siva? The Accountant Sahib told me that they have consecrated a golden nandi which was a gift of His Highness."

"So I too have heard," Rukmani replied. A nandi, a statue representing the bullock that was Siva's steed, was a popular religious symbol. "They say that when the Brahmins requested the funds for it, an Islamic scholar who was at the court remonstrated with the Nizam for encouraging what he called idol worship. Mahbub Ali Pasha rebuked him, saying, 'The wealth of the Asaf Jahis is not for the Muslims alone; it is for all my people equally.' Yes, let us go there one day and see it."

Chapter XI

The People

THE DELHI DURBAR had little meaning for the common people. For those who had heard of it at all, it was an occasion when a king "from across the black waters" was coming, and for that occasion they must have the new clothes or other supplies ready for their own nobles who would go to receive the visitor. For the common people, the watershed was the great flood of 1908. It was that which dated the events of their lives, gave drama to their conversations, and provided the stuff of their nightmares.

Who were these people? Let us meet four of them, representative not of the very poorest but of the working class: a servant, an agriculturist, a craftsman, and a clerk.

*   *   *

Govind, a groom's son. I was born in Karimnagar, the home of my maternal grandfather. As is usual among Hindus, my mother had gone to her father's home for her confinement. My father was in service as a groom at the palace of Nawab Fakhr ul Mulk.

When I was very small, I was taken to the palace, and I grew up there. We lived in a hut in the palace compound. While my father attended to his duties in the stables, my mother looked after us children and cooked the food for the family.

My childhood was spent playing about in the palace grounds, at the back where the servants' quarters were. The children of the servants all played together. We played kabbadi, which is a kind of football, and swam in the tank. During monsoons there were a lot of those black slugs with the little horns. We children used to line them up and have races. We put salt on their tails and as the slugs were always wet, the salt would fizz a bit and oh, my, how fast they went when they felt that fizzing on their backsides! At other seasons there was something we called touch-me-nots. They look like a large earthworm, except that they have hard shells. When you touch one, it coils up tight and you can roll it like a hoop.

When I was about eight, there was a milkman keeping buffaloes down below the Iram Munzil grounds who employed me to graze his herd by the side of Husain Sagar (tank) at a salary of two rupees a month. I did this for nearly four years, and then I started doing daily labor on building works, earning two annas a day carrying stones and mortar.

One day when I was returning home, Fakhr ul Mulk's son, Rais Jung, saw me. He was cantering about doing polo practice when he happened to notice me and thought I was a decent-looking lad, so he decided to take me into service. I was made groom to his son, whose pony I looked after for two years. For this work Nawab Fakhr ul Mulk paid me a salary of six rupees a month and Rais Jung used to give me another two rupees every month. After two years he took me into his apartments in the palace. At first I used to dust and clean shoes, but gradually I came to be his dressing boy, his butler, and even did some cooking for him. Being inside the palace, I could watch what the other servants were doing and soon picked up their work.

My day started very early and, as I had to be on duty whenever my master was at home, it rarely ended before 10:30 at night. But the work was very light and I never had cause to complain. There were so many of us that nobody was heavily burdened and we had time to nap or to sit and chat for quite long periods at a time. The younger, newer servants had time to learn other work from those more experienced and so better their prospects, like I myself did.

When I became valet to Rais Jung, my salary was raised to 14 rupees a month and he often gave me tips. His friends, too, tipped me and I was very well off. My marriage took place in Iram Munzil, for which my master gave me a gift of 300 rupees. When I took my bride to salaam Nawab Fakhr ul Mulk, he gave each of us five rupees, as he always did with the newlyweds who went to see him. For funerals he always gave ten rupees.

Rais Jung generally lunched at the office; I took his lunch there and served him, bringing the empty toshdan and plates home afterward. As director of veterinary service in the state he had to tour all the districts. I accompanied him and was always fed from his table on tour; I was also heavily tipped by all and sundry in the districts. He also took me on holidays to other parts of the country: Bombay, Kashmir, Delhi, Ootacamund.

When we were in the districts at the right time of year, I used to like to go watch the villagers catch the wild ducks which are sold in the markets. There is a string of villages that have big tanks, shallow enough so the grasses grow near the banks and broad enough to extend a little away from the village. About the time the ducks are expected to come from Siberia to spend the cold season here, the villagers float clay pots on the water, upside down so the air is trapped inside.

The ducks land on the tanks and become accustomed to seeing the pots among the grasses or being pushed across the water by the wind. When the ducks have been there a few days and feel quite at home, the villagers cover their heads with similar pots, made with eye holes, and slip into the tank. Keeping the rims of their pots just touching the water, they can walk right into the midst of a flock of ducks without alarming them. They seize a duck's feet and with a quick snap of the wrist pull the bird under the water before it can make a squawk. Then they transfer it to their left hand, which is kept down by their side, and reach for another bird. In this way a man can harvest a whole crop of ducks and the other birds are not aware that anything is happening.

Every summer we used to go on a month's shikar for big game, living in tents in the jungle. Once we went deep in a dense forest, where there was a small lake which was the watering place of tigers. Beaters were hired to drive the animals toward where the hunters were. Rais Jung was sitting in a machan, a platform in the tree, and Zahid Ali, the groom, and I were up another tree. Suddenly Rais Jung gave a low whistle and we saw him climbing down from the machan. We got down and found him covered with soldier ants, which bite painfully.

We brushed them off and then the three of us sat in the open clearing, facing in different directions. I had a muzzle loader, Zahid Ali had a double-barreled gun, and Rais Jung had a .500 Express. Just beyond the clearing there was some tall grass. Suddenly the tiger bounded out of it. Rais Jung took aim and fired quickly, but the bullet passed through the tiger's nose. The tiger stopped and shook its head, as though it were shaking off a fly, before it bounded away. Hearing the shot, Shah Nawaz Jung, his brother who was also along on the shikar, came up. The brothers talked together briefly and then sent us and the beaters back to camp. Taking one Lambadi tracker, the two of them followed the wounded animal on foot and shot it the next day. They were true hunters.

A number of children were brought up in the palace. These were babies, mostly girls, who were sold by their parents for nominal sums like five or ten rupees. This was quite a common thing at that time and many households had these children. They were brought up as servants—slaves, really, because they had no pay, but I never heard of any who were ill-treated in any way. They were taught to read and write Urdu by Islamic scholars appointed for the purpose and to pray regularly. When the boys grew up, they were given jobs of the better sort, with salaries, and they ate in the palace and lived in the quarters there. Some of them became drivers, some clerks, and so on. Their marriages were performed at the palace, and their children were looked after. There was nothing to bind them to Iram Munzil; they could have left and sought work elsewhere if they had wanted to.

The girls, of course, could not leave because once they attained puberty they were put into purdah. Some of them were married out of the palace and the rest to better-class employees of the palace. They were never made to work in the sense of being allotted specific tasks. While they were children, they played like all children. When they grew up, they did things of their own accord. Sometimes a son might take a fancy to one of them and take her as a concubine. Why not? They had been nicely brought up and had good health and good manners. This happened in all the big families and was regarded as perfectly normal in those days. One son had a concubine like that; she was treated with every respect, and she bore him six children, all of whom were accepted and brought up in the palace as Fakhr ul Mulk's grandchildren. Another son had a wife and a concubine living together in the same apartment and they got on very well together. The wife had no children but the concubine bore several, and both women brought them up.

Chandriah, an agriculturist. I was born in Chandaipet village, Medak District, where our family house was, although our lands were scattered in several villages. My father was of the toddy-tapper caste (tapping juice from a particular variety of palm tree to make toddy, a beverage taken either fresh or fermented, was a low-caste occupation). He had fifty acres of wet land and fifty acres of dry. I was the youngest of three brothers, and I had three sisters as well. Until I was about nine years old, a master used to come to the house to teach me Telegu, Urdu, and arithmetic. After that I used to walk a mile to Makkarajpet village to a small school run by two teachers, one a Muslim and the other a Hindu.

They did not charge us any fees, but the government used to give them yearly about five or seven rupees for each pupil. There were about fifty children, coming very irregularly, and after my first year they began to collect a half anna a month from each child.

I studied with these teachers until I was eighteen and then started learning revenue work by serving as an apprentice to our patwari (local official) for three years. At the end of each year we had to take a government examination, ten papers altogether, covering the land records, revenue, and police work. At the same time my father made me learn the art of ayurvedic medicine from a well-known practitioner who lived in our village.

At that time there were only thirty or forty people in our village who owned land, and as there was much vacant land it was possible to let fields lie fallow for a season. Every household had animals for milk, for draft, and for the plow, and sheep and goats by the hundred. Shepherds, too, had their own flocks. The result was plenty of organic manure to be had and the shepherds used to rotate among the landowners, penning their sheep for a time on the land of each person. My father had 50 animals for plow and draft, 50 for milk, and 200 goats which used to be penned in one field after another when the crops had been taken in. A goat cost two and a half rupees, so we could often afford to have meat to eat; we gave people milk and buttermilk to drink free.

After I completed my apprenticeship and got my government certificate, I accepted employment as manager for the jagirdar in our village. After several years I exchanged that post for a similar one with the jagirdar of my wife's taluqa (sub-district), and later for patwari. To that I added an excise contract and so got on very well. In middle age I gave up these kinds of work and went back to look after my lands, but that was much later.

Tasduq Hussein, a master craftsman. A shadow fell across the doorway of the shop. The young craftsman sitting cross-legged before his work bent a little lower to see the faint lines of the pattern outlined on the metal in front of him and gave a few more taps of his hammer on the chisel to finish the swirl he was carving. Then he looked up. As his eyes accustomed themselves to the sunlight in which the visitor stood, he leaped to his feet to salaam the Dewan with a deep bow. Maharajah Kishen Pershad returned the greeting and then moved about the shop examining the completed articles which stood about or which were presented for his inspection by the maker and his assistants. All the while he kept up a flow of light conversation: "Is all well with the master craftsman? This piece is very beautiful. Has his work received the appreciation due to it?"

Having accepted a cup of tea brought hastily from the bazaar, the Maharajah turned to the craftsman with a smile. "Well, Hussein Sahib," he said, "all of this bidriware is mine." Hussein bowed. The Maharajah signaled to his secretary to take care of the account and took his leave. After him, the secretary added up the prices asked, without comment, and counted out the coins, while the assistants packed up the articles and stowed them in a carriage waiting outside. Not even a collar button was left in the shop.

Curiously, Hussein inquired whether the secretary could say what the Maharajah does with the bidri articles he buys. Three or four times already his shop had been cleaned out by the Dewan in this way. "Certainly," the answer came unhesitatingly. "As the Dewan tours the districts he presents them as gifts to the officials whom he visits, to the hosts who entertain him, and to those who ease his journey."

The craftsman whose morning had developed so satisfyingly was Tasduq Hussein, master of the art of making bidri. This was an ancient art which had come from Persia with the invaders. It was no longer practiced in Persia, and Bidar, the town from which the work took its present name, was the only place in India where it was still done. Indeed, only by a combination of good fortune and someone's good foresight was it continued there. The art had been dying out, known only to a few old men. The youngest and best of those, Ramana Master, had been under pressure for the last dozen of his seventy years to divulge the secret of the art, but he had refused to teach it to anyone. Finally, in return for gifts of money and some land, Ramana had agreed to teach it to an occasional apprentice.

At this point fate stepped in. A district official of Bidar, who had helped establish a government school there, had what was at that time a novel idea. Believing that the youngsters of the town ought to be exposed to arts and crafts, he persuaded Ramana Master to teach in the village school for one hour a day. Bidri was one of the skills that was less popular with the pupils, for it required painstaking work. First a mold was made for the article desired, and then metal, chiefly an alloy of copper and zinc, was poured into it. After the metal had hardened, it was taken from the mold, looking like steel. Next it was blackened with soot and a design was sketched on it, to be carved laboriously by tiny hammer blows on a pencil-sized chisel. The grooves thus made were filled with silver and thoroughly rubbed so that the surface felt like a single smooth piece. The final step was to smear the whole article with a paste mixed by the master craftsman, heat it, and dip it into a pail of cold water, from which it emerged as if magically transformed, with the silver gleaming against a matte black background.

So painstaking a craft was bound to be shunned by most of the active boys exposed to it. The only one in school at the time who was sufficiently interested to follow the process all the way through was Tasduq Hussein. After he had mastered the techniques, he went on to take training in drawing and in design work. By then he knew that this alone could satisfy him as his life's work.

Hussein's family was horrified. His grandfather had been a respected teacher of Urdu and Arabic, to whom pupils came for private lessons. His father had studied diligently until he was not only an able accountant, but was also fluent in the Urdu, Kannada, and Maratha languages, an especially useful combination as Bidar was located in an area where these three languages came together. He became administrator of the Bidar jagir belonging to Raja Shamraj Bahadur, one of the Umra e Uzzam, or Great Nobles, and thus had a position of very considerable local standing. Every few months Shamraj Bahadur came to Bidar for three or four days to look over his estates and to confer with his administrator. The family was closely knit and continuously together in Bidar except for the father's absences when Shamraj Bahadur summoned him to Hyderabad on business matters.

In time, however, the two daughters were married off to small officials and sent away with bright prospects. Only this single son remained at home.

He had given his parents cause for anxiety early in his life, when he suffered from convulsions. His grandmother used to burn a turmeric root and apply it to his forehead between the brows: the shock of the heat would bring the child around. After several such seizures, the grandmother proclaimed that the child must be protected from any further depredations by the evil eye. At birth he had been given the name Duresh Mohiuddin, but the grandmother decided that he must be renamed in order to put him under the protection of a powerful saint, Husain, grandson of the Holy Prophet. Accordingly a ceremony was performed in which the child was renamed Tasduq Hussein, meaning "an offering to Husain to ward off the evil eye," and thereafter the boy was healthy. He continued to be the center of his family's joy.

But his developing interest in bidri was a cloud on the horizon, and his father tried to discourage him from pursuing the art. "Why do you want to pass your days working with a hammer?" he kept asking. "Do you not realize you are spoiling the family name? Who will want to give his daughter to a fellow who pounds with a hammer all day?" His objection was prophetic. Tasduq Hussein reached the age of twenty-eight years before he found a man who was willing to give a daughter to him in marriage. For the ceremonies and festivities surrounding the marriage, Hindu friends rubbed shoulders with Muslims and joined with equal freedom in the merrymaking. Marriages, funerals, holy days, were all observed without communal differences, and everyone who wished took part as his preference dictated.

By the time of his marriage, Hussein had trained others to work for him and had begun to make a name for his art. Later on, Mehdi Nawaz Jung, a Nawab from Hyderabad who had become acquainted with Hussein's work while visiting Bidar with Maharajah Kishen Pershad, whose associate he was, gave 15,000 rupees to further the revival of the craft.

Looking back, Hussein says, "Although we lived a little distance from Hyderabad, we always felt that Mahbub Ali Pasha was our protector. Anyone could approach him, rich and poor alike, and always get help from him. To some he gave lands; to some, money; to some, a decision. When he was touring in the districts, anyone at all could speak to him. He understood the people.

Sometimes Mahbub Ali Pasha used to go about incognito with his pockets full of gold. Once he had a narrow escape when he spoke very disrespectfully of the Nizam, thinking to learn some tongawallah's opinion of his reign by abusing himself, but they beat him up for saying such things about His Highness. Another time he disguised himself as a tongawallah and something about the way he handled his tonga or his horse, or perhaps the way he spoke to a customer, made another tongawallah a little suspicious that this fellow was not a genuine driver. So he began speaking to him, and after a while he realized that it was the Nizam. But Mahbub Ali Pasha said to him, "There's nothing to be frightened about—please don't give me away," and sent him off. Afterward the fellow discovered that His Highness had quietly put a handful of gold coins in the tonga. That was like him.

Bunsiraja, a clerk. Even the highly stratified society of Hyderabad was not without its rags-to-riches stories. Everyone in Hyderabad is familiar with the dramatic rise of Sir Afsur ul Mulk, the young noncommissioned officer who, by a skillful combination of competence, charm, and an eye for the main chance, rose to become commander in chief of the Hyderabad army and an intimate of Mahbub Ali Pasha and of British royalty. There were others who somewhat less spectacularly advanced in station.

One such person was a young man named Bunsiraja, who came from a very ordinary Kyasth family. (Kyasth is a caste; several Kyasth families came with Asaf Jah I and their descendants constituted the Hindu nobility in Hyderabad.) In fact, it was such a very ordinary, run-of-the-bazaar family that no one now even recalls his father's name. But Bunsiraja was not content to remain a nobody, and in his determination to better his position he studied hard. He learned to do accounts. He learned to write and speak Persian and steeped himself in Persian literature until he was fluent in the most courtly phrases of that beautiful and flowery language. Eventually he found employment as a clerk in the estate office of a jagirdar named Raja Durga Pershad. Gradually his responsibilities increased as he demonstrated his capacity and willingness to take them on. Raja Durga Pershad had no son to manage his affairs, to which he himself could scarcely attend as he spent all his time in attendance at court. Consequently he was delighted to employ this able young man, who presently became what an acquaintance described as "the whole and soul of Durga Pershad's household."

In time the Raja brought his protégé and confidant to the notice of Sir Salar Jung, who found many occasions to employ Bunsiraja's talents. What particularly impressed him, not unnaturally for a Dewan who was constantly in demand for a great variety of public occasions, was Bunsiraja's ability to compose graceful speeches in Persian.

As Mahbub Ali Pasha grew old enough to take over more and more public functions from the Regent, Bunsiraja's services were employed in his behalf, thanks to the recommendation of Sir Salar Jung. The young Nizam was as pleased as the previous patrons had been, and over the years he gave tangible expression to his appreciation in the form of official positions and then command of troops with jagirs to support them, and eventually the title which elevated him to the nobility, "Mahbub Nawaz Wunt, Raja Bahadur." That Mahbub Ali Pasha granted him the honor of naubat at his deori was the crowning symbol of the degree of success that this nobody had attained in becoming somebody through talent and hard work.

Chapter XII

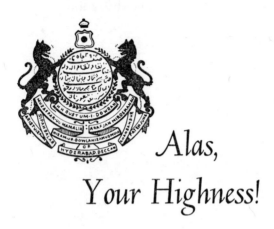

Alas,
Your Highness!

ONE DAY in late August, 1911, Begum Fakhr ul Mulk sat in the
baradari, tears streaming down her face. Normally in that handsome, airy room the delicate plaster work—pristine white flowers
and leaves and tracery soaring above the pale blue of the walls
and high, fluted arches—made her spirits soar, too. It was a happy
room, used for gay family parties, for ceremonials for a bride, for
amusements when the singing girls delighted men and women
alike with their grace and beauty. It was used also for the annual
Majlis, the prayers during Moharrum when devoted Shias beat
their breasts and wept real tears in sorrow for the tragedy at
Kerbela centuries before. Today also her tears were real and
copious and expressed grief and apprehension of a tragedy closer
to home. News had come that Mahbub Ali Pasha lay in a coma,

and that Fakhr ul Mulk had ordered his household to shift from Iram Munzil, twelve miles out, to their deori in order to be in the city, nearer to the palace.

In a moment she would go and give the necessary instructions for moving the family. But first she turned to the baradari for a moment of privacy for her feelings and to say a prayer for Mahbub the Beloved. Then, struggling to compose her features, she went to do what must be done. "God gives life and in His time He takes it again," she murmured. "Huzoor, when shall we see another such as you?"

In another part of the city, the eagles swarmed in the cloudy sky and broke off to swoop onto the roof of Maharajah Kishen Pershad's deori. They had gathered there every day for years at just this hour, waiting for their tidbits. Maharajah put down his book and made his way to the rooftop, where a servant stood in the doorway holding a tray of raw meat. Maharajah threw big chunks high into the air and watched the great birds take wing, catching the meat before it fell and then soaring away with the booty.

The durbar of poets and writers, painters, and musicians had ended early that day. It was the first day of Ramadan, the month of fasting, and the crowd had been smaller than usual. In a little while Maharajah's children would come to greet him and then he must hurry to Falaknuma Palace, where Mahbub Ali Pasha had been staying for several days, having left Purani Haveli in an ill temper. Reports said he was drinking more heavily than usual, eating very little, brooding by himself.

As Maharajah descended the steps, an aide from the palace on his way up stopped and saluted smartly. Behind him, Maharajah's secretary, who had been guiding the aide to the roof, bowed in a low salaam. Maharajah looked at them quizzically, returning their greetings. "His Highness is not well, Your Excellency," the aide reported. Maharajah felt his heart miss a beat. A bad mood was nothing to worry about; Mahbub Ali Pasha would come round and distract himself quickly enough. But this? God

grant his beloved sovereign health and long life! Not long before,
Maharajah had composed a couplet:

> A hundred thirty years and a day, O Deccan King;
> This is the span your servants pray your fate will bring.

Maharajah dressed in a hurry and sped to Falaknuma Palace.
The doctors trained in Western medicine were there, and the
hakims and vaids, the medical men of each kind in a separate
little group, talking in grave whispers among themselves. Standing somewhat apart at one side of the long room was Sir Afsur ul
Mulk, tall and erect, his nearly seventy years proclaimed by his
white hair. As Maharajah entered the room, his eyes met those of
Sir Afsur; the two men salaamed at the same time, and came
toward each other. "It is nothing much, they say," the older man
replied to Maharajah's unspoken question. "He was restless and
disturbed yesterday and complained of headache. Today he
seemed drowsy and listless. Perhaps he has been overdoing it.
The Hakims says he requires quiet and have forbidden any of us
to visit him."

Maharajah stayed an hour and left. There was so much to do.
The arrangements for the trip to Delhi in December would have
to be ready soon, to allow plenty of time for preparations. He
must take another look at the plans for the extension of the new
drainage and water-supply schemes and discuss them with Ali
Nawaz Jung, the chief engineer; Dalal, the engineer who was
to supervise the construction of the new dams, had already been
given an appointment. He must scrutinize the application from
the Christian church for funds for the leper asylum. The Cabinet
Council was to meet in the early afternoon. Somehow he must
make time to see his publisher before going to the wedding of his
servant's daughter and then on to Nawab Fakhr ul Mulk's for
dinner—though perhaps that would be canceled.

Throughout the day he telephoned at intervals to Falaknuma.
"His Highness's condition is about the same," came the answer.
The day dragged on. Early the next morning the doctors reported

that Mahbub's condition had deteriorated, and with hope fading they yielded to the pressure from the nobles to see their sovereign.

All day, carriages and cars passed and repassed along the graveled drive, and the palace was full of the great nobles: Mumtaz Yar ud Dowla, who had been Mahbub's schoolmate and had managed his program for feeding the flood victims; Murli Manohar, companion of his youth; Salar Jung III and the other great Shia nobles; Rameshwar Rao II, the quiet young Raja of Wanaparthy; the men of the Shiv Raj and Sham Raj families; and a host of others, all perturbed and distraught by the news.

Nawab Fakhr ul Mulk stood looking down on the still form, deeply moved. He had been at the bedside for some hours, immobile, unable to find the strength to depart from this man. As playmate and sovereign, Mahbub Ali Pasha had been the focus of his life for as far back as his memory stretched. Fakhr ul Mulk glanced up as a stir at the door betokened that the Resident and his staff had come. Like others in the room, he eyed the Britisher. If the worst should happen, thank God there was an heir, or this man's presence might signify the end of the state.

As news of Mahbub Ali Pasha's illness spread, a hush fell over the city. Maharajah was aware of it as he tossed all night on his bed, waiting for the next bulletin, dreading the message that he had already seen written on the faces of the doctors, wrestling with God for his sovereign's life. Early in the morning on the third day of Ramadan, he hurried to Falaknuma. The news was as bad as he had feared: Mahbub was sinking.

Just after eleven, the Heir Apparent arrived. When it was clear that there was no hope of Mahbub's rallying, Osman had been rushed to the palace. But, once there, he hesitated and turned back at the threshold. Restrained by the gentle touch of the courtiers at his elbows, he allowed himself to be led to his father's bedside. He had barely reached it when Mahbub Ali Pasha opened his eyes wide for one last look around and closed them forever. Shaken as by an earthquake, Osman fled; brought back to the room, he flung his dastar to the floor and threw himself on his father's feet. But he was too racked by emotion to remain there more than momentarily, and he quickly left Falaknuma. Before Osman's car had reentered the King Kothi gates, the shivering had started. He hurried to his room with barely time to throw himself on his bed before convulsive shudders took possession of him. The mound of bedclothes heaved and quaked with the tremors that racked his frame. At his command two personal attendants added their weight to hold down his twitching limbs. By late afternoon the paroxysm had passed and he returned to Chow Mahalla for the last salaam. By tradition he was debarred from attending the funeral.

Meanwhile, at Falaknuma, the death chamber had been crowded with subjects who longed to support Mahbub's failing strength with their own. When the dread word came, "He is no more," the nobles present reacted with grief expressed according to their various temperaments. Some knelt in silence by the dead sovereign while the tears washed their faces unnoticed. Others threw down their dastars and sobbed aloud. A few tore their clothing. Maharajah felt the earth slip away from under his feet. He fell to his knees and his whole body trembled as his mind fought to reject the news. Presently he felt calmer and moved out of the room. Nawab Shahab Jung approached him. Even in the presence of death the courtesies must not be lost; the two men salaamed each other. "Word must be sent to King Kothi," Shahab Jung said. "Mir Osman Ali Khan must be proclaimed . . ."

In the back of his mind each man finished the sentence, "before the British can swallow the state." They quickly designated two of the elder nobles to go to King Kothi palace and formally notify Osman Ali Khan of his accession. Life in death! While the funeral arrangements for Asaf Jah VI were in progress, the royal procession of Asaf Jah VII was being prepared. The king is dead; long live the king!

In the afternoon Maharajah sent for Faridoon Jung, Mahbub Ali Pasha's private secretary, and Maulvi Abdul Aziz, his own office superintendent. Nawab Shahab Jung and Sultan Yavar

Jung, the Kotwal, arrived just before them. Between them, the five decided not to seek the Viceroy's sanction before they proclaimed the new ruler. Maharajah undertook to secure Ujjala Begum's promise not to press the claims of her young son, Salabat Jah; a long regency at this time was unthinkable. For the continuity of the state it was essential that the succession not be contested. The announcement must be soon and positive. From Char Minar and from every city gate, the public must hear what they already knew. Maulvi Abdul Aziz took up his quill to compose the announcement. Maharajah and Shahab Jung altered a word or two and Maharajah signed the corrected copies.

The public knew. Since yesterday a silent city had kept the death watch. Now each house mourned the passing of a loved one. Rukmani sat with her hands in her lap, preparations for the evening meal forgotten, for Keshow Rao had returned home early, red-eyed and tight-lipped, with the news that Mahbub Ali Pasha had died. Rukmani herself had seen him walking the devastated areas and weeping at the plight of the people at the time of the flood, and she had often heard her father tell how His Highness had stepped into the swirling waters to do arati to the river goddess and immediately the flood had begun to subside. Sathi's family lived in one of of the new houses that Mahbub Ali Pasha's government had built for those who had lost everything. Together the husband and wife sat, desolate, praying for the soul of their departed sovereign, weeping quietly.

Outside the city gates, young Mahboob Narayan was struggling to comfort his grandmother. The five-year-old and the old woman had been returning from a visit to their village. When their rath had been halted at the closed city gates, the guard had given them their first inkling of the news, and now the old woman was weeping as though it were her own son whose breath had left him.

By ancient tradition the city gates were closed and barred on the death of a Nizam, presumably to prevent any outside interference in the establishment of the succession. They were reopened only on the proclamation of the successor, which had often been the first official confirmation of the passing of the incumbent. Following this tradition, the gates were closed just before noon on the 29th of August and were kept closed until Nawab Shahab Jung had proclaimed Osman the new Nizam.

Once the announcements had been signed by the Dewan, Shahab Jung, as minister for police and therefore responsible for law and order, had mounted his horse and led a solemn procession to Char Minar. Reaching there, he replaced his turban with a white handkerchief and called out in a loud voice: "The state belongs to God and the grace and the power to Mir Osman Ali Khan Asaf Jah VII!" The announcement was followed by a roll of drums. In this manner he proceeded to each of the twelve gates, proclaiming the new Nizam at each. Then the gates were opened.

Meanwhile the body of the dead ruler was taken to Chow Mahalla in a limousine. Its progress was slow, for all along the route people ran out of their houses to touch the vehicle, to take darshan of their ruler one final time, and to share their anguish. Women, many of the Muslim ones without having thought to don their burqas, smashed their bangles as a symbol of widowhood and threw the pieces at the car. Men wailed, "Hai! Your Highness! We are lost!"

At Chow Mahalla the body was dressed in full regalia with the jewels of state. Then began the agonizing process of the last salaam, first for the ladies of Mahbub's zenana, and then for the long procession of nobles and officials who had served him. Finally everyone was sent away except the Paigah nobles, the Dewan, and the men of the household, in whose presence the body received the ritual bath and accompanying prayers by the people whose special occupation this was, and then it was wrapped by them in the shroud. The wall between the palace and Mecca Masjid having been broken, he who had put his shoulder to so many biers was raised tenderly onto the shoulders of others and borne into the mosque, there to be included in the congregation for the nighttime prayers.

A great concourse of people had gathered there, spilling out onto the road on either side as far as the eye could see—mournful, tear-stained faces of men lit by the glare of torches. At eleven, the funeral namaz started and Mahbub the Beloved was lowered into the grave that yawned among the white marble tombs of his ancestors.

Lieutenant General His Highness Asaf Jah Muzaffer ul Mulk, Wul Mumalik, Nizam ud Dowla, Nawab Sir Mir Mahbub Ali Khan Bahadur, Fateh Jung, G.C.B., G.C.S.I.—which means, "Lieutenant General His Highness the Sixth in Line Equal to the Rank of Asaf, Victor of the Country and the World, Regulator of the Realm, Regulator of the State, Lord Sir the Honorable Mahbub Ali Khan the Brave, Victorious in War, Knight Grand Cross of the Bath, Knight Grand Commander of the Star of India"—or, as he once signed himself in his youth, "Mir Mahbub Ali Khan, May God Forgive Him," was dead. It was the end of an era.

• Delhi

Calcutta •

Bombay •

Hyderabad
•
ANDHRA
PRADESH

Madras •

Epilogue:

Hyderabad Today

In the early 1960s a mixed group was reminiscing one evening about the old days in Hyderabad. An eminent professional man concluded the discussion with a sigh. "Now that the Muslims have no more money," he asked rhetorically, "how are we poor Hindus to live?" It was a question being asked in one way or another by a great many people. Basically it referred to whether the reciprocally dependent relations between different communities and classes would be replaced by competition. One is tempted to say that in Mahbub's Hyderabad, Muslims and Hindus had lived together happily without regard to religious differences, but that is so cheap a generalization as to be an untruth. They lived together happily precisely because each paid careful regard to the other's religious sensibilities, and this sense of respect strengthened the underlying unity. Traces of it survived even the fanaticism that swept the nation in the thirties and forties.

"These Reddys," said a Muslim on our evening of nostalgia,

251

voicing a popular thought about many middle- and upper-class Hindus in Hyderabad, "are Muslim in everything except their religious ceremonies. They live just the way we do."

"The Muslims here," a scholar rejoined, "practice a much Hinduized form of Islam. Hindus have a pantheon of Gods, Muslims of saints. One takes images in procession, the other alams. And we join each other's celebrations."

The survival of that tradition is attested by a report in the *Deccan Chronicle,* a Hyderabad English-language newspaper, for March 8, 1971: "Moharrum, the tenth day of the martyrdom of Imam Hussein, in Kerbela, was observed in all solemnity in [Hyderabad] today. . . . Over a lakh of mourners participated in the main procession of the Bibi Ka Alam which started after the Zohar (noon) prayers. . . . Prince Muffakam Jah tied the 'dhatti' to the Alam on behalf of the Nizam. The Special Officer of the Hyderabad Municipal Corporation, Mr. C. N. O. Sastry [a Hindu], also offered 'dhatti' to the Alam at the Corporation office. . . . By the side of the roads . . . people of different castes, creeds, and communities eagerly waited to witness the scene in large numbers."

No one claims that the communal harmony is at the level of Mahbub's day, or even near it. One ninety-year-old describes the decline by saying: "In the old days when two chaps of different communities had a fight, it went around the neighborhood that Ramiah and Hasan Ali had fought. Now they say a Hindu and a Muslim fought, and we old people think it is terrible." Still, the lack of tension is significant, compared to many parts of India. This contributes to and is perpetuated by the tendency of the Mulkis to maintain the old culture, although ground is fast being lost by the growing influx of people from areas where that culture never made any impact. More of the ill-feeling today is between Mulkis and the "outsiders" than between Hindus and Muslims from the old state. Hyderabad remains, despite these other influences, primarily a city of homes and families. There are very few good restaurants and almost no night clubs to tempt even the younger generation to experiment with a more independent social life.

To see what else has remained of the Hyderabad of Mahbub Ali Pasha's day, or what has changed in the intervening sixty years, we begin with a drive through the city. Now that Hyderabad has completely filled out its common border with Secunderabad, the million and a half inhabitants of the twin cities have begun to refer to the original walled area as "The City."

We start there, at Mecca Masjid. Except that the chandeliers have been wired for electricity, it is much as Mahbub left it. But next to it, the graveyard has been roofed over and the royal graves have been connected by a single long platform of polished white marble. On it, idlers stretch out to absorb its coolness in the heat of the day. Mahbub would have liked that. As our eyes accommodate themselves to the gleaming expanse, one fact clamors for attention: one grave alone is decorated in any way. Against one end is leant a peacock feather fan, the mark of a saint's tomb. On the other end is a faded turban containing flowers, mostly roses and jasmine, stemless blossoms with the loose petals scattered over the grave in the way homage has been offered since time immemorial. It is Mahbub Ali Pasha's grave, which has become something of a place of pilgrimage for villagers, both Hindu and Muslim, from the old Dominions, when they come to the city. The grave is never without flowers; even at two o'clock in the morning, among the fading blooms of the day before will glisten a few fresh ones.

Turning away from this scene, we walk the few steps to Char Minar, noticing that the four roads leading into it are still lined with the array of bazaars and shops, selling much the same selection of goods as was familiar to the people of Mahbub's day. But inside the structure itself, where the public scribes sat to serve their patrons, are bicycle stands, ugly but functional evidence of the pressure of the increased population.

The carriages of the nobility, preceded by buglers and outriders to 'clear the streets, have given way to the cars of the politicians, flying minister's flags, or the governor's car with an escort of motorcycle police. At any rate, they do not often come to the City. The great deoris are gone or neglected, and it is a long time since Purani Haveli and Chow Mahalla have seen any sustained activity. The latter palace is about to become an Institute of Islamic Studies. Osman Ali Khan, Asaf Jah VII, was indeed the last Kulcha, as foretold in the legend. The palaces, the jewels, the responsibility for the Nizam's staff and dependents, and the empty title have descended to Mukkaram Jah, grandson of Osman Ali Khan. Most of the time he lives away from Hyderabad, in Europe, usually at his home in London. The palaces are closed and visitors are not admitted. There are rumors that Falaknuma, that fairy-tale palace on the hill, is being converted into a hotel, with a helicopter landing-pad for speeding the modern elite to the places of tourist pilgrimage.

Despite the absence of the rich and powerful in the City, the streets are thronged. The boast of more elephants than any other city has given way to that of more bicycles than any city except Copenhagen. To this can be added the probability of more cycle rickshaws than any city in India, and they in turn are being supplanted by automobiles. Both trends become apparent as we thread our way through streets crowded with vendors, pedestrians, cyclists, children, cars, cows, motor scooters, dogs, lorries, and busses. On the other side of the river, traffic thins out a bit as the wide street allows for some lanes for motorized traffic and others for that which is humanly propelled. Here we drive through the new center of the city, the modern business district on Abid Road, past the State Handicraft Emporium which sells, among its many wares, the vases and lamps, cigar boxes and desk sets and plates in bidri such as Tasduq Hussein has made for so long.

When Hyderabad State was divided by the Government of India into three parts in accordance with the linguistic majority, Bidar went to Mysore, and Tasduq Hussein moved into Hydera-bad City. In 1969 he was called to Delhi for a four-day trip as the guest of the government. There he was given an elaborate bronze plaque engraved with the legend, "To Tasduq Hussein, who has kept alive the old traditions of Indian crafts by doing bidri work, a national award for the artistic quality of his handiwork." Accompanying the plaque were a Kashmiri shawl—the ancient token of honor—and an award of 1,000 rupees.

Hussein's son is also a master craftsman and has given demonstrations of the art of bidri making in countries as far away as France and Australia. The chief drawback of bidri has always been that the slightest moisture leaves white spots on the black. Now the son claims to have developed a somewhat modified process which allows bidri even to be washed without harm. "This is an eight-hundred-year-old craft," he says proudly, "and my research has made the first major change in all that time." But his father, asked what he thinks of this new process, shakes his head like traditional fathers since Abel showed Adam a better way to pick apples. "I am the master craftsman," he says with a deprecating smile. "Is he now trying to teach me about bidri?"

A brief swing to the left takes us past the clock tower, which replaced the cannon as a means of announcing the time to the populace, and to the Public Garden. That place is no longer the home of the zoo to which Waliud Dowla donated his tiger cub, Suraiya; the zoo moved to a garden south of town, one of the few things to have moved in that direction. Here in the Public Garden, among wide green lawns, well-tended flower beds, and stately old trees, is the Idgah where Fakhr ul Mulk and the other Umra e Uzzam attended festival prayers. Here also are a museum, including a health museum, and the Legislative Assembly, which in Osman's time was the Town Hall. Any of these buildings looks like a child's conception of a palace, shining white with towers and domes and pillars and terraces in fanciful profusion, as remote from the functional concrete of newer buildings as Mahbub Ali Pasha's manners were from the chief minister's.

The chief minister's official residence, with symbolic appropriateness, stands farther along our route, neatly balanced between

Purani Haveli and Secunderabad Cantonment, as though to demonstrate the union of these two power centers in the modern government. Detouring slightly on our way to it, we pass the Secretariat, nerve center of the state government. Behind handsome wrought-iron gates, its stateliness is marred by latter-day extensions tacked on here and there like canvas pockets tacked onto a couturier suit. Inside work many former jagirdars, products of Jagirdars College, a school run on English public-school lines which was established by the Jagirdars' Association in 1927. Funds were obtained by assessing every jagirdar two percent of his revenue, whether or not he sent sons to the school. This proved to be a far-sighted measure. Many boys went on to earn college degrees, studied abroad, and competed for the Hyderabad Civil Service or went into banking and industry. They have had few problems in adapting to the changes of the past twenty years, in comparison to the jagirdars' children who did not attend the school or obtain an equivalent education. The Jagirdars College is now called the Hyderabad Public School.

Some of those who started with the Hyderabad Civil Service are no longer there. For instance, a grandson of Fakhr ul Mulk transferred to another state when the Nizam's Dominions were divided, and has worked his way to the top echelons of the service there. Some are on loan to the national government. A few, like some of Sir Afsur ul Mulk's descendants, have migrated to the West and given up Indian nationality altogether. A great number of younger sons carried on the traditional occupation of military service and were the officers of the Nizam's state forces. Many of them were in action during World War II. When the state was integrated with the rest of India, the army was disbanded and a number of officers were transferred to the Indian army. Since then, Hyderabad has contributed to the nation one president, five governors, and two ambassadors. Interestingly enough, these all came from among the families of officials, not of nobles.

But it is not only the descendants of the privileged who report to the Secretariat in the mornings: many a Grade IV employee was helped to secure his government appointment as a noble's last act of responsibility for family servants and their dependents. It represented the nearest approach to security that their masters could achieve for them before the lands, the income, and the influence on which all their livelihoods depended were washed away in the rising tide of social democracy.

One such person was Govind, who was a peon here for a good many years. He obtained a certificate which set his birth date back ten years, commensurate with his looks, and thus bought himself a few more years of income before compulsory retirement at the age of fifty-five. Despite daily contact with the new ways of doing things, he finds himself bewildered. "My youngest grandson is at the Hyderabad Public School," he says. "Imagine! and at the top of his class! My elder grandson studied up to the eighth class. He wears trousers and a wrist watch and rides a motor scooter when he goes to the cinema or the cafes. But he never brings a paisa to the house. I have no thought of what can be hoped for them. They will have what is in their fate."

Across the lake from the Secretariat grounds stands a reminder of another government: Vicar Munzil, from which Sir Vicar ul Umra governed the state as Dewan. It now houses a small engineering firm, with only a few rooms reserved for family use. On the rear its windows look out across the valley to another of the great palaces, Iram Munzil, which has for some years been the property of the Public Works Department. Processions of jeeps now chug continuously through the zenana gates where KhatijaBi once challenged every approaching male, and the lovely blue baradari echoes to discussions with contractors about widening roads, completing the new museum to house the Salar Jung collection, or an alteration to the Residency, which is now the Women's College.

The fate of these palaces is not unusual. Stripped of their jagirs, most of the nobles were left with some jewelry, some debts, and more real estate than they could afford to keep up. From landlord of a vast agricultural estate to landlord of domestic and industrial property is a reasonably short step and one which even an imperfectly modernized attitude can accommodate. The sad thing is that not one of the many palaces is being preserved to help future generations visualize this stream of their culture. All across the United States one sees vacationing families lined up for tours of restored buildings and historic sites which attempt to preserve evidence of the country's social history—possibly the more precious in America because there is relatively little of it. In Hyderabad, unless the Department of Tourism or some other agency or groups of concerned citizens can act quickly to a similar end, it will be too late. The deoris, with their successive courtyards, intricately painted arches and ceilings, their rooms paneled with mosaics of tiny pieces of colored mirror, so that a single candle could set the whole room glowing, the unbelievably delicate plaster tracery, all are crumbling like the fortunes which made them possible. So also the Shums ul Umra tombs, with room after room of intricate decorations in polished plaster. For virtuosity of plaster work, these tombs must be the equal of any in India. They are a superb but unhappily perishable example of a vanished art and as such have as little future as their caretaker, the seventh generation of the hereditary keepers of the Shums ul Umra tombs.

Most of the families who once owned the deoris and palaces no longer live in them: the descendants who have been financially successful on their own, if they remain in Hyderabad, tend to live on currently fashionable Banjara Hill, or in some of the other recently built-up areas, in houses which are somewhat more appropriate to a socialist society. More importantly, they signify an attitude that characterizes modern society: that a man is his potential. Among the descendants of the people whose lives we have glimpsed, those who represent this attitude are government servants, business executives, brokers, and professional men. Still, many of their class hold to old values. For them, a man is what his ancestors were. One descendant of the proud Paigah nobility lives in a few rooms in the slum that the deori has become, dressed in the sleazy cotton shirt and sarong of the workingman but unable or unwilling to go out and earn his living. Others of these unadapted ones whose faces are still turned toward the past have made a way of life out of litigation, constantly instituting lawsuits to secure a part of an inheritance, to recover a long-forgotten debt, to evict a squatter, or to establish a claim for a long-past service, until the court of law substitutes for the royal court in their constant attendance.

Only four from the families of former leaders have gone into politics, and they are all, perhaps predictably, from the samasthans. Two are from Wanaparthy. The younger daughter-in-law of Rameshwar Rao II was for ten years a member of the Hyderabad Municipal Council, for three of them as mayor, and for ten years a member of the state Legislative Assembly. Rameshwar Rao III, grandson of Mahbub's contemporary, better than anyone else from our story ties the past and future together. As Raja of Wanaparthy he was the first of the chiefs to turn over his principality to the new government after the police action in 1948 which brought Hyderabad State into the Indian Union. In his handing-over address he said:

Today, at least to me, is a day of mixed feelings. On the one hand I am happy that a change brings forth a government of the people by the people. I hope it will also be for the people. In the past the administration here has no doubt been for the people; but we cannot say that it has been of and by them in the modern democratic sense. It will be unnecessary to recount in detail how in the past four hundred and forty years the rulers of this principality have labored for the welfare of its inhabitants. The existing irrigation projects, wells, roads, rest houses, dispensaries, and schools are standing witness to this fact. I hope that the new administration which takes over from me today will keep in their forefront the welfare of my people and keep up the general standard of efficiency, responsiveness, and the social services to which my people have been used. . . .

Actually we are now in the process of building two irrigation projects. One is the Sarala Sagara Irrigation Project, about which all of you know sufficiently well. It is estimated to cost 16 lakhs of rupees when completed and will irrigate about 4,500 acres. We have nearly finished half of the work on this project and we had hoped that this would be completed in a year's time from now and water made available for irrigation purposes. The other is a small tank which is estimated to cost a lakh and 60,000 rupees when completed and to irrigate about 500 acres. We have been working on this small tank for now over six months and this, too, can be completed within a year from today and we hope the government after taking over charge of my samasthan would see that both these works are completed. . . .

In the process of working for the amelioration of my people we had not forgotten that education in citizenship is necessary and is after all the basis of all social polity. To this end, under the advice and guidance of the Father of the Nation, Mahatmaji [Mahatma Gandhi], and with the help of Sir Mirza Mahommed Ismail, we have drafted a scheme of village panchayats [councils] and a Representative Advisory Assembly for this samasthan. The panchayats came into being in June, 1947. . . .

Here I would like to tell my people and the staff and officers of my administration that the old order, however beneficent it be and however much you may like to continue, cannot do so in the changed atmosphere. . . . I would hence wish everyone to appreciate the necessity of this essential change in its true perspective, and understand that it is bound to be inherently good for the ultimate well-being of my people in the long run. We owe a debt of gratitude to our beloved leaders Pandit Jawaharlal Nehru and Sardar Vallabhai Patel in ushering in this change from a feudal order to a democratic set-up in this country in a peaceful, constitutional, and orderly manner.

Raja Rameshwar Rao was appointed first secretary in the Indian High Commission in Nairobi and later commissioner for the Government of India on the Gold Coast (as Ghana was then called) and Nigeria. But, as an idealistic young socialist, he felt that he was missing the exciting formative years of his own young-old nation. Having spent seven years in Africa, he resigned and went home to run for Parliament, where he has served continuously since. He has been elected by a constituency of which a third is composed of the Wanaparthy samasthan. Apart from his political activity, he has joined with associates in starting several industrial enterprises.

A few years ago he purchased the hilltop which Mahbub's government refused to his grandfather. There he has built a house in which are some of the carved wooden door posts from the Wanaparthy palace. The palace itself has become a technical training institute, endowed by a trust that he established. In Hyderabad, the home that they vacated when the hilltop house was completed is now a coeducational school, founded by his wife, who teaches there. Designed to combine the ancient culture with a modern educational philosophy, through instruction given in English, schools such as this one perform an essential service during the present period when, across the nation, government schools are being swamped with the millions of children suddenly caught in the seine of compulsory education.

In Hyderabad, as generally in India, children are being taught to read and write in the several languages which are still necessary to their lives, to do complex mathematical calculations, and to accept the responsibilities of self-government. But there is something that their grandfathers knew and these children may never know. If so, they will be the poorer. Among the old people with whom we talked there was a remarkable consensus on certain aspects of the former times, such as the existence of communal harmony. In the same way there was nearly unanimous agreement that the missing element today is the feeling of caring and being cared for, the sense of closeness to all levels of society. Both its strength in Mahbub Ali Pasha's time and its weakness now can be explained logically and even—to some minds—justified philosophically. The individual, who in Mahbub's Hyderabad as for untold centuries earlier had the security of an assured but limited place in society, now is set free or, from another point of view, is on his own, to fend for himself on whatever terms he can compete. The wastage, particularly for the transitional generation, is high; it was bound to be. For many of the younger ones, as for Govind's grandsons, the new form of society represents opportunity. But in the West, where this opportunity has existed for a good deal longer, the generation on the young side of the gap is concerned with whether technical marvels and an open society are too costly, if the price is to lose the human feeling of care and closeness. There may still be enough of that feeling left in Hyderabad to resuscitate. The question is whether organizational forms for the expression of it in ways appropriate to the present can be developed soon enough. Neither those who feed on nostalgia for a dead past nor those who turn their backs on history are apt to be of much help on this task. Part of the challenge to each generation may lie precisely here: that if there are not ways for positive feelings to bind a people together, then it will be done by negative ones, or the society will crumble. Hyderabad has given us a testimony to the positive. It may yet be relevant to the new society.

In Mahbub Ali Pasha's time, when the population was far smaller and the administration was decentralized, a personal government was possible. At times of famine, the patwari of a village knew from first-hand acquaintance which of the villagers lacked money to buy cattle fodder and which could not even buy food grains for their families at the subsidized rates. It was therefore quite simple for him to issue the necessary chits to the jagirdar, to ensure that they would be given money for buying their supplies. As those who were slightly better off knew that the burden would also be lifted from their shoulders when it became intolerable, and as they did not in any event expect to progress much beyond the condition in which fate had flung them, the temptation to graft and corruption in this process was minimized and the arrangement was supported by trust on both sides.

In British India this system of reversing the flow of revenue at times of famine did not exist. An early Resident, James Fraser, noted that, "while many thousands of people in a state of starvation fled from the Company's territory [i.e., British India] into Hyderabad, where they were subsisted for several months by public and private charity, I heard of none that came from the

Nizam's adjacent districts." Similarly his predecessor, Colonel Stewart, wrote, "During the scarcity which prevailed last year in the city and in the Company's neighboring districts, it was a subject of remark by every traveller coming here from Madras or Masulipatam that the moment they entered the Nizam's Dominions all the worst appearances of famine in a great measure ceased. They no longer saw the villages filled with the dead and the dying."

The travelers Colonel Stewart mentioned came from British India, through a fertile agricultural district which is part of the present state of Andhra Pradesh. Even there, just across the Nizam's borders, the villagers' chances of surviving a period of scarcity, or indeed of almost any other major crisis, depended largely on the time necessary for communications to thread their way through the administrative maze, as well as on the distance between the locus of decision and the place where help was needed. Today's elected government is necessarily much more like the urban-based, mass-oriented British Raj, with the result that both the personal contact and the resulting trust have decreased or disappeared.

It is this change from personal to impersonal administration that everyone we spoke with deplored, even while many understood and accepted it intellectually. The sense of caring and being cared for was a most cherished value of Mahbub's time and is what is most universally missed today. The people of Wanaparthy say to the Raja's family: "In the old days when we needed a decision of some sort from the government, we came to the Raja Sahib and he said yes or no. Today we have to go to Mahbubnagar [the district town] and there we are passed along from one official to another, to this and that office, or we wait in the court until our case is called. Why have you people gone away? Now we are orphans."

Govind expressed a similar sentiment about unofficial contacts. He said: "That was an era of gold and silver; this one now is of paper. We poor people were happier then; we were looked after like the children in the family. Plenty was cooked so we got something from the table even though our salaries did not include food. Now at most we might get half a cup of tea after a gentleman has finished his tray, but mostly they drink the pot dry. In those times, if we met with difficulties there was always someone to listen and to help. A few years ago I went to greet a gentleman whose grandfather had been kind to me in the old days. He hardly spoke to me and then sent his clerk out to give me ten rupees. When you give, you should give with your own hands, as though it were a pleasure to give, and not like a machine throwing out something. I shall never go back there again."

Even the Hijras notice the change. In speaking of their yearly treks through the villages, a Naik said, "Today they say, 'Hey, hey! Go away! What influence have you got now? The Nizam's rule has gone!' And we say, 'Was that bread given to us by the Nizam? We ate of your charity then and even now it is your charity that we are eating and living on. Then we didn't force you and now we do not force you. Even then we asked in the same way: our hand below and yours above. That is written in our Kismet, so what can one do about that?' So still they keep us."

In the city, too, the Hijras are managing to hold on. Wherever there is a birth, they still go to dance and sing and call down blessings on the new life; but they feel some anxiety for their future, and for a present in which questions about people are reduced to what can be answered by a computer. In 1969 they held a national conference which demanded that they should be listed in the census as females rather than as males, though some of them resisted either classification. A Hyderabad Hijra said: "How can they list us as women? We are not born women. But we are not men. We are separate." The conference also launched a campaign against family planning. Reflecting shifts in the Government of India policy, they began by agitating against sterilization and have since opposed contraceptive pills.

Chandriah the agriculturist, on the other hand, feels the economic pressure as much as anyone and lays it in part to the in-

creased population. He says: "Now I have no goats and no milking animals. The shepherds no longer rotate their flocks but pen
them in the lands of those who have power—our local officials,
the patel, the patwari, and the sarpanch. But the flocks are so
small now that even that is not much use. I buy meat once a fort-
night at five rupees a kilogram and peanut oil for cooking, which
we used to do in ghee. I am not alone; everybody is in this position. There are three or four hundred people now cultivating the
land in small plots.

"Even so they cannot get help in the seasons when they need it.
In the old days, the Harijan laborer was available for work and
there was plenty of labor. It is true they did not have a very good
life, but they did not starve. How could we let them starve? Even
though they were untouchable and were not allowed inside our
houses or to draw from our wells, it was something that they were
used to, just as we were accustomed to knowing that we could
not touch things belonging to a Brahmin. Now they want to
change all that, and I suppose they are right, although you cannot change people's hearts by legislation."

In Chandriah's youth, it was the voices of the elders that
counted. Today in India, as elsewhere in the world, the strenuous
demands on politicians make it necessary for a man to establish
himself during his prime, if he wishes to participate in the
decision-making process. But it is more than this reversal of roles
between the generations that Chandriah refers to, when he says,
"A young relative of our family left his studies and became a
leader of a student movement. Now he is sitting as an M.P. in
Delhi. I ask you, in what way can he represent this country or
legislate for it wisely? What does the Government of India know,
sitting there in Delhi, about what goes on in the countryside and
the villages far away?" Another old man said: "We could always
go to the jagirdar or to the Nizam with the confidence that our
problems would be sorted out fairly. Who now goes to the chief
minister?"

Perhaps the most graphic images of this change toward a sense of personal distance are suggested by the changed responses to an emergency. During the flood, Mahbub Ali Pasha stood outdoors in the pouring rain and prayed aloud to God to take him; he was ready to die if God would only spare his people. Then he walked among them distributing not only instructions to go to his palace for food and shelter, but also words of encouragement and comfort. Today the heads of government view these disasters from a helicopter, from which they then proceed to top-level strategy meetings. This latter image conveys nothing about the relative magnitude of the problems or pressures, the resources brought to bear, or the possible effectiveness of the measures taken. It refers only to the people's sense of alienation from the governing levels of society.

This contrast pertains not only to Hyderabad, but to all of India, to America, and to the world. It may be inevitable, as eyes are necessarily focused on events in the national capitals at home or half-way around the world. We all share the dilemma it reflects, for no place now can remain insulated from the problems across its borders. Rats and germs and the sweet smell of blossoms are no respecters of boundaries. So we of the West join the Hyderabadis in living with the paradox that our present, compared with a recent past, is at once more populous and more impersonal; more egalitarian and more conscious of relative deprivation; more flooded with communications and more isolated; more affluent and more constricted; more technologically efficient and more humanly inefficient. In Robert Frost's eloquent phrase, the problem of our day, on which we may be able to get some hints from the days of Mahbub the Beloved, is "how to crowd but still be kind."

Appendix I.
Hyderabad: Census of 1911

F OR THE FINAL count in compiling the 1911 Official Census for India, which was to confirm or correct the laborious preliminary survey, the instructions issued by the Census Commissioner point out that "The Census should be taken a few days before the full moon, because the light will then be available in the early part of the night and people will not ordinarily have left their homes to attend the lunar bathing festivals."

Counted in that gentle light, the people of Hyderabad State at the close of the first decade of the twentieth century were found to number about 13,375,000. The area of the state appeared to comprise 83,000 square miles (or roughly more than a third of the Deccan). There were some 2,700,000 occupied houses, probably not counting ruder dwellings. Of the persons who lived in them, slightly more than half were male. The commissioner declined to claim absolute accuracy for the population figures. First, the more wretched female servants would be ignored by many a head of household, not out of malice or deliberate disrespect so much as because they were not important enough to cross his mind. Second, many men with multiple wives shame-facedly acknowledged only one to the census taker, although the practice of having more was both legal and well known. Perhaps they feared that reporting such would advertise their prosperity to the tax collectors.

In counting women, it was common practice to understate the age of a marriageable daughter, a trick by which hardpressed parents bought a bit more time for arranging a suitable match. The total of four times as many widows as widowers suggests, in the absence of a major war during the period, considerable social support for the prohibition on remarriage of widows. Life was not unduly long, however, for anyone. The age distribution at the turn of the century peaked at thirty years, and 93 percent of the population was under fifty.

As one of the things we have noticed about Hyderabad is the relations between the communities, it should be interesting to see how they were represented numerically and their proportions in the urban population shown in table A. It is worth noticing that Hyderabad City, although the only city with a population over 100,000 in the Nizam's Dominions, had less than 40 percent of the urban total. (See table A.)

A. Numerical Distribution of Communities

Religion	Total state population		Urban areas
	Population	Percent	Population
Hindu	11,626,000	87.0	827,000
Muslim	1,381,000	10.3	439,000
Animistic (tribal)	286,000	2.1	1,000
Christian	54,000	.4	16,000
Jain	21,000	.15	4,000
Sikh	5,000		3,000
Parsi	1,500		800
Jewish	12		12

Approximately 7 percent of the Hindus, a third of the Muslims, and three-fourths of the Christians lived in the cities. No doubt related to the pattern of urbanization is the distribution of literacy, which overall approximated 4 percent: 23 persons per thousand among Hindus, 60 per thousand among Muslims, and 443 per thousand among the Christians. Of the literate Hindus, 4 percent were women, while among Muslims the figure was 27 percent.

The census also lists the number of persons speaking the major languages. In view of the post-independence decision to draw state boundaries on linguistic bases, this is interesting. The most common language was Telegu, mother tongue to some 6,370,000. Next came Marathi, spoken by about 3,500,000. Canarese followed with somewhat

B. Occupational Distribution

Occupation	Hyderabad State			Hyderabad City			
	Total	Hindu	Muslim	Total	Hindu	Muslim	Christian
I Farming or mining	8,400,000	7,456,000	667,000	49,000	32,000	16,000	120
II Industry, trade, or transportation	3,100,000	2,875,000	226,000	155,000	113,000	37,000	5,000
III Public administration and liberal arts:							
Public force	164,000	93,000	67,000	63,000	14,000	45,000	3,000
Public administration	346,000	249,000	92,000	27,000	8,000	18,000	1,000
Professions and liberal arts	209,000	169,000	35,000	24,000	9,000	11,000	4,000
Persons living on income	28,000	16,000	12,000	23,000	4,000	18,000	400
IV Domestic service	421,000	223,000	190,000	not available	not available	not available	not available

over 1,700,000. Only then comes Urdu, the court language, with 1,340,000. Fewer than 9,000 claimed English as their tongue.

The occupational census tells us something more about the communal groups that is worth bearing in mind since this was a state where a Muslim ruler had a majority of Hindus for subjects. The census classifications (here somewhat simplified) and the distribution by groups are shown in table B.

Appendix II.
A Bedtime Story

THIS IS a sample of what Nawab Fakhr ul Mulk heard from his storyteller, who sat behind the head of his bed and helped him while away the hours when he could not sleep:

Once a man who had returned from a long journey went to a merchant to whom he had given his money for safekeeping and asked for its return. The merchant denied ever having received it, but as it was the traveler's whole fortune, he insisted and an argument ensued. Finally the traveler dragged the merchant off to see the king and to beg for justice. The king listened carefully to the traveler's account and the merchant's denials, and asked, "Were there no witnesses?"

"None, Your Highness," the traveler replied.

"But there must have been some witness," the king said. "Where do you claim the transaction took place?"

"Under a peepul tree, Your Highness," the traveler explained. "We sat there at mid-day when everyone was resting. I finished counting out the money and was off before anyone came out."

"Then of course you have a witness!" the king exclaimed. "The peepul tree is your witness."

The traveler smiled ruefully. "I am afraid it is not the kind of witness that will come and give testimony, even for so august a personage as Your Highness," he said.

"Nonsense," the king replied matter-of-factly. "Of course it will come. Here, take my ring. Go show it to the peepul tree and say that the king commands it to appear and bear witness."

The traveler took the ring and bowed his way out of the room, thinking sadly that if his case depended on whether the peepul tree obeyed the king, his fortune was certainly lost to him.

Meanwhile the king asked the merchant a few more questions, glanced out of the window, paced the room a few times, clapped his hands for a glass of water to be brought to him, and resumed his pacing. Then, putting his head out the window and peering as far down the street as he could see, he exclaimed impatiently, "This is taking a very long time. Shouldn't he have been able to reach the tree and return by now?"

"No, not yet," the merchant replied soothingly.

"Then," said the king, "I shall have a Musahib read to me while I wait." He clapped his hands again.

Eventually the crestfallen traveler returned and bowed low. "Oh, Your Highness," he reported, "three times I showed your ring to the tree and proclaimed that the king commanded it to appear at court, but the disrespectful tree paid no attention."

"What do you mean, it paid no attention?" the king demanded. "The tree has been here in your absence and borne witness."

Then the astonished traveler began to weep and wail inwardly, for he thought to himself, "Arrai! What have I done? I have given my fortune to a thief and come for justice to a madman! All is lost!" Scarcely able to believe his ears, he heard the king order the merchant to return the money, but the merchant protested, "There was no tree that came here and gave witness, Your Highness."

"Of course the tree bore witness," the king said. "When I asked you whether this traveler could not have got to the tree and back by now, you said 'No, not yet.' If you had never sat under the tree with him and accepted his money, as he says, you would have replied, 'How do I know? What tree?' So you will now return the money."

Glossary

AKKA Elder sister.

ALAMS Sacred symbols representing the Prophet, his sons, and others important to the Shia Muslims.

AMARI Ceremonial howdah of a particular shape. Its use was an honor in the gift of the Nizam.

ARATI Movement of a small oil lamp before the face of an image or person as part of an act of worship.

ASHRAFI A gold coin worth about 25 rupees.

BAHADUR An official title of honor; literally, "the Brave." No longer used only for bravery; one of the lowest grades of nobility.

BARADARI Literally, "twelve doors." A room containing twelve doors which, because of its airiness, lent itself to entertaining and to large gatherings, such as Majlis. It was sometimes part of a noble's main palace and sometimes separate, as a summer house.

BHOIS Men of the fisherman caste who also carried palanquins and bore burdens on their heads.

BIDRI Handicraft practiced in Bidar, Hyderabad State. Bidri wares are of metal with silver inlay against a black finish or ground.

BUGLOOS Ceremonial belt of velvet or brocade required in the presence of Hyderabad royalty.

BURQA Tentlike garment worn by Muslim women in public to cover them from head to foot, with eyeholes covered by net.

CHAOUSH Arab mercenaries who settled in Hyderabad, many of whom married local women. Also, their descendants.

CHAR MINAR Four-towered structure built in 1589 by Mohammad-Quli Qutub Shah. It became the symbol of Hyderabad.

CHOW MAHALLA Mile-long compound adjacent to Mecca Masjid, containing 16 buildings, including the one used primarily for durbar in Mahbub Ali Pasha's time, the royal treasury, and the school built for Mahbub.

CRORE 100 lakhs; 10 million (see *Lakh*).

DASTAR Form of headdress required in the presence of the Nizam and others of the royal family.

DASTARKHAN White cloth spread over carpet for traditional form of meal service.

DECCAN Plateau covering most of the triangle of South India.

DEORI City palace built around successive courtyards.

DEWAN Prime minister.

DHOLAK Drum played with the fingers on the two ends.

DURBAR Audience of royalty or nobility; also the hall where the audience was held.

FALAKNUMA "Mirror of the Sky," the palace built by Sir Vicar ul Umra and acquired by Mahbub Ali Pasha.

HAKIM Practitioner of Unani, a system of medicine which originated in Greece, brought to India by Arabs and Moghuls.

HIJRA Member of a community of impotent males, most of whom have removed their external genital organs.

HUZOOR Your (or His) Highness.

JAGIR Grant of revenues of a particular area to a person; often accompanying a high appointment and generally for the purpose of maintaining troops.

JAGIRDAR Holder of a jagir.

KOTWAL High official responsible for internal security and for the city police; he reported directly to the Nizam.

KUMKUM Red powder used by Hindus to make the mark on the forehead and also in worship and on ceremonial occasions.

LAKH 100,000; written 1,00,000.

MAJLIS Prayer meetings held by Shia Muslims during Moharrum, focused on the martyrdom of the Prophet's grandsons; often held in private homes and open to all comers.

MANSAB Royal grant originally involving maintenance of

troops; later a periodic stipend granted from state or privy purse as a mark of royal favor.

MARDANA The part of a house used only by men; by derivation, the men occupying it.

MECCA MASJID The large mosque near Char Minar. The royal tombs were in the courtyard of this mosque.

MELA An event like a county fair, for trade and fun.

MOHARRUM The month when Shia Muslims mourn the deaths of the grandsons of the Prophet at the battle of Kerbela.

MULKI Citizen of the Nizam's Dominions; non-Hyderabadis, or Ghair Mulkis, were considered outsiders.

MUSAHIB Courtier.

MUSNUD Half-moon-shaped pillow with bolsters, often on a matching carpet or divan cover, usually of velvet heavily embroidered with gold. Also denotes the Hyderabad throne.

NAMAZ Muslim prayers recited five times a day while standing on a prayer carpet or cloth with the face toward Mecca. At certain points the person kneels and touches his forehead to the ground. Preceded by ritual ablution.

NAUBAT Ceremonial drumming sometimes accompanied by a particular wind instrument supplying a tune, usually done from a position over the main gate of a palace or deori. The right to naubat was an honor granted by the Nizam.

NAWAB Title of nobility.

NAZAR Offering of coins as token of respect and fealty; sometimes objects that were admired were presented as nazar.

PAIGAH Class of nobles that intermarried with the royal family and were given vast jagirs for maintenance of the household troops.

PAISA See *Rupee.*

PAN A savory held in the mouth and chewed or sucked slowly, consisting of a fresh betel leaf wrapped round a mixture of various ingredients such as slaked lime, condiments, spices, betel nut, and occasionally, tobacco.

PANDAN Metal box, often highly ornamented, containing the

ingredients for pan. Elaborate pandans were fitted with small boxes, dishes, and trays for the ingredients.

PARSIS Descendants of Zoroastrians who were driven out of Persia in the 14th century and given refuge in India on condition they adopt certain Indian customs and the language of Gujerat, where they originally settled.

PATEL, PATWARI Local government officials.

PESHKAR Administrative officer in charge of the royal treasury and army; required to be in constant personal attendance on the Nizam; deputized for the Dewan. In Hyderabad, a hereditary office of the family of Maharajah Chandulal.

PESHKASH Tribute money.

PUJA Hindu prayers, performed sitting cross-legged in front of a shrine, ordinarily with the use of incense, red kumkum powder, and flowers, and often the symbolic offering of food, such as a banana or some grains of rice. Usually done in the presence of fire (as, from a lamp).

PURANI HAVELI Palace most frequently used as city residence by Mahbub Ali Pasha. It consisted of an area one mile by 145 yards, containing numerous buildings.

PURDAH System of secluding women and veiling them from the sight of men.

RATH Wooden cart with canvas top, drawn by bullocks. It could be curtained for women in purdah.

RUPEE Basic unit of money. Since 1958 it has consisted of 100 new paise. Formerly there were 3 pies to the paisa, 4 paise to the anna, 16 annas to the rupee. For this reason Indian children learned the multiplication tables through 16 times 16. A Hyderabad rupee of 1903 would be worth approximately $1.60 at the 1971 exchange rate.

RYOT Peasant.

SAILABCHI Wide-rimmed, deep dish used as a portable washbasin.

SAMASTHAN Ancient principality, governed by an indigenous Hindu prince. There were eight samasthans in the Nizam's Dominions.

SHERWANI Coat reaching just below the knee; worn over pyjamas or dhoti.

SHIA A Muslim sect, roughly comparable to the Catholics in Christianity, with the Sunni sect in the role of Protestants. Shia practice involved more complex ritual, more visual symbols and processions.

SHIKAR Hunting expedition.

SHIKARI Hunter.

SUFISM Mystical sect of Islam which emphasizes the personal union of the soul with God.

SUNNI See *Shia*.

THASBI Muslim rosary.

TONGA Horse-drawn taxi with two wheels and one seat where the passenger sits back-to-back with the driver.

TOORAH Stiff gold tassel worn upright on dastars of royalty.

TOSHDAN Metal lunch-box containing a stack of dishes in a holder.

VAID Practitioner of ayurveda, a system of medicine developed by the Hindus.

ZENANA Women's apartments in a house, forbidden to males over twelve years of age except for husband and blood relatives. By derivation, the women occupants.

ZENANAY Male prostitutes.

Note on Sources

Most of the information in this book was gathered in conversations with people in Hyderabad whose memories reach back into the days of Mahbub Ali Pasha, or who have lively memories of their parents' conversations about him and life in his times. As one would expect, those memories represent the Indian point of view. Quotations giving the British point of view, except in the very few cases which are otherwise identified, come from documents in the India Office Records, of the Foreign and Commonwealth Office, London. Mahbub Ali Pasha's letter about his reluctance to accept an English tutor, as well as the one detailing his complaints about Salar Jung II, are preserved in the same place. Until 1911 the British Raj, known officially as the Government of India, had its headquarters at Calcutta. Information which flowed between Calcutta and the Resident at Hyderabad was contained in letters, telegrams, memorandums, and reports which are now in the India Office Records. We drew chiefly on the Residents' correspondence with the Viceroy and his staff or with the Foreign Department, which dealt with affairs in the Princely States.

Added to these two sources, which account for the largest part of the data, are certain occasional references. In Chapter I the accounts of the flood are translated from the Urdu of Syed Khursheed Ali in *Adeeb*, Toofan Number, September–December, 1908, published by the Sahifa Press, Chaderghat, Hyderabad. In Chapter II, Nizam ul Mulk's account of his encounter with Nadir Shah appears in Yusuf Husain, *The First Nizam*, New York: Asia Publishing House, 1963, p. 244. We have also drawn on Husain's translation of Nizam ul Mulk's will.

Sarwar Jung on palace etiquette, in Chapter III, is quoted from his memoirs, Nawab Server-ul-Mulk Bahadur, *My Life,* London: Arthur H. Stockwell, n.d., p. 171. Other quotations from the same work include the remarks about the detrimental effect of the Resident's policies, and Mahbub Ali Pasha's complaints about Salar Jung II. Clerk's remark at Windsor Castle is reported in Victor Mallet, ed., *Life with Queen Victoria,* Boston: Houghton Mifflin, 1968, p. 102. The English visitor who commented on Captain Clerk's difficulties with the Resident was Wilfrid Scawen Blunt, who referred to the tutor's strained relations in *India under Ripon,* Lon-

don: T. Fisher Unwin, 1901, p. 65, and appended several letters from
Claude Clerk. Blunt also recorded Mahbub's preference for Salar Jung II
as Dewan after Sir Salar Jung's death. The letters which Mahbub wrote to
his officials as a young man, together with one reply, are translations of
correspondence in the possession of the authors. Mirza Mehdy Khan's comments on the popular attitude toward education come from the *Census of
India, 1901*, Vol. XXII, *Hyderabad*, Part I, Hyderabad, Deccan: Venugo-
paul Pillai & Sons, 1903, p. 140. This was also the source of the instructions
to begin census taking by moonlight which are quoted in Appendix I.
Much of the material about the Berar negotiations is quoted from *The
Gazette of India Extraordinary*, Registered No. L.848, Calcutta: Government of India Central Publication Branch, April 5, 1926, pp. 141 ff.

All the poetry in Chapter V, with the exception of one well-known
couplet by Fani, was composed by Maharajah Kishen Pershad and has been
freely translated by the authors. Sir Salar Jung's advice on how to treat a
sovereign apparently impressed the young Kishen Pershad enough so that
he made some notes about it. These are quoted by Mehdi Nawaz Jung in
the biography *Maharajah Kishen Pershad* which he wrote and had published privately (n.p.) in 1950, a few years after Maharajah's death. In the
following chapter the letter from Sir Salar Jung about the famine in Orissa
was addressed to Sir John Lawrence and is quoted by Syed Abid Hassan in
Whither Hyderabad? Madras: the B. N. Press, 1935, pp. 136–37. Muhammad-Quli's line about the Angel Gabriel sorrowing for Husain is a
quotation from H. K. Sherwani, *Muhammad-Quli Qutb Shah: Founder of
Haidarabad*, Bombay: Asia Publishing House, 1967, p. 58. We have also
drawn upon Sherwani's detailed description of the founding of Hyderabad
and of the city before the coming of the Asaf Jahs.

In Chapter VII the dowry of Sultan Jehan Begum and the exchange of
letters with Osman Ali Khan about a visit from his zenana are translated
from the originals owned by Fakhr ul Mulk's great grandson, Syed Mohammad Zaki, of Hyderabad.

In the Epilogue the speech made by Rameshwar Rao III, Raja of Wanaparthy, on handing over his samasthan is excerpted from a copy which he
lent us. Two early Residents are quoted about famine conditions in the
Nizam's Dominions. James Fraser's remarks are from Hastings Fraser,
Memoirs and Correspondence of Gen. James Stuart Fraser, London:
Whiting & Co., 1885, p. 88. Similar remarks by Colonel Josiah Stewart are
quoted by Syed Abid Hassan in *Whither Hyderabad?* on pp. 100–1.

The census statistics in Appendix I are from the *Census of India, 1911*,
Vol. XIX, *Hyderabad State*, Part II. M. Abdul Majeed was the Superintendent.